With Love and Loathing

Books by John Crosby

WITH LOVE AND LOATHING

OUT OF THE BLUE

John Crosby/ With Love And Loathing

McGraw-Hill Book Company, Inc./New York/Toronto/London

Printed in the United States of America.

Library of Congress Catalog Card Number: 63-15018

14505

TO ELLIE

Contents

With Love and Loathing

Travel

ORIENT-SIMPLON EXPRESS

■ The old Orient Express from which Alfred Hitchcock's lady vanished, scene of a score of movies and plays, is finished, dead, killed by the Iron Curtain, but the Direct-Orient still runs from Paris to Istanbul and back, crossing a half-dozen borders on the way.

If you catch it from Belgrade en route to Paris, as I did, you must get up very early because it leaves Belgrade exactly on time at 4:59 A.M. Even at that hour, the Belgrade station swarms with humanity, old women in rags, young men in faded denim, clusters of families—mother, father, aunts, grandmothers, kids. God knows where they are all going. The air reeks with poverty, which has its own smell.

I go instantly to bed and when I awake at eight, the train is belting through the Yugoslav countryside in blinding sunshine. Women in long skirts in the fields, standing motionless. Beautifully shaped haystacks. A man herding geese. Crenellated towers for grain. The corn looks withered and dry, symptomatic of the bad crop failure Yugoslavia is suffering.

The Yugoslav villages are made up of whitewashed cottages with brown slate roofs. Each has its own yard fenced in unpainted wood. No grass, but vines and trees. Through the open window the heavenly smells of hay and sunshine. The roads are white and dusty, and we pass a cart full of yellow pumpkins. On the other side of Zagreb, the river runs swift and brown. The flat fields are replaced by wooded hills. The corn grows close to the tracks squeezed by the hills.

The train passes a platoon of Yugoslav cavalry on prancing horses, conceivably the last cavalry on earth, pulling a tiny cannon. Off to fight the Crimean War, I suppose. The Yugoslav Army is in great demand by the movie crowd for its picturesque, anachronistic ways; it's the subject of many gags, but I notice neither Stalin nor Khrushchev wanted to tangle with it.

Oddly for an express, the Orient-Simplon stops at many little towns, and the littler they are the better I like their stations. Flowers in baskets, hanging from the roof. Stone pots of flowers around flagstone steps. Sometimes a little grove of trees with chairs and tables for the loafers, who sit and stare, making the most of arrivals and departures.

The farewells are emotional. Twenty-five thousand young men and women flee Yugoslavia, either legally or illegally, every year to more hopeful lands like Australia or Canada. You look down at them from the train windows like in a Hitchcock movie. Kisses and embraces and tears between the fierce-eyed young men and the young girls in print dresses with plaits down their backs, leaving the old folk to tend the geese. The old folk wave and wave until you can't see them any more.

In the late afternoon the clouds come, blotting out the sun. It's cooler, thank God, and with any luck it'll rain. The ground is baked, with croppings of sunbaked rock showing through like bones. The Yugoslav border guards come in to ask for my passport. I try a smile. They don't smile back. They've seen all those movies, too, I guess, and the guards in the Communist countries never smile. Or maybe there's nothing to smile about.

At the little station of Poggioreale Campagna, we're in Italy. The Italian border guards enter in their white uniforms and white caps. Much cleaner. Much newer. Much politer. I'm a traveler, not an enemy of the people. Almost immediately the countryside is Italianate. The roofs of orange slate. The white plaster houses.

Poplars in rows. The train is climbing into the hills now. White stone fences divide the fields, line the roads, giving the land a three-dimensional rectangularity. Speeding new cars on the roads, macadam now in place of white dirt, and I recall that from Belgrade to the border I've seen only one car, a truck in the field, otherwise bicycles and carts.

Soon the Adriatic stretches out blue-gray to the right of the train. A speedboat makes white waves far below. Villas with orange roofs cling to the hills overlooking the water. A white tower on a headland stands over a tiny harbor with stone breakwater. We enter Trieste—first the old port with its quaint, pastel houses, then into the new station, very modern, smelling of new cement. No flowers in pots. No loafers under the trees. No benches, no comfort, no nonsense. We're back in the twentieth century. People in ties and suits. Exquisitely dressed Italian women. Girls in skin-tight white slacks. (What's slack about them?)

Past Trieste the countryside is domesticated, manicured, well tended, rich, much different from the untamed (and not at all unattractive) wildness of Yugoslavia. It's getting dark outside and there's rain on the window in the twilight.

Night falls and we're in Venice—the lights shining on the water. During the night the train passes through Switzerland, robbing us of some spectacular views. I awake in France.

The houses are gray with red roofs and round towers, clustered together cheek by jowl in the villages. The meadows are green with grass, the roads lined with evenly spaced trees. Even the cows look French. We pass a fierce figure with a black cloak falling to his heels, arms akimbo, guarding two cows like d'Artagnan guarding the Queen of France. Presently the Seine, lined with poplars of uniform height.

Then at 9:25 A.M., exactly on time, we are in Paris, wearing her fall colors already, the leaves in the Tuileries laced with yellows and reds, and looking, as always, serenely beautiful, even in the rain. ■

PARIS

■ Paris was the first place I came to when I started traveling ten years ago, and now, for the time being, it's home.

When I was searching for a place to live in Saint-Germain-des-Prés, a shower of rain drove me into a bookstore, and presently I found myself browsing through some gay little tomes entitled *Le Petit Cancer de l'Estomac, Psychose et Glandes Endocrines, Maladies de la Nutrition,* and (to put the titles in English) *The Woman Frigid, the Man Impotent* and—now we're getting a little more French—*The Heart, Its Maladies and Its Treatments.* This was my introduction to French bookstores, which are a world apart.

My neighborhood is awash with bookstores—and what bookstores they are! The degree of specialization achieved by a French bookstore takes my breath away. I'm used to American bookstores where they fill the window with *The Agony and the Ecstasy* by What's-his-name Stone and maybe *Ship of Fools* and that's it. But in Paris it's different, as I found out that day in the rain.

You want to know what books the bookstores were pushing in my block? Let me tell you what books the bookstores were pushing in my block.

Right down the street from the hotel where I was staying (you must ask me about that sometime; it's a gas) is Raymann's, and Raymann's was featuring in the window *Tables of Sines and Cosines to Ten Decimal Places and Thousandths of a Degree* by Herbert F. Salzer and Norman Levine. If there's anything I hate, it's people who pander to popular taste, but, by God, they're not going to level that accusation against Raymann's while I'm alive. They were beating the drum for *Sines and Cosines* like some bookstores push the works of Anne Morrow Lindbergh.

Other books that were big in Raymann's window that week were *The Mossbauer Effect, Molecular Spectroscopy, Statistical Processes of Evolutionary Theory,* and *The Motor Apparatus of the Mammary Glands*—in case the passerby was looking for Christmas presents.

Across the street from Raymann's is the Librairie de Musique, where they sell scores of all of Schumann's works and like that, but the Librairie de Musique had veered from the strict path of specialization and gone after the mass audience in what I considered deplorable ways. In their windows were books on how to play football, how to box, and how to play "*Jeu de Dames*" (for beginners), which I thought gleefully was a book on how to seduce women (for beginners), which is just what I needed, but it wasn't; it was—well, "Jeu de Dames" is checkers, for God's sake.

Down the block, though, I came to Livres Anciens et Modernes, and here the bookseller was hewing to the discipline of strict specialization. This bookstore was specializing in Stendhal. Everything about Stendhal—books by him, books about him, everything you could want to know about Stendhal and maybe some things you wouldn't want to know about Stendhal; it was all right there in the window.

Around the corner on the Rue de Vaurigard was de Boccard's little book mart, and, brother, here one's interests narrowed down to a Gallic point so fine as to almost disappear. Architecture is Boccard's big passion, and they had—well, for example, a 600-page book on sculptured doors. And, for another example, a book on the architecture of Angolid architecture in the fourth and third centuries B.C. Specialists in Angolid architecture in the fifth and sixth centuries—well, hell, *everyone* knows a million of those. But I can count on the fingers of one hand the people who know anything at all about fourth- and third-century-B.C. architecture in Angolid, including where it is.

A few doors down is a bookstore called Librairie de Médicis, whose twist is political economics. There, cheek by jowl, were a biography of Genghis Khan and John F. Kennedy's *Stratégie de la Paix*. Accident, probably, putting them together like that.

Practically next door is Corti's bookstore, which my son would love. Their specialty: terror and the supernatural. Where else would you find *Monumental Incongruities* and *Book of Monsters?*

There are probably two hundred bookstores all within four blocks of my place, and not a best seller in any of them, probably.

In an increasingly conformist society where the whole world seems to read the same six books, it's a comforting thought that somewhere in Paris a reader is happily browsing through *The Motor Apparatus of the Mammary Glands,* and the hell with Katherine Anne Porter. ■

■ The French are delightfully French about even their quiz shows, which may be the only truly international cultural contribution of this century. In 1959 I was watching a French quiz show one night with a French intellectual who was acting as interpreter.

You might say that the interpretation of quiz shows was a rather mean-minded occupation for a French intellectual—but then you don't know French quiz shows. It was a darned tough quiz show. The contestants wrestled successfully with the genius of Descartes and Pascal. The questions veered to the life of Victor Hugo.

"Aha!" said the Frenchman.

"Why *aha?*" I wanted to know.

"They're voicing their opposition to de Gaulle."

"De Gaulle? But it's about Victor Hugo."

Hugo, it was explained patiently to me, silly Anglo-Saxon that I am, was a famed and courageous opponent of Napoleon III. "But what has that got to do with de Gaulle?" I asked.

"De Gaulle is being compared to Napoleon III," said the Frenchman. "The parallel is inescapable."

Well, it was plenty escapable to me. In fact, if the Frenchman hadn't been there, it would never have occurred to me. "You mean to say Frenchmen are sitting home getting a message of opposition to de Gaulle out of this . . . this quiz show?" I inquired. It seemed a very innocuous, if difficult, quiz.

"You underestimate the subtlety of the French mind," I was told. "We did this sort of thing all the time during the occupation under the noses of the Germans." Allusions to Attila the Hun and other unsavory historical personages had been slipped into all sorts of radio programs while terribly subtle Frenchmen sat home and said, "*Aha!*"

There were all sorts of references to the perniciousness of Napoleon III on French television—all properly construed in the proper French intellectual circles. "Napoleon III was even called *mon général*—just like de Gaulle," murmured the Frenchman.

"*Aha!*" said I.

It can't be denied that the only criticism you will ever hear of the de Gaulle administration on French television has got to be by interpreting quiz-show questions. You sure won't hear it anywhere else. TV is government-operated but not at all on the English model; BBC news is renowned for its completeness and impartiality. French television news comes under the scrutiny and control of Roger Frey, French Minister of Information. This, as someone pointed out to me, is as if Pierre Salinger exercised a blue pencil over the reporting of all Washington news.

Not all Frenchmen are absolutely carried away by de Gaulle, particularly in intellectual circles, and—at least in 1959—to make these people feel they were not alone in a world of Gaullists, these veiled references were sneaked on the air. The deviousness of these digs at de Gaulle were astonishing. One device was to overpraise *mon général* to the point where the French, who appreciate moderation in all things, would have liked to throw up. This didn't mean the French were on the verge of revolt. It was not even intended to put such thoughts in anyone's mind. It was just—well—the Frenchman's way of saying he was going to think as he pleased no matter who was in the Presidential Palace. ■

CANNES

■ I was once stranded on the Riviera by a French national strike, which interrupted everything in France except pleasure.

As I lay in the sun at Cap d'Antibes, the Mediterranean was

extraordinarily blue, like a huge aquamarine, and because I am afflicted by conscience, its very blueness, the enchanting beauty of Eden Roc, just added to my discomfort. I should be home working, I kept telling myself, I shouldn't be lying here in the sun staring at a bewitching bronzed almost naked blonde striking attitudes on the diving board.

The women at Cap d'Antibes all drape themselves carefully in poses as if waiting at any moment for the cameras to click. You forgive them this affectation because they are among the most beautiful women anywhere. Eden Roc attracts beauties from all over the world—Australia, Egypt, the funniest places—and the concentration of feminine beauty, most of it in bikinis, almost overpowers you. Hedy Lamarr was there one day and, brother, in that league she didn't measure up.

One night at the Casino I was seated next to Princess Ibrahim Ali, who, a certain maître d'hôtel assured me, was the most beautiful woman in the world. The d'hôtel will have to be nameless because if he ever gave such a public accolade to any one girl, the other beauties there would scratch his eyes out.

But that's getting away from my problem, which was how to get home. It was a problem that haunted me all the time, while driving to Monte Carlo, for instance, twisting through the mountains high over the blue, blue sea, a route that must be among the most breathtaking in Christendom. It was a problem I kept turning over in my mind while sitting on the terrace at the Hotel Carlton, sipping a drink and watching the sun sink slowly into the mountains or while dancing under the stars at the Casino or while watching the Duchess of Windsor lose a packet at *chemin de fer*.

Trapped, I said to myself bitterly. Trapped like a mink. It wouldn't have been appropriate in those surroundings to say that I was trapped like a rat. Much more like a mink or maybe a sable. A strike is a terrible thing.

André Sonier, *directeur de réception* at the Hotel Carlton, enjoyed the awesome title of being the best physiognomist in Europe. A physiognomist, as you all know, of course, is a man who knows all about you at a glance—your character, your social standing, your personal habits, and, above all, how much money you have. In a resort city like Cannes, where princes may arrive dressed like banshees and bums may arrive in Cadillacs, it's a priceless gift, especially at the Carlton, which has had more than its share of both.

The daughter of a Spanish grandee once arrived incognito at the Carlton and demanded to be shown her room. An attendant asked for her card of identity, and the lady, outraged at not being instantly recognized, swept out to the Majestic. Naturally that sort of thing is to be avoided at all costs, and if Sonier had been there, it probably would have been.

Sonier himself denied his own reputation as something invented by journalists. "I know many people," he would tell you with a shrug. "That is all there is to it. But there are difficulties in this business. Right now, there are too many girls. They arrive—girls of a certain profession. They are well-mannered. They are well dressed. They have money. They look no different from the countesses or the movie actresses." He paused a moment, then added quietly, "But I never make a mistake about a girl."

"Now, that's the proudest boast I ever heard. How do you manage that?"

"The voices. The manners they can acquire by imitation. The dresses they can buy. The voice is not so easy."

"That blonde," I asked. "Who is she?"

"Nothing much," said Sonier.

"French?" That's what I would have taken her for.

"American," said Sonier wearily. "I don't know what she's doing here."

The physiognomists, you'll be happy to learn, are not always infallible. Next to Sonier, the most noted physiognomist in this area was André Sella, the proprietor of Eden Roc at Antibes. One day a grubby old man with a beard showed up and was shown the door immediately. Turned out to be Bernard Shaw. ■

RAPALLO, *ITALY*

■ There was a little excursion boat that left Rapallo twice a day, crowded to the gunwales with German, Swiss, and Italian tourists, and it chugged placidly down the coast to Santa Margherita and Portofino while the passengers—more middle-class than anything we know in America—gazed fondly at the *castelli* of the rich that dotted the cliffs, and took endless photographs of them, heaven knows why.

After the little boat stopped briefly at Portofino to pick up more passengers and more cameras, it headed out to the Mediterranean again and then there were no more *castelli.* In fact, there wasn't much of anything to look at except towering cliffs of gray rock. (The Germans took pictures of the gray rock too, which must have been terribly interesting to their friends and relatives when they got home).

Just about this time I began to wonder why I'd come. (I was aboard the craft solely because my children wanted to take a boat ride.) As far as the eye could see, there was nothing but gray rock—no houses, no villages, no anything. Suddenly there was a break in the gray seawall, which could hardly be discerned from a hundred yards away, and presently the little boat slipped into a tiny cove entirely surrounded by massive and terribly unfriendly cliffs. At the foot of the cliffs, clinging to the rocks at the edge of the sea, was the little—well, hell, minuscule—town of San Fruttuoso.

San Fruttuoso came into being around 1100 or 1200 and could hardly have been much smaller then. Today it boasts a tiny, wretchedly poor fishing village, the seven-hundred-year-old convent of San Fruttuoso, now deserted, and the tomb of the Doria family. The Dorias, one of Italy's most famous families of navigators (and now a princely family of great wealth), sprang from Genoa, but because they were a seafaring family they wanted to be buried by the sea and there they are. Like a lot of Italian coastal villages, San Fruttuoso can be approached only from the sea. The mountains, which ring it, severely discourage road building or even path building.

We clambered—the Germans, the Swiss, the Italians, and our small contingent of one American family—up some steep rock steps into a little café to get some coffee. It was terribly crowded at the bar so we went to the end of the room and there, perched on the seven-hundred-year-old walls, was an American television set and darned if it wasn't turned on. It happened to be Easter Sunday, and while we sipped the coffee, we watched a tremendously impressive Easter service, broadcast from Milan.

San Fruttuoso may be cut off from the rest of civilization—I greatly doubt that there is a bathtub in the whole place—but, by gosh, it's got television. It can take its religion—like the rest of us—by remote control. Just push the button. Outside on the walls of the convent are a couple of plaques commemorating disasters that have struck San Fruttuoso. In the early twentieth century, the place was swept by fire, and a couple of the sisters lost their lives saving others. Then came a disastrous flood from the mountain peaks.

And now, I thought, television has struck. The sisters fled in the nick of time. The unfriendly mountains and the narrow aperture of seawall kept the pirates out—but it didn't keep television out. And in large numbers the people of San Fruttuoso are giving up their siesta, a tradition of centuries, to look at it. ■

ARANJUEZ, *SPAIN*

■ "All the good bullfighters have a writer in their *cuadrilla* now. Three *banderilleros* and one writer. Dominguín has Peter Viertel and Ordoñez has me," explained Ernest Hemingway with only the suspicion of laughter in his blue and marvelously candid eyes.

Hemingway and his friend Bill Davis had been following his favorite bullfighter, Antonio Ordoñez, around the bullfight circuit for six weeks, and his face was flaking slightly, the result of much sun, much wine, much laughter and maybe not many baths.

We were lunching in a little inn by a swift brown river. Like all Spanish towns, Aranjuez is aflame with red roses hung on white walls, but it has some distinctions of its very own. It harbors the spring palace of the Spanish kings, the best white asparagus in Spain—we were eating some at the moment—and a little jewel of a bullring which is very old and very beautiful. The town was bursting with *fiesta.* Across the road from us a woman and her pretty daughter sold strawberries packed like a display of red rubies in wicker baskets ornamented with green leaves, and down the road a girl sold that American concoction, Eskimo pies. A man stopped by to sell us a toy fighting cock made of real cock feathers, and another man shined my shoes for ten pesetas, which is three times what he would have charged if there had been no fiesta. Suddenly it occurred to me that I had never been in a Spanish town when there wasn't a fiesta. The Spanish are always celebrating something, at least when I'm there.

"The small ring is better for watching," said Papa Hemingway. "In a big ring a bad fight is just bad. In a small ring the bad things are still bad, but you can see the fear in the bullfighter's face and that's intarrestin'." Thirty or forty years' residence abroad had not curbed or in any way altered Hemingway's Midwestern accent, a sure mark of strong character.

"I had lost all interest in the bulls until this man came along. Antonio, you know, is the son of the bullfighter in *The Sun Also Rises.* He fights in the classic way. There has not been anything like him since Manolete. You'll like him, I think. After the fight, he'll drive us to Granada, where he fights tomorrow." There was the barest hesitation. "If everything goes well, he'll drive us to Granada. First, he must fight the bulls."

As it happened, Ordoñez was not destined to drive us to Granada, but that's getting ahead of the story.

"We have not had any interest in bullfighting in years," said Bill Davis, who has seen (according to Papa) literally thousands of bullfights, "because of what the crowd was demanding of the bullfighters."

It is ever thus. What the crowds demand, they usually get. Shakespeare gave them Gloucester's eyes in *King Lear* and a stageful of dead bodies in most of his plays. Dominguín had been giving the crowd "the telephone." In this spectacular bit of nonsense, when the bull was sufficiently confused, Dominguín leaned one elbow on the bull's forehead and made like he was telephoning a girl. It was very brave and in very lousy taste.

"When Ordoñez fights, the cape moves very slow," said Papa simply, "and it has a little bit of immortality. We will not drive far tonight—only to Manzanares, about two hours—because I do not like to drive far after a fight. You forget the fight."

A few tables away a couple of American girls were staring hard at Papa, who—even in a Spanish town in fiestatime—was pretty picturesque. There was the white beard which was just as famous as Alfred Hitchcock's stomach and much more beautiful and respectable. In addition, Hemingway combed his hair right down over his forehead like the beatniks in Montparnasse. This haircomb was certainly picturesque and it drew many stares, which Papa frankly enjoyed. He was a big lovable ham about being stared at, was Mr. Hemingway.

The American girl leaned forward and in an audible whisper to her companion said, "That's the man who wrote *Of Mice and Men.*"

"She might at least have given me credit for *Tortilla Flat,*" muttered Papa. "Come on—let's go to the fight."

The best bull of the afternoon was Ordoñez's second one, the fourth of the *corrida*—best of many afternoons, said Bill Davis. It was a superb animal, charging straight and fast and without warning.

"A good bullfighter prepares his bull for death and makes him love what he is doing," said Hemingway. Ordoñez prepared the fine beast with loving care, just enough of the cape, just enough of the pic. "Good! Very good!" said Bill Davis of the picador's lancing. "But now he should pull it out." And at the precise moment, the picador pulled out the lance.

A fine *faena* loomed; then an *espontaneo* jumped in the ring and messed things up. An espontaneo is an amateur who has had some experience with bulls and who dives into bullrings—some thing like the nuts who charge out of the stands and slide into second base at ball games—to attract a little attention and maybe a contract. The only other espontaneo I had ever seen—at Seville some years before—had been killed by the bull in just under a minute.

This one did better. He made three passes, pretty good ones, too, teaching the bull a few things he shouldn't know and unlearning some of the careful Ordoñez instruction. But the crowd roared approval. Then the matadors lured the bull away with their capes. The cops landed on the espontaneo, but not before Antonio clapped him on the back and offered to pay his fine. This was fine and generous of him, since any matador would like to murder an espontaneo for messing up his bull.

The last act between a fine bull and a great matador began. The lines of the passes became very simple, very slow. Just as a good painter eliminates and eliminates and eliminates, so a classic matador scorns the rococo trimmings. The bull's charges—one leading into the next one, all part of a master design—have both grandeur and simplicity like the lines of the Parthenon. Cape, man, and bull blend into a single composition that hangs there in air and imprints itself on the retina of the mind like the anguish of an El Greco.

This was one of the moments that the true *aficionado* lives for, suffering through countless bad fights and mediocre fights huddled in the exquisite discomfort that the Spaniards build into their bullrings to test the mettle of the true lovers of the bullfight and to scare away the others. In moments like this—when bull and bullfighter and crowd, too, are caught up in a mutual breathless wonder—the passes get a little bit of immortality.

Disaster struck without warning. Ordoñez was going backwards, which he shouldn't have been doing, and the bull for a split second glimpsed the man (a lesson taught him by the espontaneo) on the ground chopped up and made rough by the hoofs of horses and other bulls which the attendants should have smoothed but didn't—and all these tiny misdemeanors slowed the cape just a fraction of a second too long.

The horn caught Ordoñez in the left cheek of his obscenity and deposited him on the whole obscenity. "We're not going to

Granada tonight," said Papa Hemingway almost before his bullfighter hit the ground.

Ordoñez was on his feet in an instant. The other matadors lured the bull away, as Ordoñez's manager and handlers charged in, trying to pull their bullfighter out of the ring.

"Is he bleeding?" said Bill Davis.

"He's bleeding." The blood was staining the black-and-red trousers in a neat round way.

"Bad luck," muttered Bill Davis.

Ordoñez pulled away from his handlers, limping, holding himself very erect, moving very slowly. The handlers, still pleading, backed out of the ring. The crowd was hushed, respectful. To square his bull, Ordoñez made a slow pass, agonizingly slow. The bull charged, wheeled, and was still—his forefeet well placed and together. Ordoñez sighted down his sword and with his ebbing strength went in over the horn. It was a marvelously clean and beautiful kill, and as his banderilleros carried him from the ring to the waiting ambulance, which took him to the hospital in Madrid, he was awarded both ears and the tail of the brave bull he had killed. ■

TORREMOLINOS, *SPAIN*

■ Five years (six? ten?) before I visited Torremolinos, it was a sleepy little fishing village with all the charming poverty that so entrances visitors from America: bullocks pulling water carts through the streets; fishermen fishing in their adorable little boats, their lights winking through the darkness all night long (a twenty-hour day is tough on the fishermen, but, God, it's picturesque).

Word of all this unbearable charm—the bullocks in the street, the quaint fishermen's houses, the twisted streets—spread throughout Western Europe, bringing rich Swedes, rich Germans, not so many rich French (because they have their own quaint spots to overrun), rich Americans, and rich English. The charm began to be heavily encrusted with money. Property values began to rise, and the charm began to dwindle.

Ten years earlier, you could rent a house there for five dollars a month, they'd tell you. That is, those who had been there ten years before, if you could find any such. In August, 1962, you were more likely to pay $250 a month for something overlooking the sea. The bullocks were fast vanishing, to be replaced by the Mercedes Benz. The fishermen were still out there, their adorable lights winking most of the night, but the price of their delicious fish was rising, and soon, alas, the time would come when they wouldn't have to work all night to earn a living, and the lights would disappear.

In 1960 servants were $8 a month. In 1962 they were $25 a month, and for that they would work only from 7 A.M. until they put away the last dish after dinner. Maybe 11 P.M. Another couple of years and the Abundant Age would really catch up to them, I thought. They'd be demanding a day off, for God's sake, and might be up to $40 a month in wages.

That's the trouble with prosperity; everyone wants to share it. And it was already making things very tough on the people who got to Torremolinos first, when things were so cheap and so quaint and life was difficult only for the poor Spaniards.

When did the charm of Torremolinos begin to dwindle? The answer would depend on when you got there. Last August I thought it was still pretty nice. Our house hung on a cliff overlooking the sea. The sky was blue. The sea was a deep and satisfying green, and it pounded in our ears all night. (What else would you want? Egg in your beer?) But, of course, I was a newcomer and didn't know any better.

"You should have seen it two years ago," the Old Hand told me. (Or five years, or ten years, depending on when he got here.) "That street wasn't there, then." It was a street of shops for tourists. And "That store there," he would tell you indignantly, "with the suede coats and the handbags. Right there was once one of the most beautiful houses on the southern coast. Handhewn beams. Fountains. Most beautifully proportioned rooms. They tore it all down to make that awful shop. The desecration!"

I didn't have the heart to tell him the desecration was his. As I said, I'd just got there; I found it a charming spot. But I supposed it wouldn't be long before I was an Old Hand.

One night I went to a farewell party for a house. It was a beautiful old Spanish house surrounded by a high white wall covered with purple bougainvillea, with an ordered inside court of date palms and reflecting pools. The rooms were magnificently proportioned, high-ceilinged, thick-walled, and cool. And it was going to be torn down for an immense and modern and lucrative hotel. Ah, woe!

Next year I knew I'd be telling a newcomer, "You should have seen the house that stood where that hotel is! Most beautiful gardens! Hand-hewn beams! And they tore it all down to make that awful hotel! It's a desecration." ■

TANGIER, *MOROCCO*

■ In the days when Tangier was a free port, you could scarcely push your way through the Zaco Chico at 4 A.M. for the money-changers and smugglers and black marketeers. When I was there last year, the only recent large crowd in the Zaco Chico had been caused when Anthony Quinn sat down for a cup of mint tea and almost caused a riot.

I asked Paul Bowles, the novelist who has lived there for many years and written about Tangier with love and authority, whether Tangier was indeed, as they said, dead.

"I suppose it is," he said sadly. "People are still coming here, but with different ambitions, different expectations. There's no longer any element of a colony."

The money-changers had left, but now the beats, from everywhere, were pouring in because they'd heard they could smoke pot and be left alone. "The *Village Voice* runs ads for cheap houses in the Arab quarter. They come here to paint and write. Most of them don't make out here because it takes more perseverance than they possess," he said wryly.

The American beats were coming on Yugoslav freighters where the fare was $110, the cheapest way—short of swimming—you could get across the Atlantic. Well, the beats ("I call them the Eighth Street Knicks," said Bowles. "The beats no longer exist.")

arrive, and they are not a hundred feet from the Yugoslav freighter before they are loaded down with pot (or kif or marijuana or tea or whatever name you like to give it) and paying six times what it's worth.

Tangier has an international reputation as a place to go to pot in, but then you run into someone like Bowles. Bowles has not only not gone to pot, but he gets enormous amounts of excellent writing done, more than he would get done anywhere else.

"Tangier doesn't make a man disintegrate," said Bowles, "but it does attract people who are going to disintegrate anyway. Life is so easy here, so cheap, and the climate is so marvelous. If you're going to go to hell, you can do it here more pleasantly than in Greenwich Village."

Kif is embedded in Arab culture as alcohol is in Judaeo-Christian culture, and in Tangier the two meet—the Christian alcohol drinker and the Moslem smokers of kif—and exchange substances. Neither is very good for the other.

"This is the beginning of the herbal world that stretches from Africa to the Far East," my friend William told me as we padded through the native quarter, which was dark and silent and closed in. The houses on the narrow streets were barred and shuttered, and so, in a way, were the people who lived in them.

We stopped at a door, and William banged on it hard. "Peter! Open up! Open up!"

Minutes went by and he kept banging, and presently Peter opened up. He was an American, dressed in dirty white canvas pants and a shirt and sandals, and he wore a thin rim of beard.

"Hello," he said without warmth or coolness, neither inviting nor rejecting us. It's symptomatic of the kif smoker that he can be truly neutral, truly removed from external passions, wrapped up in his interior visions. Peter was, as they say, stoned.

"Can we come in?" asked William.

"Sure," said Peter. There was again neither invitation nor rejection. He truly didn't care whether we did or we didn't.

We went into the cool Arab house with its tiles and arches that Peter was renting for $30 a month, and sat on a rug on the floor because there was no place else to sit. On a crate in the center of the room was a typewriter, and scattered about one end of the room were letters, papers, pocket books.

Peter pulled out a cigarette made of kif and lit it and passed it around. Everyone except me smoked it, me wanting to keep my perceptions clear and sharp, and kif is not kind to anterior perceptions.

"Where's Robert?" asked William.

There was a tremendously long pause. "He's around," said Peter finally, as if he had examined all the possibilities and that was the only way to suggest where Robert was. There's a tremendous desultory quality about kif-laden conversation that is hard to suggest in print.

Presently Peter's wife came in, a rounded, lovely girl with dreamy eyes. She was stoned, too.

"Could we see the house?" I asked.

She smiled her dreamy smile and led me around without a word. We went out on the roof under the stars; we looked at the sleeping children, two little girls, asleep on a mat under a blue light. (There wasn't a stick of furniture in the whole house.) Then we went back to the room where the kif smokers were having another stick and talking their desultory talk.

Peter is a writer, and presently he showed us his latest writing: "Out of the vortex, the entrails spilling red, stars like diadems exploded, purple, green, curving and tearing the eyeballs like vomit into a dissonance like distant symphonies, wah wah wah, inchoate and undulant."

That's kif writing, like kif talk, full of sounds and smells and visions and incoherence. There's a whole literature of it being turned out on egg crates in Los Angeles and Greenwich Village and the Arab quarter of Tangier, and being unread everywhere.

Soon we were out on the narrow, twisting streets again. "He's smoking three hundred pipes a day, staying stoned like that all day, every day," said William, who smokes quite a lot of kif himself.

We went to a bar in the European sector where the European and American lushes hang out. The lushes were stoned, too, but on the Judaeo-Christian substance of alcohol. Aggressive, noisy, gregarious, where the kif smoker is dreamy, pliant, ungregarious, totally self-sufficient. The aggressive ones we view with amused tolerance in our country. The dreamy ones we throw in jail. It's a puzzlement, as Yul Brynner said in *The King and I.*

Bowles has written that the literature, the music and much of the architecture of the Moslem world have been evolved with marijuana-directed appreciation in mind.

"In wintertime, a family will often have a hashish evening," he says. "Father, mother, children and relatives shut themselves in, eat the [marijuana] jam prepared by the womenfolk of the household, and enjoy several hours of stories, song, dance, and laughter in complete intimacy. 'To hear this music you must have kif first,' you are sometimes told. Or: 'This is a kif room. Everything in it must be looked at through kif.' The typical kif story is an endless, proliferated tale of intrigue and fantasy in which the unexpected turns of the narrative line play a much more important part than the development of character or plot.' "

Just like television. The expression on the addict's face is the same: jaws slack, eyeballs dull, idiot look. ■

■ It was Paul Bowles who took me to Sidi Kacem (which is the name of a saint, the name of the place where he's buried and the name of the fiesta held once a year in his honor), 18 miles outside Tangier in a huge grove of ancient olive trees bordering one of the finest beaches on the Atlantic Ocean. It was about 10:30 P.M. when we got there, and the main thoroughfare was already jammed with Berbers who had come down from the hills with their donkeys and horses and children for the revelry.

The main thoroughfare was lined with what they called cafés, improvised of sweet-smelling fir branches, and you could sit on the ground and watch the dancers in their infinitely seductive arm and hip movements, which are, to Western eyes, infinitely monotonous. I watched three of these dancers at three cafés before I found out they were not girls but boys, beautifully trained in the arts of dancing and homosexuality. (Twelve is the best age, and at thirteen you're already on the way out and down.)

A line of outdoor bazaars sold (or rather didn't sell, since I saw no one buying) figs and Arab candy (huge mounds of a poisonous red-and-white stuff) and sweet muffins, which were delicious.

A bit farther on there was gambling, which was fairly mild. Six playing cards were tacked to a table. You put your money (a franc was a big bet) on the card of your choice, and the dealer threw dice. If it came up your number, you won. I played three times and won three times, and quit, absolutely convinced that this was the only gambling joint I ever saw in which the house had rigged odds against itself.

Next to the gambling, a holy man was selling teeth, of which he had a large and tidy mound. When he saw me taking notes, he threatened to turn me into stone.

About 2 A.M. the drums took on a new and wilder and higher note, and Bowles, an expert in these matters, said to me, "Now it begins. They're getting into a trance."

We watched the dancers, bobbing and weaving and jerking, both men and women, in convulsive movements of agony or ecstasy, which, when you come right down to it, are the same thing.

"They can keep it up for as long as twenty hours. They're possessed—not, they think, by devils but by God."

Just the same, a relative would occasionally step into the mob and drag off a screaming, bobbing woman and tell her to stop making a fool of herself, she's upsetting Mother. I asked Bowles why, if they're possessed by God, anyone should want to stop it.

He shrugged. "These dances are pre-Moslem. They are ashamed of this primitivism."

At 4:30 dawn was breaking. The rhaatas (the rhaata is a sort of Arab clarinet) were still wailing, but there were fewer of them. Dawn everywhere has its own smell, its own feeling of a beginning and ending. As the sky brightened, the Berbers headed, like lemmings, toward the sea, thousands of them coming over the immense dunes, outlined in black against the roseate sky like the last scene in *La Dolce Vita.* It was an immense white beach, a thousand feet wide, and the Berbers came right down to the edge and stared at the waves. The bolder ones went swimming in the cold water. The young boys started a soccer game on the white sand.

It was six in the morning when we started back. The main thoroughfare was now almost empty, the fig sellers still not selling any figs. But there was a single, silent crowd gathered in the center of it, listening in rapt silence (that any actor would have loved) to an Arab storyteller. I asked the Moroccan artist, Ahmed Yacoubi, what story he was telling.

"The story of Moses coming out of Egypt," said Yacoubi.

"A strange story for a Moslem to be telling," I said.

"Why? It's a good story," said Yacoubi. ■

LETICIA, *COLOMBIA*

■ Upon my first glimpse of the Amazon River, four Indians were pushing a dead racehorse into it. The animal, which had been valued at $5,000, slid slowly off the bank, and within one foot of the shore it was totally submerged. The Amazon gets awfully deep awfully quick.

Considering its great depth—even at Leticia, 2,000 miles from the Atlantic, the river is about a hundred feet deep—and two-mile width, the current is very strong—around ten miles an hour—which makes it one of the world's most efficient disposal units. People who fall into the Amazon, they will tell you in the local saloons, don't even come up once. They just disappear. Bodies are almost never recovered from the river even when a search is started immediately.

Just what happens when the waters close over is a matter of intense speculation but no real knowledge. The water is muddy, and witnesses right on top of the scene can't see below the surface. There are the deadly little piranhas down there and snakes and alligators, and huge catfish that are supposedly man-eaters though that is very much a matter of conjecture, too. Or maybe the current just swirls people to the bottom. Nobody knows what happens to people or racehorses except they disappear.

What was the racehorse doing there in the first place? Leticia is a small river town of about 3,000. By upper-Amazon standards, that makes it a huge metropolis, but still you don't see racehorses there very often. This one was being flown from Montevideo to Bogotá. Since the field at Bogotá closed at sunset, the airplane put in at Leticia for the night. Some time during the night the horse slashed itself on barbed wire and bled to death. A terrible end for a fine animal and a rather gruesome introduction to a great river.

But—come to think of it—appropriate. The Amazon has a strong streak of grue in its otherwise splendid makeup. Along its banks live some of the world's least friendly Indians, some of the world's most deadly snakes like the fer de lance and the bushmaster, to say nothing of the world's largest snake, the anaconda, and hordes of poisonous insects.

But, after making allowances for these minor discomforts, the river has great charm. Life along the great rivers—the Nile, the Amazon, the Mississippi—has great points in common. Life moves slowly, very slowly. The women move with a stately grace, and after a few days of the steamy climate you find your own walk gets pretty stately, too. The river is dotted with tiny communities whose people remind me strongly of the Cajuns at the mouth of the Mississippi. Like the Cajuns, everyone in town is a blood relative of everyone else. Like the Cajuns, they're friendly, laughing people, and also like the Cajuns, their life centers around their boats.

Most of the little towns are built on stilts to protect them from the river, which the stilts don't always do. (The Amazon when it gets in a nasty mood can rise thirty feet, a tremendous rise for so broad a river.)

Leticia, I ought to explain, is at the confluence of three countries. A fifteen-minute walk through the woods puts you into Brazil, where you encounter not only different currency but a different language (Portuguese). Across the river is Peru.

Even in Leticia you run into that sort of snobbery we have at home for anything imported from France or Italy. For instance, if you buy some of the local whiskey, the bartender will tell you with great pride, "It's from Peru." That just means it's from across the river, but it's supposed to give the booze some magical quality.

I was with the cast and crew of *Zoo Parade*, which was photographing a series of television shows on the animals and reptiles and fish of the upper Amazon region. It was not only a long way from home for me but a long way from home for them. *Zoo Parade*, after all, had started in May, 1949, as a local Chicago show with a couple of live cameras, a one-page script consisting largely of cues reading "Go to next" and ad-lib questions and answers between Marlin Perkins and a reporter named Jim Hurlbut.

It was a very pleasant, very informal, very local show designed simply to bring the zoo to the homes of children whose parents were too lazy to take them to the zoo. Seven and a half years later, *Zoo Parade* was 2,000 miles up the Amazon, seeking new sights for its viewers, largely because it had run through most of the zoos in the country and each year sent it farther and farther in search of new material.

"Before long," I told Mr. Perkins, "you guys are going to be looking for snakes on the moon."

Marlin Perkins, the curator of the Lincoln Park Zoo in Chicago and star of *Zoo Parade*, was essentially a reptile man, and he handled snakes with the tenderness most men reserve for their wives or perhaps other men's wives. With Mr. Perkins, Ross Allen, another renowned snake catcher, whose body was covered with crosshatches left by snakes which resented his interest in their welfare, and Mrs. Allen, no mean snake catcher herself, we pushed off in a little aluminum boat one night on the starlit Amazon, which was black as ink and broad and still and terribly empty.

Unlike the jungles of Africa, where the lions and hyenas liven the night with a splendid chorus, our night noises were relatively small noises—the chatter of the barking tree frog (which can make a hell of a racket for so small an animal), the sudden squawk of birds disturbed by snakes, even the sharp *huh* of the fresh water porpoises as they came up to breathe. And sometimes for minutes there was utter silence when you could hear your own breathing.

When you hunt at night, you turn off the main river body into the little lakes which the Amazon creates behind its banks. At the edge of the lakes you plunge right into the trees. When the water is high, there are water trails through these trees for hundreds of miles. The trees rise straight out of the water, some of them forty feet around and a hundred feet high, creating a sort of arboreal cathedral. In the branches and thick ropelike vines which brush against your face are the snakes.

You hunt snakes at night with a miner's lamp fastened to your forehead. It casts a strong beam in which a snake's eyes gleam red as rubies, a spider's as green as emeralds, an alligator's a sort of fiery orange. When you spot the proper gleam, you head straight to it, remaining quiet as a mouse. The lamp stares at the snake and the snake stares back. When an animal doesn't know what to do, it does nothing. By the time you get close you can determine whether it's a poisonous snake, in which case you take it with a snake stick, which keeps the mouth at a good safe distance, or nonvenomous, in which case you just reach in and grab it with your hands.

It was Marlin Perkins who did all those things. On snake hunts, I'm strictly an observer.

In their constantly widening quest for new material, *Zoo Parade* had, the year before, gone to British East Africa to photograph the lions, leopards, elephants, rhinos and the grazing animals such as the antelopes and zebras of the great plains. The same crew found the problems on the upper Amazon immeasurably more difficult.

Next to an anaconda, the African animals are a bunch of hams.

They parade around the wide plains or relatively open forest glades in broad sunshine like movie stars, and with today's long lenses it's no great problem to take infinitely detailed closeups. Where we were, though, the animals and reptiles lie in a jungle far denser than that of Africa, mostly in deep gloom. In fact, many of the little furred animals or birds or reptiles would die if you left them in the scorching sun for more than a minute or two. Only mad dogs and Americans go out in the Amazon sun.

Many of the most interesting of the Amazon fauna are the fishes and reptiles and mammals which lie under the muddy waters of the river completely out of the range of the cameras. It's a shame you can't photograph their capture, because reptile hunts are fairer contests between man and animal than most hunts. It's the hunter's wits and eyes and hands pitted against the animal's instincts and eyes and fangs and claws. In every regard except wits, theirs are sharper than ours. The age-old joy of hunting is there reduced to its most primitive level. Take 'em alive and take 'em with your own hands. Frankly, I consider this form of hunting a kind of insanity, but those people it afflicts get an enormous satisfaction from it.

The madness is likely to strike anyone. Jim Hurlbut and I were coming home one evening from the little Brazilian town of Esperanza, a few miles downstream from Leticia, where we had been testing the Brazilian beer which was both strong and delicious. Our boat was putt-putting upstream against the strong Amazon current in an orange sunset which suddenly outlined a snake swimming the other way.

His hunting instincts inflamed, conceivably by the beer, Hurlbut reached out and hauled in the snake and instantly had eleven feet of bitterly protesting green racer wrapped around his neck. A green racer isn't venomous—something Hurlbut didn't find out till later—but that doesn't mean it hasn't got fangs. It has, and it sank them into Jim's wrists with great enthusiasm. Between us we stuffed the snake into a plastic shopping bag, which my housekeeper had purchased for other purposes, and bore the beast home, angry but alive. Hurlbut's glow of triumph was a fine thing to see. ■

■ The airplane came in only once a week, bringing people and supplies and also—theoretically—mail from Bogotá. But one day they forgot the mail. I suppose the pilots had other things on their minds.

The way I reconstruct this scene, it went something like this. These two pilots, whom I promptly dubbed Orville and Wilbur after getting a glimpse of what they were flying, are pelting along at 8,500 feet, and Wilbur says, "Orville, what did you do with the mail?"

And Orville says, "I didn't take the mail. I thought you took the mail. It was lying there on the counter next to you."

And Wilbur says, "Well, it's still lying there, then. Aaah, well, we'll be back next week."

Neither snow nor sleet nor gloom of night—but only occasional lapses of memory—will keep these couriers from the swift completion of their appointed rounds, I kept saying. Postponing everything to *mañana*, which is a tomorrow that never comes, is a well-known characteristic of Spanish-speaking peoples, and one they resent being accused of, but that incident of the mail is as pure an example of it as I know.

There were some other notable examples around Leticia. One was a large Italian freighter named the *Cucutah*, which rested at anchor just at the foot of the hill outside our hotel. It had been resting there for eight years, slowly rusting away. Its cargo of asphalt had been loaded wrong, which made unloading difficult. So for eight years the problem of unloading had been discussed from all angles until the ship ceased to be operable. At the time I was there, the ship was slated for the scrap heap in Germany, but just when it would get there was a moot point. It was supposed to have started the 2,000-mile jaunt upriver under tow before I left, but it was still sitting there, awaiting another *mañana*. ■

■ One day I found myself sitting cross-legged on a split-bamboo floor in a large palm-thatched hut on the Atacuari River in Peru, playing chess with a missionary named Herbert Grings.

My purpose in being up the Atacuari, a tributary of the Amazon and quite a large river in its own right, was to look for Indians, not to play chess. There had been reports of a tribe of Yagua Indians in that area, but on the Amazon such reports are largely conjecture, and if you want to find out the truth, you simply have to go look for yourself. So, in an aluminum boat powered by a 30-horsepower outboard, a couple of us went up the broiling Amazon a hundred miles, took a sharp right turn and went another hundred miles up the Atacuari to find out, firstly, if the Indians were there and, secondly, if their costumes and customs and dances and pets and handiwork were interesting enough to justify sending a camera crew up there to photograph them.

The Indians weren't there. Señor Aguirre, a plantation owner who is *patrón* of these particular Indians, told us regretfully that his Indians were on a two-day march into the jungle, cutting chicle. The patrón operated what amounted to a company store. That is, the Indians bought, say, a shotgun from him and then worked a year for him to pay it off, but, as the missionary explained, if it weren't for the patrón system, the Indians would never get a shotgun.

It was fortunate for me that the missionary, Mr. Grings, a white-goateed man, tough as wire, had been missionarying through Africa and South America for thirty years, living with the wildest tribes on both continents, and it was only occasionally he ran into someone who could play chess. (He won.)

The upper Amazon teems with missionaries, all of them marvelously resourceful fellows. Along with bringing the word of God, they must know how to take an Evinrude apart, heal the sick, teach the children, rescue the flooded, speak two or three languages and half a dozen Indian dialects, and do about a million other things only dimly related to the Gospel.

Grings was just passing through this little stretch of river in pursuit of the same Indians we were seeking. The next day he loaded his pack on his back and plunged inland on foot—there is no other way to travel in that area—through roadless and almost trackless jungle to find his Indians. If I wanted to come along, he said, I'd have to take my shoes off; otherwise, I'd slip and fall in the cataracts that lay ahead.

I told him I didn't want to see the Indians that badly. He wanted them for God. I just wanted them for color television and —well, frankly, there weren't—and still aren't—enough color sets out yet.

The traveler, I always say, should not only broaden his knowledge of other cultures but should scatter a little of his own in the countries he visits. I decided to help Eloisa, a waitress at the hotel, with her English. It all started when Eloisa, in pursuit of learning, asked Jim Hurlbut and myself whether *muchas gracias, en inglés,* was not "many thanks"—or, as she expressed it, "money tonks."

We told her this was archaic English; the proper translation of *muchas gracias* was "thanks a million." As Eloisa said it, it came out "Tonks a meellion," but at least she was headed in the right direction. After that, her education progressed by leaps and bounds. We taught her that the proper English for *Vámonos* was "Let's blow this joint" (Les blow dees join') and that the proper way to say *Es muy bueno* was "It's real gone" or "Just crazy, man, crazy."

Like all newcomers adrift in a foreign language, she had occasional trouble with her genders, and we had to remind her constantly that a "cool cat" was a *caballero,* not a *dama* (slick chick, of course, or "sleek cheek," which is the way she said it and which I think is even better). She was not at all *estúpida* (square); she was very *inteligente* (hip). And I'm sorry we weren't there long enough to move on to some of the more advanced English constructions like "That's the way the cookie crumbles," which I planned to teach her as the proper translation for *Que será será.*

When she wasn't studying her English, Eloisa was reading a *novela,* or comic book. It wasn't like our comic books in that it was about four inches thick and in Spanish, but in all other regards—the too-handsome and muscular men, the wasp-waisted full-breasted women—it could have been interchangeable with the junk that festoons all our candy and stationery stores. The spread of the comic book is an international blight. ■

BUENOS AIRES

■ Somebody remarked very wisely about Argentina's lovely metropolis that it resembles a city which has just emerged from an enemy occupation. It's beautiful, modern, European, bustling, cosmopolitan—but just a little down at the heels. The buildings are grimy, there are holes in the streets (while I was there a taxi fell through a hole, severely injuring the occupants) and gaps in the sidewalks. People will tear down a building, intending to build another one in its place, run out of money, and just go away—leaving a hole that resembles bomb damage in London. But what a lovely, bustling, alive place it is. You sit in the sidewalk cafés and watch the people marching briskly by (the pace is like New York's), chattering Italian, English, German, French—as well as Spanish. Marvelous city. I felt very much at home there. Very alive. Full of beans. (This euphoria, I'm told by the older hands, lasts about a week; then one begins to see the holes in the cement.)

Argentina is the Texas of South America. And not simply because of all the cows. The Argentines think Buenos Aires is the greatest city in the world. Their frontier mountains are the highest, their pampas are the widest and their women the most beautiful. Their pride is overwhelming. *Dignidad* (dignity) is immensely important all over Latin America, but the Argentine preoccupation with dignidad is extravagant even by Latin-American standards. The Mexicans, who hate the Argentines—the loathing is mutual—have a joke which goes, "The way to get rich is to buy Argentina for what it's worth and sell it for what they think it's worth."

"I don't know whether it's more hazardous to travel by foot

or by car," a friend told me in Buenos Aires. Both are extremely dangerous in B.A., not because the Argentines are bad drivers exactly, but because temperamentally they are very different from Anglo-Saxons. Just as we'll never understand their politics, we are not likely to understand their driving. Driving is not only a means of transportation, as it is in the United States, but much more than that; it's a game, a sport, a test of one's manhood, one's courage.

About the only word of advice I can give you timid Anglo-Saxons is, for heaven's sake, be careful crossing streets. But how? Buenos Aires' streets, like those in Paris, are frequently the junctions of three streets. Since the Argentines have not yet been cursed with one-way traffic, that means cars are bearing down on you from six different angles. And there are no traffic lights. (There are only about six traffic lights in all of Buenos Aires, which is the eighth-largest city in the world.) Suppose Columbus Circle had no traffic lights and all the streets and avenues converging were two-way streets. It's 5:30 in the afternoon and you are a pedestrian trying to cross from Eighth Avenue right across the center of the circle to Central Park.

I defy anyone to look in six directions at once. There was an intersection near my hotel that I tried to cross for twelve minutes. I'd venture out, scuttle back, venture out, scuttle back. I'd just about resigned myself to never getting across that street, when I saw a child of six get across. How did he do it? He just walked firmly out there in that maelstrom, chin up, eyes scowling, and defied them to run him over. There was a screeching of rubber against cement, a few Latin curses, but he made it. Anyhow, if that little child did it, I had to try. And I made it, too!

I asked a man at the foreign office about how cars fight their way through these triple intersections. He took me for a drive to show me how it was done. You plunge into an intersection; another car on the intersecting street plunges right at you. Someone has to give way. Both cars jam right at each other. At the last moment the other car slams on his brakes and you slip triumphantly through.

"The front of his car dipped," said my friend, still flushed with his victory. "That means he had his foot on the brake a little bit. His nerve was cracking."

You must realize that these contests of will, of nerve, of sheer bravado, are not necessarily just between two drivers. On the bigger intersections a man has to face down not merely one driver, but maybe six different drivers.

And the cars they're driving are positively antique. If you like old cars, spend five minutes on a busy street corner in Buenos Aires and you will swoon with rapture. You will see old Chevrolets the like of which cannot be found anywhere outside or inside the Smithsonian Institution. You will see Reos, you will see Marmons, you will see Graham-Paiges. Now, I ask you, when was the last time you saw a Graham-Paige in full possession of its faculties tearing—well, tottering—down a road?

An American told me that the Argentines must be the world's greatest mechanics to keep these wrecks running. An Argentine told me you see 1923 Fords, their brass radiators gleaming, their canvas tops spotless and without holes, purring along with that special clicking sound the old cars had and the new cars haven't. However, if you think you can go down and start a collection of vintage cars to rival James Melton's, forget it, unless your name is Henry Ford.

Those battered but durable old wrecks are still terribly, terribly valuable. Anything that runs, the oldest of Fords, will still bring $2,500 in the open market. New cars in these inflation-ridden countries are out of sight. I saw an ad in Buenos Aires for a new Chevrolet Impala—asking price $25,000. The seller probably got it, too, although that was a little high. You can buy a nice Chevrolet or a Ford for as little as $15,000; a compact goes for $7,500. If a Detroit car brings in that kind of dough, what, you may well ask, do Rolls-Royces sell for under that wacky economy? Well, a Rolls was auctioned off for $150,000 not long ago. The rich there are very, very rich and the middle class can't afford cars.

The Kaiser car, which was such a flop in our country, is a big hit in Argentina. Kaiser took his old tools and dies out of Willow Run and moved them down to Córdoba, where his factory is now one of the greatest money-makers in the world. It's now the biggest single manufacturer in Argentina, with a current annual volume of $100 million.

The manager of the plant, James McCloud, estimates that the current average age of cars on Argentine roads is fifteen to twenty years. That's the average. McCloud feels there is a need for at least a million cars in Argentina. In the meantime, the old ones will have to do—and at simply getting you there, they do fine. You hail a cab, an ancient but proud vehicle creeps up, and you sink into leather cushions and give the address. Then you start noticing things.

The first thing you notice is that the seats are very comfortable. The second is that the roof is comfortably high, that you have enough legroom, and that the seats are off the floor. But, of course, it's a 1934 Cadillac. Of course, the seats are a little worn, the windows may be cracked, but it gets you there, which is more than some of the new cars do. An employee of our Embassy in Buenos Aires told me of his spanking-new American car brought in from the United States, whose make shall be nameless. In the first 200 miles the driveshaft broke and he's waited five months for the company to send him a new motor. He's very bitter about new American cars and is shopping around for an old American car—the older, the better. I found a beauty—a Durant, I think it was—made in 1922: leather seats, beautiful canvas top, ran like a dream. But I couldn't afford it. The owner wanted $3,000. ■

■ I visited one of the shantytowns of Buenos Aires. Everyone visits them, and everyone comes away muttering, "Something must be done."

They are much like our own Hoovervilles of the Depression. The one I visited (there are dozens in Buenos Aires holding maybe 400,000 people) is, its inhabitants told me wryly, the oldest in the city. You get to it through the beautiful and rich northern suburbs, driving past Palermo Park, certainly one of the world's great parks, down an avenue whose mansions remind you of those on the Avenue Foch in Paris. Then you turn left two blocks and there is Misery Town, an enormous city block surrounded by a concrete fence like a walled castle of old. There are occasional breaks in the cement, and at each of these, faces brown, sullen, and suspicious.

At one, a little girl of maybe five stood eating a peach and clutching a peso. I asked her if she'd summon the leader. You don't get very far unless you talk to the leader, generally the oldest inhabitant, who is offically designated to cope with the police who occasionally raid the place, as well as fend off other nuisances. The little girl vanished and presently reappeared with the leader, a burly, hearty, gentle fellow who looked like Anthony Quinn. "Come in," he said. Inside the cement fence it was a rabbit warren. Dirt paths darted off in all directions just wide enough for one or two people.

Each shanty had a little yard eight or ten feet square. The shanties had been constructed with monstrous ingenuity of wood or tin or tar paper or beaverboard by the inhabitants, who live rent free because the government is ashamed to evict them. Inside the huts there were plants on the wall and pictures of the Virgin Mary and birds chirping in cages. It was lunchtime and a family of six was seated around a tiny table on which were wine and bread and cheese and fruit, the classic lunch the world over.

"Everyone here works," said the leader. (This is not true in other parts of Latin America, but in Argentina there is a labor shortage.) "The average wage is a hundred and fifteen pesos a day [roughly a dollar-and-a-half], up to five thousand a month [roughly $62]."

"I would like to visit some of the houses," I said.

The leader shook his head. "The men are at work. They don't like their womenfolk to see men while they are away."

Instead he took me to his house, which he explained was better than most because it had two rooms and a shower (he laid the pipe from the city water system). He had lived there ten years.

"I came from the camps," he said (the "camps" are the ranches), "because the wages are better in the city. If I could get the same wages, I would go back to the camps." He exercised racehorses at the racetrack nearby for a living.

"What do you do for amusement?" I asked.

"If I took a drink," he said, "we wouldn't eat. If we went to the cinema, the children wouldn't have shoes."

What did the children do for amusement?

"There are playgrounds in the parks and swimming pools," said the leader. "Perón built them. I was a Peronista and I still am. Life was better under Perón."

We walked down the paths, peering into yards, into a barbershop with its one stool, the cement floor cleanly swept and flower boxes on the wall. We met a tiny, laughing blond girl about five years old who insisted we see her house and took us there by the hand.

"Some well-dressed gentlemen have come to visit us," she told her mother.

The mother told us she had come from Paraguay when her husband—a bachelor of arts, she said proudly—had died. She had brought her eight children, ranging in age from three to twenty-eight, to Buenos Aires. There was one fairly large room with three beds in which the nine of them slept.

"There's nothing in Paraguay," said the women. "No jobs. No money. No food."

"There must be some good things?" I asked the leader.

"The friendship," he said instantly. "If you get sick everyone takes care of you."

At the corner of the shantytown was a grocery store which sold bread and wine and olive oil to the 2,000 people of the block. The proprietor, a short round man, told me he had been there eighteen years since the squatters rushed in.

"I had a little cart and I sold bread. Now I have this. I take in a hundred thousand pesos [$1,250] a month, of which twenty thousand [$250] is profit." Not bad, considering he lives there rent free with free electricity and water from the city. "These are good people," he said.

"Wouldn't you like to get out of here?" I asked.

"Of course," the man said. "The bank is building houses and I have been on the list for ten years." He laughed wryly. "But the people rushed in and sat down in those houses and the government can't get them out." ■

■ On a visit to the Zemborain *estancia* on the pampas, one of the oldest in the Argentine, I sat in a room that was chalk-white with black beams, beautifully proportioned as are all Spanish rooms. Around the walls hung paintings of the family ancestors—grandfather, great-grandfather, great-great-grandfather, great-great-great-grandfather.

A dozen children, an assorted mixture of cousins and brothers and sisters, came in carrying a wooden cage with two small birds in it, chattering like bluejays. They presented brown cheeks for me to kiss, assuming, I suppose, that I was some kind of cousin since everyone was.

"We let a man hunt on our property," explained the mother of three of the children. "In return, he gave the children the birds." The children showed off their birds and then flew off like a flock of starlings to the horses which were placidly chomping the lawn. The horses wore the Argentine saddle—sheepskin with the wool still on it, over layers and layers of leather and wool, very comfortable for both horse and rider.

The children scrambled on (children here ride without stirrups and scramble is the only word for the way they get on a horse) and disappeared into a flock of eucalyptus, whooping. "They run wild all day," said their mother. "Here they are safe. Nothing can hurt them. The workers have been with the family thirty or forty years."

The idea that strangers are an ever-present danger is one of the peculiarities of the Argentine and helps explain the tremendous drawing together of family, standing together against, as it were, a hostile world. Estancias are constantly being broken up into smaller units as they pass down from father to sons and daughters. But they stay in the family. The Zemborain estancia is one of the smaller ones, only 10,000 acres. (Some Argentine estancias are 200,000 acres, 350 square miles.)

"The children love it here," said their mother. "In the wintertime they go to school in Buenos Aires where we live. But even in winter, we come here every weekend because there is nothing for the children to do in Buenos Aires except go to the cinema."

We drove to a different house, that of another cousin, all part of the same estancia, for luncheon. For fifteen minutes we drove across the open pampas, the sea of grass—then brown under the hot February sun—past herds of Black Angus steers. "My father was the first to introduce the Black Angus to Argentina," said Mrs. de Torres.

A double row of towering eucalyptus trees threw the driveway in deep shade against the hot sun. Behind the eucalyptus stretched rows and rows of tall privet which join their branches thirty feet up, forming a little natural cathedral. Near the house were a magnolia tree with its shining green leaves, forty feet high, and a ceibo tree which grows the red ceibo flower, the national flower of Argentina. The house was guarded by two stone lions and on the gate was a sign: RUE DE BANDALIDA.

"My grandfather had a street named after him in Paris," said Mrs. de Torres. "The boys got one of the street signs and put it on the gate." In the nineties, the owners all lived in Paris on the profits from the estancia and came home only once in a while. Some of them still do, but not so many. In the patio were a dozen more grown-up cousins and aunts and uncles, and scattered around the lawn a dozen or so more children. The talk flowed on in English, in Spanish, in French, and now and then in German—the Argentines being great linguists.

After lunch, they showed me the stable. A gaucho in his *bombachas,* the traditional baggy pants falling over soft leather boots, with his flat round hat and trim jacket, was saddling horses and some little Argentine ponies for the children. The bridles were made of untanned leather, beaten and worked until they were hard as wood.

"They never rot," explained one of the cousins, Michel Ganay, who is half French and half Argentine.

The gaucho's horse had seven layers of leather and wool and felt on it. Across it hung the *boleadoras,* the two lead balls covered with hide, attached to a rawhide rope, which the gauchos use for hunting. The lasso was of rawhide, harder to throw and stiffer than the nylon ropes our own cowboys used, but they last forever.

Later, we inspected the pedigreed Black Angus with their short legs and their pleading baby faces.

"These have been an experiment," said Ganay. "I've been crossing Black Angus with Frisian heifers. I get two calves instead of one and they grow very fast. Within nine months and fifteen days after they are born they weigh as much as their mother." He shrugged. "Mostly the Argentines don't like experiment. They like to leave everything as God made it."

A nine-year-old boy on horseback, son of the *cabañero* who tended the blooded cattle, was driving the Angus out of one pen into another, helping his father proudly.

"They go to school on horseback," explained Ganay. "Four or five little ones on one horse. You go to school and there are twenty-five horses tethered there."

One of his own children scrambled on a horse and galloped off to the swimming pool where he jumped off and dove into the water. The horse started to graze peacefully.

"They leave the horses all over the place," said his father. "They run off and forget a horse sometimes as much as two, three days." Like an American child, I thought, littering the lawn with bicycles.

One of the mothers spoke up: "I think this must be like the life they led in your South before the Civil War." ■

RIO DE JANEIRO

■ Crossing streets in the beautiful city of Rio ought to have been less hazardous than it was in Buenos Aires; Rio was full of traffic lights. But who paid attention to traffic lights? The wildest drivers in Rio last year drove the *lataçãos,* which are little buses. The lataçāo drivers liked to fill up their buses and then drive hell-bent for election to the end of the line, stopping for nothing—passengers, traffic cops, traffic lights, small children.

There was a police crackdown in process against these lunatics while I was there, and the latação drivers got so angry at being arrested that they were threatening to strike. Police Chief Segadas Viana protested that his men were not being especially severe. In fact, the cops were arresting bus drivers only if they committed nine violations of the traffic rules in one trip. If a bus driver committed nine violations, he was hustled off to police headquarters where, among other things, his eyesight and his mental health were tested.

Brazilian teen-agers had—and may still have—their own lighthearted game on the roads—a form of Russian roulette. Along about one in the morning, with a few drinks under their belts, they would steal cars and then race them as fast as they would go through intersections. If another teen-ager happened to be playing the same game at the same intersection at the same time —well, they both lost. ■

■ After seeing one of the shantytowns that are the Buenos Aires slums, I was interested in visiting one of the *favelas* of Rio de Janeiro. So I took a walk up the steep stone steps of the particular favela that was once photographed by *Life,* which ran in a perfect crescent up a steep hill, the blue and pink and white shanties festooning the hill like lanterns. They were made of wood and tin and sometimes cardboard, and the rooms were tiny, but a cool breeze swept in from the blue sea below, and there was a clear smell of salt and fresh laundry in the air. A swarm of brown children scampered up and down the steep steps like goats.

A favela dweller named João Pereira de Oliveira took me in hand and showed me his place which he had built ten years before with his own hands and where he was living with his wife Joanna and their three children, two of whom had been born there. There was a tiny room with a table and chairs, a cage full of canaries hanging from the ceiling, a tiny bedroom with one double bed (in which, I guess, everyone slept), a little kitchen, and a balcony overlooking the blue sea. Small but picturesque. If the houses had been made of somewhat sturdier materials—stone or concrete—this favela would be in fifty years the artist colony of Rio, and then all the chic *avant-garde* crowd would try to get in and the rents would go sky-high.

The rent was exactly nothing—and you can't hardly find rents like that any more, especially in the heart of town overlooking the Atlantic Ocean. Of course, there was no sewage and no water in the house, but a common water faucet was fairly close.

Pereira was a baker. His wife worked, too, making shirt-waists, and they were a cheerful couple. Living there was not so good, he said smiling, but it was not so bad either. He would have liked an apartment, of course, because the children were growing up; and how could you raise children all in one room that way?

Later, Pereira led me down the steep, narrow steps. In the house just below his, three men were listening to a football game on the radio and drinking beer. Just below that was a minute bar where a couple were drinking and telling jokes. We had to hug the wall at one point to allow passage of a couple of men who were helping a drunk up the hill, and I thought what a terrible hill to climb drunk. At the foot of the hill there was a little evangelical church and, so help me, they were singing hymns, beating out the rhythms as only a Brazilian can beat them out.

If Josh Logan ever sees this place, I thought, it'll be another *South Pacific* and it'll probably run twelve years. ■

■ Travel is a Good Thing, and I recommend it to all the paranoiacs in this country who regard every other country with fear, or even just suspicion.

The redoubtable Samuel Johnson, who toured the New Hebrides with Boswell in order to reduce his own hysterical anti-Scottish feelings, once said, "The use of traveling is to regulate imagination by reality, and instead of thinking how things may be to see them as they are."

Just as Robert Kennedy was returning to Washington from Indonesia and Japan and Ted from Israel, Ireland and other points, Jacqueline took off for India and Pakistan.

At a Presidential news conference, May Craig flung Bobby's around-the-world trip at the President's head as if he'd stolen the money. I saw Bobby Kennedy's home movies on NBC along with millions of others and I thought he acquitted himself extremely well. One of the great ways to reduce paranoia is to get out of the house. If you go visit your neighbors, whether they be in Indonesia or next door, you are likely to discover—as Johnson did about the Scots—they're not plotting against you; they're getting and spending and whistling at the girls like everyone else.

And, of course, while reducing our own paranoia, travels are useful to reduce the other side's distrust of us. I found Bobby Kennedy particularly refreshing in asking Indonesian students to step forward and state their grievances against Americans. No one would. Just having Kennedy there proved Americans haven't got horns.

One of the hopeful characteristics of Khrushchev is that he gets around, unlike his paranoid predecessor, Mr. Stalin, who sat huddled in the Kremlin imagining monstrous conspiracies against himself as if he were Robert Welch. All this travel tends to let in fresh air. We send Benny Goodman to Russia. They send the Ukrainian Dance Ensemble here.

The idiot fringe, of course, will denounce the Ukrainian Dance Ensemble as a nest of spies. But I'm of a trusting nature. I can't help thinking that a Ukrainian folk dancer is probably the last person in the world the Russians would send over to spot our missile sites. He's got enough on his mind keeping time to the music. ■

Jargon

■ The trouble with advertising jargon is that it's contagious. Today's idiom of the ad agencies becomes tomorrow's vernacular. My friend Jim Mainwaring and I were kicking it around one day a few years ago, just seeing how far we could make it go, and a good deal of what we said to each other—on that occasion pure advertisingese—is now, you might say, common parlance.

"Television," said Jim, "is pricing itself out of the market." That was as good as any cliché to start with, an ad agency truism that had seen good service and yet was as up-to-date as *Variety*, where it got kicked around pretty thoroughly from time to time.

"You mean, moneywise, the whole picture has changed?" I inquired.

"You're tuned in on my antenna," said Jim, who knew every agency cliché in the book. "Only it's not moneywise this season. It's dollarwise."

"Dollarwise, then, the whole picture has changed."

"Dollarwise and agencywise and copywise and talentwise," said Jim, warming to his task, "television is pricing itself out of the market."

"How do you know?" I asked him. "The precincts aren't all in. You're sitting around Ad Alley thinking that outside New York it's all Jersey. You gotta check the trade and get out in the field.

Or else you're talking to yourself. You're not tuned in on *my* antenna."

"You mean, it doesn't jell with you?" asked Jim.

"I mean I won't buy it."

"Well then," said Jim, who also was an expert at the Machiavellian maneuver, "well then, let's spin the compass and see where we're at."

Right away, I saw what he was up to. And he was.

"The ball's in your court now," said Jim firmly.

I toyed with it a while, not knowing whether to run with it or kick.

"Let's start from the top," I said cautiously. "If television is pricing itself out of the market, then the big play goes back to radio."

"It figures."

"It figures?" This was high praise from Jim. "You mean I'm tuned in on *your* antenna?"

"Well," said Jim cautiously, "not quite. Let's take this ball of wax and mother-hen it. Let's woodshed it. Let's iron the bugs out of it."

The ball was back in his court. "O.K.," I said, "let's do all of those things. Let's think on our feet, shall we? Let's put wheels on it."

"Well," said Jim, venting a new expression that didn't quite know its way around yet, "I'm allowed one crazy idea a month and this is it. If you'll just let me run off at the mouth a bit."

"Go ahead, big boy, fill me in."

"Well, I was talking to a guy on a plane from Cincinnati—I realize this is just a one-man survey—and he updated me on a couple of gimmicks he's got in the hopper."

"New wrinkles on his pitch, eh?"

"Yeah, but he hasn't quite cleared it with the top brass. So I hope you're soundproof."

"I'm deaf and dumb. Update me, big boy."

Jim lowered his voice to a whisper. "He says dollarwise the Big Act has got to go co-op. That's straight from the upper echelons. Of course, plans haven't been finalized yet."

"You mean they haven't covered all the bases?"

"No, but he's trying to get the client to firm up. It's just possible he may put the wrap-up on it next week. You think it figures?"

"Well, I can only call 'em as I see 'em, and I'd like to have the research department dig out the facts and take a good look at the numbers before I make a firm commitment, but—just thinking on my feet here—I'd say it comes off, though not perhaps from every angle or when the overall picture is considered."

"Good boy," said Jim with admiration. "That's one of the most beautifully qualified statements I ever heard. You really hit me where I live."

Next time I saw him, "Television," he told me, "is people. Television comes right into your living room."

"You're just talking off the top of your head, I presume," I said.

"I'm just throwing it on the table for what it's worth," he corrected me. "Television comes right into your living room," he repeated. "And when I invite a guy into my living room, he's got to be a real guy. I mean you can like him or dislike him, but he's got to be real. Television will detect a phony every time. Television looks right through a politician's chest at his heart."

"Let's start from the top," I suggested, which is ad agency parlance for "Where were we?" "Television, you say, is people. You're just thinking out loud, I assume."

"Television *is* people," said Mainwaring firmly. "Television is fourteen million truck drivers and bank clerks and little guys and their wives and their children. And when you criticize television, you're criticizing the American people."

That had been the philosophical defense of radio for a great many years and one with which I violently disagreed. But, of course, you can't say you disagree. Not in that league, you can't. I put it into English: "I can't go along with you there."

"You mean you won't buy it, don't you?"

"I won't buy it. Or any part of it. It's for the birds."

"Well," said Jim defensively, "it was *just* an idea." He underscored the *just* heavily, putting the proper disparagement on ideas, especially his own.

To talk pure ad agency with real skill one must deprecate an idea before it is hatched. One must never get into too exposed a position. Wholehearted endorsement is foolhardy.

Most ideas are prefaced with a thick screen of hedging. "I don't know where this will take you but. . . ." Then, suitably hedged, out comes the idea. "This is probably wrong but. . . ." That particular gambit divorces the author from all responsibility before he even states whatever he has in mind.

In this half-light, an idea—any idea at all—appears shamefaced from the outset. It is, as it were, a sustaining idea; it hasn't got a sponsor. When you throw an idea on the table for what it's worth, you're divesting it of a good deal of its value. Most ad agency clichés are a form of timidity. "Let's pool our brains," for example, can be roughly translated as "Don't forget we're in this mess together."

There are a good many gambits for climbing out from under responsibility for a suggestion. A man will be—shall we say—thinking out loud, and he suddenly perceives they're not buying it or any part of it. Right there he says, "Seriously, though." He means that everything he has said up to that point is arrant nonsense, and that he knows it as well as the rest of them.

"Seriously, though, let's pool our brains." (Or, in English, "Why the hell doesn't someone else make a suggestion?") "Let's start from the top." ("Why don't I learn to keep my big mouth shut?") "The way I look at it, we want a show with a track record." ("Let's buy *Gunsmoke*. After all these years, how can it go wrong?")

Well, the language over there on Mad Ave doesn't resemble anything in your experience unless, of course, you're in the advertising dodge yourself.

There is one agency type, so help me Hannah, who opens every meeting with the announcement: "Let's up-periscope and look around." What does it mean? Well, it means everyone present is to give everyone else the benefit of his forward thinking, and if you don't know what that means, you don't belong in this advanced class.

After everyone has up-periscoped and looked around, conceivably an idea germinates in somebody's skull, and then you might just casually say, "Let's go on a fishing trip with this." That means, of course, let's play house with it. Let's pool our brains. Let's put wheels on it. Let's spin the compass and see where we're at.

After you have been on a prolonged fishing trip, presumably the idea develops into something approximating a usable proposal, ready for submission to the client. Then you turn to one of the junior executives and remark, "Terse it up a bit and put it on a chunk of paper."

Your really hip ad boy can talk this way indefinitely without once subsiding into coherence. It's not easy.

There was once a confab at one of the networks on how to cut costs, and one lad who shall be nameless delivered himself of a peroration which one of my spies took down as well as he was able to do in a dark screening room. Went like this:

"The time has come to put the compass on the table and see which way is north. Fight! Hit that line and hit it hard! I'll just talk off the top of my head, but I know you'll get the picture. We're all a team, a big team; we're all fighting for the same thing —better shows. You say no business like show business, but, men, if we want to stay alive we've got to make more money. Cut costs, cut them intelligently. That great leader of us all, our big coach in Washington, is showing us the way. We're little men, but we can do our part, too. And now I'm gonna pass the ball to our quarterback." *

After a couple of years of this sort of exhortation, some men find it difficult to talk any other way. To them the ball is always on the fifty-yard line and let's get in there and fight, fight, fight. Your real expert at ad agencies can take a sentence and make it double back on itself so you don't know what the hell he means.

An ad man once assigned a junior to a project, and when asked when he wanted it, declared, "Well, I'm in no particular hurry about it, but I wish I had it now."

On Madison Avenue, when tackling a problem, a man never says, "Well, we're getting somewhere." That's much too easy. You have to trick it up a little. One ad-agency executive—so help me!—ended a conference with, "Well, the oars are in the water and we're headed upstream." That may well be my favorite

* This peroration was first recorded during an earlier national administration, but I discover that the sports imagery is also used in touch football.

sentence since Jim Mainwaring surfaced with "Let's up-periscope and look around."

On Madison Avenue ideas are inspected, sniffed at, mulled over and tormented more than anywhere else and naturally this has brought forth language of unique beauty. One ad man, sniffing away at a program idea, turned to his colleagues and remarked, "Let's drop this down the well and see how big a splash it makes."

Then there was the network executive who, when confronted with an idea which demanded some cogitation, declared, "Let me take a temperature reading on this and I'll get it back to you." And another network executive, trying not to commit himself too deeply on one of his own ideas, qualified it with "Mind you, I'm only giving you a side-saddle opinion."

One crazy mixed-up ad agency man, nosing around a projected program, murmured, "Let's guinea-pig that for size." Meaning, I guess, let's try it out on a small scale before getting stuck with it on a large one. As I say, I guess that's what it meant.

There was, too, the case of one ad agency man trying to talk down the ideas of another one. Snarled the second one to the first one, "Don't low-bridge me."

(And in this connection, though outside the agency field proper, there is an expression which I'm very fond of over at one of the news magazines called "the diagonal nod." When the boss man over there gives an idea "the diagonal nod," it means his opinion falls exactly halfway between "It's great" and "It's lousy." So, naturally everyone over there knows exactly where he stands.)

Of course, Madison Avenue isn't the whole story. You can find ad men all over the place—Chicago, Milwaukee and, naturally, Hollywood—and, while the general tenor of metaphor is the same, there are certain regional differences which I'm sure you students of language will find interesting.

In Hollywood, for instance, you will encounter the expression: "We were blown out of the tub," which means simply that the agency has lost a client or an account. When you want a junior account executive to handle detail work, you tell the personnel department, "Get a boy to carry the grips." There is a slightly larcenous practice out there (and elsewhere) concealing added charges in production fees, which increases the agency take above the ordinary 15 per cent. This is known as "honking a live one." (The "live one" is a client with a fat wallet.) And when a guy fails to make a sale or land a new account, he is said to have "burnt off."

Out in Chicago they have an expression: "Keep your pores open on this one," which means don't do anything hasty. (That, of course, is the general direction of almost all ad agency talk. The idea is for heaven's sake, be careful. Don't go rushing into anything.) And when you have finally decided the idea is definitely lousy, you "pull the chain on that one."

Madison Avenue rolls with the blow; it watches carefully which direction the cookie crumbles. This is not to accuse it of being ahead of the times or affecting in any real way the veer of change. But it is aware that things are different. Take this, overheard:

"Things have really changed. Today you've got to give a guy incentive to get him to go out and kill himself."

But one of the finest little sentences to come out of an ad agency conference in years was proclaimed at a Friday afternoon meeting, to wit: "Let's kick this around over the weekend and Monday morning we'll get together and cross-pollinate." Sex has been creeping into everything.

Another and rather franker expression that you could encounter around the networks these days is "snake talk." Whenever a man's in a spot where he doesn't want to make a decision but has, regrettably, to say *something*, he indulges in "snake talk," which is to say he wriggles back and forth from "yes" to "no" through "maybe" in such a way as to keep everyone hopelessly confused as to where he stands.

Another expression which is coming up fast, my spies tell me, is "the dramatic plus." You can make quite a score with this one. Let us say someone is outlining before your little group an act whereby a guy dives from a 100-foot tower into a damp washcloth. From the back of the room you speak up quietly and say, "But where's the dramatic plus?" This indicates a great zest for perfection and, at the same time, tosses the ball into the other guy's court very nicely. Men have been known to make vice-president on less than that.

And if you're seeking new ways to say "I like it but let's, for God's sake, go slowly"—as who isn't on Madison Avenue?—here are a couple that should get you through a day or two: "Let's smear it on the cat and see if she licks it off." Or: "Let's send it on a local and see if it comes back express."

Once a client asked an account executive, "Why did you decide to do it that way?"

"At the time we decided," said the account executive crisply, "we didn't stop to figure out why."

I have here just one other example of Mad Ave prose. I haven't any idea what it means but it has haunted me for nigh on to ten years: "I don't think we'll baby that agency any more. We'll just force-feed them." As I say, I don't know what it means, but I like the idea of an agency being force-fed. It's high time.

From one of my spies in Chicago comes word that ad agencyese is developing what he calls the triple redundancy. He swears he heard an account executive tell a client, "We'll send this letter to all physicians, doctors, and M.D.s."

There is generally, in some of the later Madison Avenue patter, a note of pessimism, if not downright cynicism, in their gropings with the spoken word. Take this one, for example, which is a very real example of Mad Ave: "Let's roll some rocks and see what crawls out." Obviously the boys are not expecting much. In the old days, they used to "mother-hen" an idea or they'd say, "Let's incubate this and see what hatches," and this, with its intimations of maternity, was kind of sweet and touching. Now they're rolling rocks, and you know what crawls out from under those. ■

■ Now, do not let it be said that—simply because I am talking about language (O.K., call it that) in this chapter—I am tracing any interrelationships or anything like that. I am merely a reporter. Furthermore, the UN is blocks east of Madison Avenue, and Foggy Bottom is practically an hour away by airplane.

Lately I've been listening to the diplomats around the United Nations, and all I can say is on Madison Avenue they're amateurs at dodging an issue.

The first word you have to learn around the cookie pushers is *position.* You don't have a point of view; it's a position. And if you harbor it long enough, it hardens into a posture. But it's never your position or posture; it's ours, which means you and the United States (if you're an American diplomat) or theirs, if it's anyone else like Russia or Sweden. In other words, he or I don't have a position—*they* do or *we* do. Or to put it another way, it takes two to take a position or strike a posture.

Actually, you don't take a position; you *have* a position or you *review* a position. If we haven't made up our weak minds about our position on something, it's because the situation needs to be "carefully delineated" or: "We'll require more clarification." (That's "Whadd he say?" in diplomatic language.) Or: I think we better wait for them (friends, enemies, anyway, the other guys) to "spell it out in formal detail."

After they have spelled it out in formal detail and we still haven't a position or don't want to spell it out yet: "The United States has some thoughts on the matter." That means "We're working on it. Leave me alone." Or, if you want to go further or wordier: "There were consultations and some discussion on that and we plan to meet with the British next week."

That doesn't commit you or the British to anything beyond the fact that someone is going to have to pay for lunch. After the "consultations" or "meetings" or "discussions," you might very well say that the "British went along" with our position, which is one way of saying that the British have so little interest in that particular area that they don't have any position about it at all and the American position won't get them into any great trouble in the areas they are interested in.

Or then again maybe it will. In which case, the British and the American delegates had "a fruitful discussion." ("If you're going to ruffle all those Portuguese feathers over Angola, keep us out of it.") Or maybe you have had "a useful discussion," which is another way of saying nobody said anything.

On the other hand, you and the British (or the Swedes or the French or anyone except the Russians) can really let your hair down and have "an exchange of ideas." Then you're really getting somewhere. That means he did not disagree. Of course he did not agree either. But he listened. And that's something. (The Russians don't always do that, even. Sometimes they take the headphones off.)

To go even farther down the sunny path of international harmony, you come on the phrase "cooperate to the utmost." That means the British won't yield an inch, but again, they'll listen quietly. You must be grateful for small favors in international relations.

"Consultations," "meetings," "discussions"—these are things one has with one's friends. With one's enemies one takes "soundings," which doesn't mean these are necessarily unrewarding. Sometimes you can learn a lot more from "sounding" than you can from "a fruitful discussion."

Now, sir, let us say you are a newsman and you ask a U.S. diplomat what our position is on President Ngo Dinh Diem's obstinacy in Viet Nam, the answer might very well be something like this with the proper translation: "We're trying to get a priority on that. (We're passing the buck to higher authority in the State Department.) We have the resolution under consideration. (We can't make up our mind about it.) The whole report has not been digested. (We don't know what the British and French think about it either.) There are various people in the process of reading it now. (What do you suppose we do for a living here except read all these damned cables?) We'll have nothing to say (the situation is chaotic enough without adding fresh fuel) until we consult with our friends (who haven't made up their minds either), but we'll push for negotiations (we'll prod them to say *something*). Meanwhile, we have no comment. (We know damned well what we think, but we don't want anyone else to know.)" ■

■ In the increasingly crowded field of jargon that is pure gibberish, the psychiatrists are still well out in front, but that's because they took an early lead. The sociologists are gaining steadily on them and, I confidently predict, will be able to talk gibberish just as well if not better than their mentors. I have my own computing machine here, which I made out of hairpins discarded by emancipated women (which means they are polarized against common sense), and it tells me that the date on which language will become totally unintelligible—when, in short, obscurity becomes total blackness—is 2086. I'll be dead then, thank God.

The darkness is closing in fast. Here's a quote from a sociologist named Bernard Berelson of the University of Chicago. Sociology, he says, has become (hold on to your hats; we're entering a tunnel, fellows) "technical and quantitative, a-theoretical, segmentalized and particularized, specialized and institutionalized, 'modernized' and group-ized.'" Whee! ■

These changing times

■ I think we are in the middle—or perhaps just at the beginning—of a quality revolution which is not really understood and is even resisted by our businessmen and our artists. In the finest play around, *A Man for All Seasons,* one line in the opening monologue always gets a chuckle: "The sixteenth century, the century of the common man—like all the other centuries."

But I harbor the suspicion and the hope that we are on the threshold, if not already inside, the century of the uncommon man and even more importantly the uncommon thing. At least in this country, I think we are. Today it's the mass man and the mass thing that are in trouble. The mass magazines are in terrible trouble, floundering around to find a formula to fit a mass man who seems to be not as responsive to formulas as he once was. Meanwhile, the quality magazines—*The New Yorker, Harper's, The Saturday Review*—are coining profits.

The mass movies are finished, and of the eight giant movie companies that once dominated the world, only two—Twentieth Century-Fox and Metro—are producing movies in the old mass consumption ways and both are in awful trouble. Meanwhile, United Artists is coining money. With what? Quality movies, produced on an individual basis by quality producers buying quality books and plays and stories.

The automobile industry felt the bite of the uncommon man when he started to buy foreign cars in uncommon numbers. The industry responded (belatedly) with the compact car, which wrested the market back from the foreigners. But only temporarily. Now the foreign cars are coming back strong. There are more different *kinds* of cars—foreign, compact, standard—on the roads than there have been in many a moon. Remember when all cars looked alike? They don't any more, and the urge to be different—if nothing else, to have different-color seats—is spreading outward from the more sophisticated centers. It's all part of the common man's desire to be uncommon.

The common man's desire to be uncommon started, I have a hunch, when he discovered how common he was. And he found that out from Vance Packard's books—*The Status Seekers, The Hidden Persuaders* and *The Waste Makers*—mass books, all of them. Mass man decided commonality was all right for the herd but not for himself, and he started deserting the herd in great numbers—attending art theaters, going to museums, buying Fiats, reading *The Atlantic Monthly.* It's a cloud no bigger than a man's hand—well, actually, it's about the size of his arm—but it's going to get much bigger, the urge to quality. ■

■ In building, I'll admit, the mass building is still king—the ant-hill structures which are sprouting all over the earth—but the outcry against them is mounting in volume. In Chicago, in Philadelphia, even in New York, there are signs of a reversal, if only in the recognition of the problem.

In New York, of course, the replacement of small quality structures by big mass structures is worst.

Frankly, I don't know how they got all these tall buildings built in New York's climate. The Sahara at high noon in August has nothing on New York in September and you can quote me, bub. I don't know how they got the Pyramids up either in that hot but dry climate, but they had whips. We got nothing but money.

Still, the buildings seem to go up. O. Henry used to say it'd be a great city when they got it finished, but I'm not so sure any more. The high apartments are the shape of the future not only in the United States but everywhere. They were building a twenty-story job right next to my hotel in Monte Carlo, and they were in such a hurry to get it done, they started the hammering at 7 A.M. and kept it up until 11 P.M. The only time you could get any sleep was from noon until 2 P.M. when the workers knocked off for lunch.

Around the outskirts of every city anywhere in the world the same tall, square, depressing buildings are going up. I think the architects of the world have let us down. I do think something more stimulating than these upended cigar boxes might be contrived. I'm starved for the sight of a curve in a building. Do we have to have all those straight lines and knife-edged corners? Is it just possible that Louis Sullivan was dead wrong when he said, "Form follows function"? Why should it? I think not only that these cigar boxes are lazy architecture but also that the architects are going to make themselves unnecessary with these rectangles. Anyone can draw a rectangle. Who needs an architect?

Most of the ravages in New York and elsewhere are caused by the tax structure. This is a worldwide problem. Municipal revenues the world over are inadequate because they are almost all based on real estate taxes. They are monstrously unwise for two reasons: first, they don't provide nearly enough money; second, they tear the guts out of a city in the ever-increasing pressure to produce more and more revenue from a foot of land.

This is why we tear down lovely old structures on Park Avenue and erect hideous office buildings in their place. Thus we destroy our past, and create a huge traffic problem, housing problem, and parking problem for our future, all to live marginally and increasingly uncomfortably in the present. I think our great cities in fifty years will, at this rate, become almost uninhabitable.

In the ancient world a city was essentially a meeting place for minds and for ideas and not just a great merchandising center. Today our cities are left to the rich, the poor, the juvenile delinquents and the ward heelers.

We have become a suburban society, a nation of Scarsdales.

If Socrates had lived in Scarsdale, he'd never have become "intellectually the acutest" man of his age. He'd have been too busy catching the 5:13 to have had any long thoughts. Once he got to Scarsdale, there would have been cocktails with the Flemings, the PTA meeting, and on Sunday the grass to cut—all activities safely calculated to blot out philosophy.

Also, if Socrates had lived in Scarsdale, he'd probably never have known Aristophanes or Xenophon or Plato, because that crowd would have been living in Greenwich Village, and he wouldn't have known Pericles and Aspasia and that government bunch, because they would all have been living in Washington. He spent most of his life on the streets and in the marketplace of Athens, which were peculiarly suited to lounging and talk, and he talked incessantly to the local politicians, the shopkeepers, the writers, the soldiers, the students, and while he did much to shape their minds, they did more to shape his.

The old cities were the meeting ground of soldier, merchant, statesman, philosopher; they were the only places where all could meet, hone their minds on each other's disagreements. Out of these explosions of mind came the grandeur that we call civilization. Today we not only have the suburbs, the haven of the middle class; we also have the specialized cities: Washington, where the lawyers talk like senators, and Hollywood, where the lawyers talk like the late Jerry Wald.

London, Paris and Rome are not only the financial centers of their countries (as New York is) but also the seats of national government, the centers of literary and intellectual life, and also the places where movies are made. This has enriched every field: government, books, movies, finance. Most importantly, it has enriched the life of each individual in it.

What we have to do is make New York habitable again for something besides banks and insurance companies. But then we must build meeting places for the people—parks, playgrounds, coffee houses, theaters. There is no place in New York where people can rub elbows except saloons. We must have wider sidewalks with benches to sit down on, if we have to tear twenty feet off every building in Manhattan. Meeting places are important;

the property rights of real estate people are not only unimportant, but usually hopelessly evil. (You may set it down as Crosby's Law that all lobbies are despicable but real estate lobbies are the most despicable.)

There's another change in American cities that makes me unhappy: I think we were entirely too hasty junking our streetcars for buses. I'm crazy about streetcars, especially the new postwar jobs. Munich, Geneva, Stockholm, Belgrade have new swift streetcars that are almost noiseless. I recall the old-style streetcar that made a hell of a racket. The new ones make no noise at all except when crossing another set of rails. They're very fast, easy to operate and they don't fill the atmosphere with carbon monoxide. Also they're cheap.

There's almost nothing noisier, dirtier or more uncomfortable than a bus and they're terribly hard to operate, considering the guy also has to make change, tell old ladies where Bleecker Street is, and tell us all to step to the rear. Let's go back to the streetcar. ■

■ President Kennedy, speaking at a National Football Foundation dinner, put his finger on one of the fundamental problems of our age when he said, "The sad fact is that it looks more and more as if our national sport is not playing at all—but watching. We have become more and more not a nation of athletes, but a nation of spectators."

We certainly are. In more ways than one. The whole tenor of life is toward nonparticipation. If, for example, one goes back fifty years, the average boy would be a farm boy (we were largely a rural population then) who could do everything—milk the cows, shell the peas, play center field. Today the peas arrive picked, shelled and frozen and the boy watches Mickey Mantle play center field. Participation is left to the experts; the masses watch.

More and more our plants are being automated, and the worker —if he's not tossed out altogether—is reduced to the role of watcher. In the offices, the business machines do the computing and the filing and the memorizing. If that infernal machine which understands a few words, and types them, gets perfected—and it almost certainly will—the machines will take dictation, too, replacing all those rounded, nubile girls with a lot of nonaesthetic knobs, a perfectly horrible thought.

Democracy itself, it sometimes seems, is getting to be largely a spectator sport—the great majority of voters deferring altogether on the complicated problems to a few experts in the Rand Corporation who make the decisions and do the thinking.

What's to do about it? Well, I think the first step is to call attention to the condition so that we all become aware of it. I think that both as a nation and as individuals we should ask ourselves how much time in any given week we devote to being spectators and how much to actual participation.

I must lay down some rather arbitrary rules here. Reading a newspaper, for example (worthy as that operation is), is a spectator sport and so is looking at television. Arguing politics with a dinner partner is participation; reading about it in the newspaper is nonparticipation. The first requires opinion, facts, interest—well, participation. The other is a blotting-up operation. Going to the movies, watching television, watching a computer do the work—these are all spectator activities.

A participant activity is something in which you use your vocal cords, your muscles or your mind or preferably all three at once. It's quite possible, in this television-automobile-movie-automated world, almost to get through life on a 100 per cent nonparticipation basis.

A good many years ago Fred Allen gloomily predicted that the way things were going, the human race would eventually have no minds at all "but eyeballs the size of cantaloupes." Fortunately, there are some hopeful signs. Television is so bloody dull that a good many nonparticipants have fled to the saloons, where at least they argue, or to the cellar, where they build boats or do some other do-it-yourself activity, both healthy participant exercises.

There are two inexorable movements in the direction of action rather than nonparticipation. 1) The servant class is rapidly disappearing, not only in America but all over an increasingly affluent Europe, so until somebody automates bed making, you'll have to do the housework with your very own hands. 2) And if our streets get any more choked with cars, we may have to get out of them and walk to work. ■

■ Although President Kennedy didn't mention it in his speech, we have also become more and more not a nation of smellers, but a nation of nonsmellers. They've been taking away the God-intended, freedom-sustaining smells we used to have. This first came into focus for me in October, 1960, when I read a marvelous article on the South Pacific by Eugene Burdick in *Holiday* magazine.

"There is another aspect of the Pacific which for reasons I do not understand is almost never remarked," wrote Burdick. "That is the smell of the Pacific. In America we have deodorized our culture and our land. Fertilizers are non-organic and hence farmlands odorless; factories such as breweries and bakeries which used to give out great redolence now have their smells snatched up by blowers and either absorbed chemically or shot high into the sky. And so it goes with almost every smell in America. It is tamped down, obliterated, extinguished."

I like smells. Preferably good smells, but even a bad smell, I think, is better than no smell. After all, the sense of smell is one of the five senses and why, oh why, did we ever decide simply to do without it? The villain, I strongly suspect, is Mr. Milton Feasley, who warned that even our best friend wouldn't tell us and advised us to use Listerine. It was given further impetus by the monster who invented B.O. for Lifebuoy. What is the matter with body odors? In moderation, body odor is one of the sweetest and most urgent of smells.

"In the Pacific . . . things smell," wrote Burdick. "Some of the smells are fundamental, vast, seductive and exciting. Others are shocking and almost beyond the capacity to endure, though one does endure them and finally even ignores them."

Smells, like music, have that achingly familiar power to evoke the past; a good strong whiff can stab you to the heart with pain and longing and remembrance. But what is the child of today to remember if there are no smells? My eleven-year-old city-bred daughter and I were riding through the fall countryside on our bicycles; suddenly she said, "What is that smell, Daddy?" I was shocked. It was the smell of burning leaves, an odor as traditional to fall as a turkey to Thanksgiving, as fir trees to Christmas. But how do you explain that to a child who has never smelled burning leaves? You can't really. You just have to have smelled burning leaves every fall for thirty or so years. It's something far beyond meaning, deep in the realm of feeling.

I'm from Wisconsin and the smells of an old-fashioned nondeodorized barn are part of my heritage—the acid fragrance of manure, mingling with the sweetness of the hay, the distinctive lime smell of whitewash, the very clean sharp odor—almost a taste—of leather. It makes me sound a thousand years old, but I can remember, too, Grandmother baking bread, the smells filling the whole house.

"There are dozens of places in the Pacific that a blindfolded old hand could identify merely by sniffing," wrote Burdick. Describing Suva, the capital of Fiji, he said, "There is everywhere in the Pacific the sweet scent of copra which from a distance reminds you of a freshly opened jar of dried coconut but which grows more unpleasant as you come closer.

"Then there are the smells of curry, of unwashed bodies, of garlic—and that is the Indian section of Suva. There is also the odor of fresh-cut grass, tiny but persistent, wafted off the lawns of Grand Pacific Hotel and Government House. There is the smell of beer from dockfront pubs and restaurants. There is also the smell, low and soft and muted, of rotted sugar cane coming from the husks of crushed stalks. The last smell is from the fish markets and then you are in Suva itself."

Well, we'll fix all that. First come the missionaries; then the traders; then comes the Hilton Hotel chain and finally the Air-Wick people, who'll make the air pure and antiseptic. And dead. ■

■ The homogenization of the world is proceeding apace, clearly. Even Spain, *Variety* reported, as early as 1961, was outlawing its ancient working and sleeping hours to bring it into tune with the rest of the civilized world. In Spain, as everyone knows, one used to dine at 11 P.M after a good, long siesta and then stay up half the night. But not any more.

By government decree, film houses and theaters that used to operate two performances a night, one starting at seven and the other at eleven, now turn out the lights by eleven-thirty from October to May and half an hour later between June and September. "Time-worn habits that have made the country unique for late-hour dining and diversion," reported *Variety*, went out the window in a sweeping government move to establish a working and playing day that compares with the rest of civilized society, come what may....

And why does Spain have to get to bed at the same hour as the rest of the world? I recall seeing little children still up snapping their castanets at 5 A.M. during the fair at Seville. Their normal bedtime was something sensible like 1 A.M., but since it was fair time they were allowed a few hours extra. Charming custom.

Of course, you can't reasonably blame the reform—if reform is the word for it—on Americans. Practically nobody else had hours like the Spaniards either. But I'll bet we are being blamed for it. It wasn't until the Americans got bases in Spain that the Spanish started tampering with their ancient customs.

The French have put bowling alleys in the Bois de Boulogne. They have a drugstore (known simply as Le Drugstore) on the Champs-Élysées. The Italians have our quick lunch. So have the French. And the Spaniards are going to bed before midnight.

(Well, at least the government has been trying to push it down their throats.)

And another thing: the women of the world are one and all wearing pants. From Belgrade to Stockholm, from Scotland to Munich, the womenfolk everywhere more and more are in trousers. In St. Tropez and St. Moritz I have seen them wear pants for evening wear and I rather suspect the habit will spread. They'll be wearing them to the office next. In fact, I'm willing to lay plenty of eight-to-five that in a hundred years skirts will be worn for only extreme ceremony. Girls will get married in skirts and maybe get buried in them. The rest of their lives they'll spend in pants.

Where will it all end? As Nancy Mitford points out in her book *Don't Tell Alfred,* it was not so long ago—not more than thirty years, which is just an eyeblink in recorded time—when every nation had its own costume, its own architecture and its own food, all distinctive and unique. Today the sun never sets on Coca-Cola or the cigar box, modern architecture or neckties and nylons.

Tomorrow what? I can close my eyes and see the Congo looking like the Mosholu Parkway with palm trees fringed by hot-dog stands. Drugstores at the corners selling Vance Packard's *The Waste Makers* and practicing it all over the rest of the store.

I suppose it's inevitable that the rest of the world should pick up our bad habits. But why don't we pick up some of theirs? If Spain is going square, why don't we go Spanish? I think America should adopt the siesta, which is one of the more civilized habits of the world. In fact, apart from Americans and the English, I can't think of any peoples who don't enjoy siestas. No other animal stays up sixteen solid hours without dozing off. Why should we?

I think we ought to lock up Macy's and Gimbel's for a couple of hours after lunch, pull the shades, and everyone cork off for a couple of hours. It would improve the disposition and put us all in tune for a nice late dinner. Say at 10 P.M. ■

■ The automobile, we all know, is responsible for many changes, some of them good but most of them bad. The latest one to come to my attention was pointed out to me by a countess I met in Paris only last November.

"There is not time for *l'amour* any longer," she said, and sighed. "It is the traffic."

"The traffic?" I said.

"These things"—she sighed again—"require time. The *cinq-à-sept* is very difficult under these conditions. It is the traffic."

The cinq-à-sept (as if there were any among you who did not know) are the hours sacred to profane love in Paris, the hours of dalliance with someone else's wife or with one's own light of love. At the hour of five, the businessman departs his office, telling his secretary he'll be back after his *apéritif*. The secretary knowing, of course, that the apéritif has red lips and round arms. At seven, he's back in his office just in time for the call of his wife, who wants to know when he will be home for dinner. At least that's how it was.

"But now there is no time, no time," murmured the Countess. "It is the traffic. Until a few years ago one could get almost anywhere in Paris in fifteen minutes. Now"—she shrugged—"forty minutes, especially between five and seven. The traffic is terrible. That leaves no time."

I saw what she meant. In the old days, the gentleman took fifteen minutes to get to his light of love; later, fifteen minutes to get back to his office or perhaps to go home. That left an hour and a half for dalliance, which is only correct. Otherwise it becomes, not l'amour, but something else, something hurried and not at all French, and not at all l'amour. French cooking requires lots of butter and lots of time. *Quant à l'amour,* you don't need the butter; you do need the time.

I took the matter up with a gentleman I know who has maintained a succession of lights of love in apartments around Paris.

He sighed heavily. "The traffic is terrible. Until last year, I could take a taxi. Fifteen minutes. Then it became twenty. Then thirty. Then it became impossible."

"Well," I said, "there's always the Métro."

He snorted. "My dear John, have you ever tried going to the light of your life in a subway at five o'clock? I have been doing that for two months. Have you any idea what hell a subway is at that hour? Children coming home from school. Wives coming home from the shops. The hurry. The rush. The noise. One arrives—nerves exacerbated, irritable, distraught. For the next ten minutes, just to calm down, one tells the lady how terrible things are. One complains. This is hardly the proper spirit."

He lit a cigar, slowly and carefully, and puffed on it, very slowly. This is what Mae West used to like, a man who takes his time.

"But the worst part of this situation," he said finally, "is the contemplation. The anticipation. You must realize that the most important part of l'amour is anticipation. 'Ah, if I only had her in my arms right now,' you think. To plan, to dream, this is part of l'amour—the most important part." He shuddered. "You know, all day long I think of that damned subway ride, dreading it. The next thing—it hasn't happened yet, but it will—I'm going to hate the girl for putting me through that ordeal. And when that happens—well, that's hardly l'amour, is it?"

The automobile has much to answer for. But to kill l'amour in Paris may be that blackest crime of all. ■

■ On the national scene we've observed another new phenomenon: a change in the nature of the Presidency, not the least of the legacies President Eisenhower left President Kennedy. That is, government—or, to be more accurate, non-government—by popularity.

A bare three months after he assumed office, the Gallup Poll showed that Kennedy was approved overwhelmingly (73 per cent) by a populace that remained resolutely indifferent, if not downright hostile, to his policies. I suspect that Jacqueline Kennedy would get even higher than 73 per cent approval. Caroline Kennedy is a smash with the Democrats, the Greenback party, the Goldwater Hardshell Republicans as well as the Rockefeller Softshell Republicans, and, I imagine, even the Birch Society. As for little Prince John. . . .

Prince John! What am I saying?

Well, why not? The only enduring governments in the world besides our own are Britain's and Sweden's and Denmark's—monarchies, all of them. France hasn't been able to keep a government in power for more than twenty minutes (except dictatorships like Napoleon's—or de Gaulle's government, which smells strongly of dictatorship) since they beheaded Louis XVI.

I always felt that Eisenhower would have made a much better monarch than President. He did all the things Queen Elizabeth does at least as well and sometimes better. His foreign travels were the greatest triumphs scored by the West during his administration. So resounding was his visit to India that the Communists stirred up all that trouble in Japan to prevent him from scoring another one there. This is Foreign Policy by The Visit. The Presence—just like Elizabeth and Edinburgh.

In a couple of other respects the Eisenhower administration resembled monarchy much more than Presidency. For one thing, Eisenhower stayed resolutely out of politics. In fact, you could get up a pretty good argument that Eisenhower stayed farther from politics than some British monarchs. Like the British crown, Eisenhower was the symbol of America and all it stood for. Also, like the British crown, Eisenhower was almost totally removed from the area of criticism.

By abstaining with such chilly aloofness from anything that resembled political activity, Eisenhower left some rather sticky problems in public relations to Kennedy, who has other ideas about the office. There is a body of opinion—larger than you think and especially prevalent among women—that politics is not seemly for the President of the United States. He should be above all that. There's something awfully vulgar about getting into argument over unemployment, taxes, and that sort of thing.

Eisenhower never demeaned himself like that and—you can hear it whispered in the women's clubs—he was perfectly charming to everyone, no matter who they were.

I think we have had a secret hankering for monarchy for a long time. Not having royalty to look up to, we do the next-best thing. We elect the richest men we can find to public office—Rockefeller to the Governorship, Kerr to the Senate, Kennedy to the Presidency. All these people live regally. They haven't the titles but they have the emoluments. Today, practically the worst thing that can happen to you in politics is to be born in a log cabin. (The modesty of his birth didn't help Nixon; it hurt him.)

And there's another thing. I think monarchy would have a strong snob appeal inside Russia. The Russians haven't had a monarch since 1918 and monarchy is always most attractive to those who have never known it. I'm convinced our stock would soar among the Russian bourgeoisie if we were a monarchy and not just a democracy.

In America—so well conditioned had Eisenhower left us—I can see no serious resistance to the idea of an American monarchy from anyone. Except Kennedy, of course. He wants to be President. ■

■ When Adlai Stevenson was named Father of the Year in 1961, he said the American father "has come on sorry times. He is the butt of comic strips; he is the boob of the radio and TV serials and the favorite stooge of all our professional comedians. Let's face it. Father has become a dodo, a simpleton, an object of mirth."

Mr. Stevenson was out of date. Father *had* been all those things, but the image had changed—and is still changing. It started with Robert Young in *Father Knows Best,* who was the wise, deeply understanding parent, a sort of mixture of the Pilgrim Fathers and George Washington. Now the symbol of fatherhood on television is the parent of Dobie Gillis, who says simply and with deep feeling of his son, "I'm going to kill that boy."

I favor the immortal words of Sam Levenson, patron saint of fatherhood in most of Brooklyn (except in some pagan parts of Flatbush where they are still worshiping at the shrine of Daddy Browning). Sam Levenson declared, in words that should be cast in bronze all over the Father's Day Committee, "When I was a boy, I used to do what my father wanted. Now I do what my boy wants. My problem is: when am I going to do what I want?"

That comes closer to the spirit of American fatherhood as of right now. I have been taking the pulse of fathers on my block, and "If Africa can be free, why can't we?" is what they're saying. (Well, there are a lot of poets in the neighborhood and they talk that way.)

In short, revolt is the spirit of the times among our real up-to-date fathers. It was Robert Paul Smith, who, in *Where Did You Go? Out. What Did You Do? Nothing,* said that all this togetherness between father and offspring was not only impossible but unwise. Warfare is the natural state between father and child, and don't you forget it. My own candidate for Father of Any Year was the late Moss Hart, the author of those inspiring words which all fathers should clasp to their breasts: "It's our house and we're bigger than they are."

Anyway, I was happy when Adlai Stevenson was named Father of the Year. It made me reflect that with a Catholic in the White House and a divorced man as Father of the Year, there should be no limit to the possibilities for tolerance in this hemisphere. ■

■ And now let's examine the startling and downright disturbing change in the image of us newsmen. The American Newspaper Publishers Association was in New York fairly early in 1961, and while they worried over at the Waldorf-Astoria about rising costs, diminishing revenues, television competition and other dark matters, I was worrying about something else. I mean, fellows, Our Image. It's gone plumb to hell.

The newspaperman used to be cast in the image of Hildy Johnson. Hell of a fellow. Drank up a storm, but in all other regards he was thoroughly admirable. He could devastate the mayor with a witticism, outwit the chief of police, unmask the renegades and usually get the girl. In *Roman Holiday* the newspaperman was Gregory Peck and he gave up his story for love. I doubt that any publishers would have approved of *that*, but, damn it, the chap was likable, to say nothing of handsome, dashing, intelligent, and charming.

It's been a long time since newspapermen have been cast in any mold that Gregory Peck could fill. Three conspicuous recent examples pop into my mind. There's the third-rate journalist—that's how they bill him—in the movie *La Dolce Vita*. Marcello is good-looking but if he has any other good qualities, they are not discernible. He's a small-time gossip columnist, spineless, unfaithful, lecherous, in the end totally corrupt, and pretty dumb. That hurt the worst—the dumbness. Fellini was once a newspaperman himself so we cannot say he's totally uninformed in those matters.

Still, lousy as Marcello was, he's at least personable. The others aren't even that.

In *Don't Tell Alfred*, Nancy Mitford has at the profession with a perfectly deplorable journalist called Mockbar, who works for a newspaper which bears a suspicious resemblance to Lord Beaverbrook's *Express*. And what a little horror he is! Constantly lashed by his vicious master for larger and larger scandals, he squeezes out misinformation and large-scale misrepresentations. Even when he gets the facts right, he wildly misinterprets them.

However, that's the very least of it. Inaccurate. Sensational. Scurrilous. We've been called all those names before. Miss Mitford goes on to level a far worse charge. Ineffectual. No one really takes Mockbar seriously, and the man he's writing about principally in *Don't Tell Alfred* doesn't even read him. That's the worst thing you can say about a journalist: that he's sensational and unread.

The other journalist on display in recent popular fiction is in Graham Greene's *A Burnt-Out Case.* This one embodies all the vices of the others—sensationalism, disregard for the truth, and all that—and in addition he's monstrously fat. Aw, now, gee whiz, Greene! If we are to be represented as all that depraved, we might at least be reasonably proportioned.

Of all the portraits of journalists now on view, Greene's is the least appetizing but the most expert as a piece of fiction. This rat—in addition to being unprincipled, inept, ungracious, physically repellent and lazy—has a sickening maudlin sentimentality about him that will revolt all newspapermen. Oh, a lovely man!

As I say, gentlemen, our public relations in the popular arts have never been worse. The only comfort I can offer is that all these newspapermen are foreign—one Italian, two Englishmen. One added crumb of comfort: bad as our public relations are at the moment, Madison Avenue's are worse. ■

■ In London not long ago, the last double bed, a huge Victorian brass affair, departed the Ritz Hotel, that splendid hostelry whose bathrooms are among the most beautiful chambers in the whole world. Ah, woe, as Judith Anderson used to say in whatever Greek play she happened to be in at the moment.

"It is the end of an era," said Edward Schwenter, the hotel manager. "I don't know what Grandfather would have said about this deterioration in our social habits. But it's a fact that few people require double beds these days. They say double beds are unhygienic, or unaesthetic or something."

Ah, woe!

Of course, what the Ritz considered a double bed is not what the ordinary housewife would consider a double bed. It was big enough to house a small family or perhaps stable a couple of horses. I remember with an ache of bitter nostalgia the *single* beds at the Grand Union at Saratoga, now only a memory. The single beds came, of course, two to a room. They had oak headboards roughly eight feet high and could sleep three people easily. And they were single beds, mind you. You could push the two of them together and have a basketball game, which the drunks at Saratoga sometimes did, annoying the horseplayers in adjacent rooms who were bent over their form sheets.

All gone, alas! ■

■ It's not just that the old values are changing. The whole established order of things has gone cockeyed. On some TV show or other some time back, the hero had tracked the murderer down and was explaining to him—that's half the fun, telling the killer just how you figured out it was him all along—when a sweet little old lady sent a bullet past the private eye's ear and into the killer's black heart.

That's the way little old ladies have been behaving on television these days—like homicidal maniacs. As a matter of fact, the whole female sex is beginning to act like that on TV.

Back when I was a boy, it was smart to keep your eye on the butler in a whodunit. He seemed so harmless that he was almost certainly the one who was blackmailing Sir Roderick. But nowadays, we who are wise to the thought processes of TV writers are automatically suspicious of any babe—even sweet little old ladies. The more helpless, the more wide-eyed she is, the more you should watch out. They're cunning, the vixens.

On one show the blonde came to a tough-minded private eye for help, and in the course of aiding her, he mowed down the character she had craved protection from. It was only later that he discovered the girl had planned it that way all along.

That's the pattern to watch for. The sweet little things come in saying, "I need help." After that, watch out, brother.

This is raising hell with all the dramatic values I learned at my mother's knee. When I was a growing boy, a widow was a widow

—the natural prey of unscrupulous operators who wanted to buy up her land to sell back at fabulous profits so they could run the railroad through. You could trust the widow to be decently helpless. Her dramatic function was to play minnow to the sharks. Today the minnows chase the sharks into shallow water and eat them alive. It is upsetting what I was brought up to believe was the law of nature.

Another dramatic value that has got itself thoroughly twisted upside down by television is the role of the American Indian. Every schoolboy in my set was brought up to believe that the only good Indian was a dead Indian. In my boyhood, Injun Joe in *Tom Sawyer* was considered typical of the whole Indian nation —a liar, a scoundrel, a menace, the very model of a villain. That was Injun Joe.

On contemporary television, though, the Indian has almost taken the place of the widow. He's the born victim. Somebody is always trying to steal the Noble Redskin's land, or throw him unjustly off the reservation, or rob him of his birthright. Even when they're bad, the Indians are regarded as juvenile delinquents. They don't know any better, and if they'd been raised in a nice clean city like the scriptwriters, instead of those woodsy slum areas where they grew up, they'd be just like white people. This is liberal thinking, I guess. Frankly, I think it has messed up the land of make-believe beyond recognition. ■

Reviews

NOTE:

■ I started column writing as a reviewer of radio, later of television, and later I occasionally reviewed Broadway shows, books, even fashion shows. Here I've picked out a few reviews, partly because I think some should be in the book, but partly for other deeper reasons.

These reviews of television dramas show how far television has gone, mostly straight down, from the Golden Age of television around 1955. *A Night to Remember* was that old almost forgotten thing—live television. Thirty-one sets, and 107 actors all doing it in front of your very eyes at the moment you saw it. I don't ever think we'll see anything like that again in straight drama on television.

Rod Serling's *Requiem for a Heavyweight* introduced (actually, it was the second show but it was the one we all think of) that great series *Playhouse 90* which is long gone. Used to be on every week, a different ninety-minute play, many of them originals like *Requiem.* Most of the playwrights who wrote for *Playhouse 90*—and the directors—have long since fled to the movies or the stage, but television bred them and they gave great glory to the medium for a brief spell.

Sound of Music and *Do Re Mi* were both Broadway musicals.

The first was a monstrous money-maker. The second never made back its production costs, although it got reviews which were much too kind. I throw these in because these two shows indicate the direction Broadway is taking toward bigger, more expensive, more derivative and just plain bad musicals, bad money driving out good. The review of *Marienbad* was included simply because far-out movies are the coming thing and I thought this might provide movie reviewers with a clue as to how to grapple with the avant-garde good-naturedly. ■

■ The greatest single thing about Kraft's marvelous 1956 production of *A Night to Remember*, the tale of the sinking of the *Titanic*, by Walter Lord, was simply that it was done at all on live television. A few years earlier it would not have been possible, at least not possible with this marvelous attention to detail and flawless technical direction.

This was far and away the most complex production in television history. The show was done from what was at the time the world's largest TV studio, the NBC studio in Brooklyn. There were thirty-one sets and 107 actors with a total of seventy-two speaking roles. Seven sets were constructed in duplicate to be shown at first dry, later with rising water. Sets included a portion of the hull and absolutely authentic reproductions of the interior, including the bridge, radio room, café, crow's nest, captain's quarters, grand staircase, lifeboats. Every detail of the set was exact. A marine engineer and a draftsman were employed to translate the original blueprints of the *Titanic* into the real thing.

I bring up all this technical detail because it contributed enormously to the show's impact. Suddenly we were all transferred backward in time to April 14, 1912, before either World War had accustomed us to disaster. For the *Titanic* was a disaster in its day almost unimaginable in ours. Yet Walter Lord, who spent twenty-eight years in research on his book, re-created that moment in history with such painstaking fidelity that we suddenly were back in 1912.

Lord's respect for fact was faithfully adhered to by the director, George Roy Hill, who did a miraculous job of cutting back and forth from bridge to engine room to steerage to cabins. From his unwieldy cast, Hill got splendid cooperation. Actors cut in and out with marvelous precision, some of the scenes being only a few lines long.

In fact, it was this that kept us rooted to our chairs. The *Titanic* was an immense craft, and the great drama of the occasion—as Lord made full use of in his book—was that a fact that meant one thing in one part of the ship meant something quite different someplace else. This, incidentally, is something characteristic of all disasters, as anyone who has ever covered one can tell you.

Five minutes after, say, an explosion, you will get twenty-five different stories from twenty-five different witnesses. The character of the witness enters deeply into what he saw, or believed he saw. As the stark truth came home to the many passengers on the *Titanic,* they each reacted with gaiety or gallantry or cowardice in their special predestined way, and this is what gave the play an awe-inspiring dramatic punch.

There were many high moments, but my own favorite was when the ship designer Andrews explained with simple mathematics that the great ship was doomed. The line "The ship must go down" had the simple lucidity of a pistol shot.

The end—with Andrews going down with his unsinkable ship, the great chandelier crashing all over him—was so sudden I couldn't quite believe it. (With three thousand gallons of water to play with out in Brooklyn, I don't know how they got through it without drowning at least one actor.)

The closing words bear repetition: "Had any of these 'ifs' turned out right, every life might have been saved. But they all went against her. And never again has man been so confident. An age had come to an end."

So enthusiastic was the response to this show that Kraft repeated it, showing the kinescope. Commented Chester Bahn in *Film Daily,* "Television shows of the entertainment calibre of

A Night to Remember presented on the Kraft Television Theater constitute a far greater threat to the motion picture theater box office than either our old features now on the video market or shortly to be on it or toll television." ■

■ The second of CBS-TV's *Playhouse 90*—also in 1956—was called *Requiem for a Heavyweight,* and it had the distinction of being the first hour-and-a-half drama written especially for television. It also had the distinction of packing an awful wallop and setting a pace for casting, direction, settings and production that I could only hope would be a regular thing.

Requiem for a Heavyweight, by Rod Serling, took a hard, cold look at the fight game, and a grim, grim business it made of it, too. At the time there seemed to be a small ground swell in this direction, the movies having belted the pugilistic dodge around considerably in *The Harder They Fall* with Humphrey Bogart. After *Requiem* I couldn't imagine any young man embracing the career of fighter with any great enthusiasm. Or at all.

But then, if the play was at all accurate, fighters are hardly the sort of people who look at this sort of drama or do anything much more intellectual than hang, slack-jawed, around saloons and talk about their old fights. Hero of this gay little romp was Mountain (powerfully and poignantly played by Jack Palance), a Tennessee mountain lad who apparently went straight into the ring from ninth grade and who, at the beginning of the play, was threatened with blindness and was washed up as a fighter.

The play opened like a thunderclap. A winning fighter surrounded by cheering well-wishers and himself exuberant with health and victory came down a ramp and disappeared into a dressing room. After a long, long moment, the loser (Mr. Palance) tottered down the ramp supported on one side by his manager (Keenan Wynn) and on the other by his trainer (Ed Wynn). He was a battered hulk on the fringes of consciousness. There followed a scene with an old fight doctor (Edgar Stehli), retiring after thirty-eight years of patching up unglued fighters, who talked about the ring in slaughterhouse terminology.

The kid's washed up. Washed up with him is his manager, who has been living off him for fourteen years and who is up to his eyes in debt, too. (He had bet the kid wouldn't last three rounds and he lasted seven in his last fight.) So then where does he go and what does he do? Palance was given the role of a man who is just short of being punchy—the stammering speech, the jerky movements, and all that—but underneath the faltering speech lies an essential decency and humanity that command your respect and affection. Both author and actor collaborated here to create a genuinely moving and real person.

Serling contributed a whole gallery of fight characters, most of them pretty unappetizing—the fight manager, who is not above trying to make a clown of his fighter in the wrestling ring in order to get out of hock; iron-faced gamblers; a punchy fighter (Slapsy Maxie Rosenbloom), who endlessly recounts his old fights; a sleazy wrestling promoter; the trainer who genuinely loves the fighter. They moved through a dreary succession of locker rooms and corridors and fifth-rate hotels in which you could almost smell the sweat and dirt. The settings by Al Heschoug and lighting by Bill E. Grams did much for this story.

Once he stated his premise, Mr. Serling had to get out of it somehow, and here he brought in the love of a good woman (though love is perhaps too strong a word), and he lost me a little bit here. However, the woman was played with great economy and heart by Kim Hunter (it was a hell of a cast all the way around), and Mr. Serling went to great lengths to keep the thing plausible and unsentimental.

"I don't think I ever had a date before," says Mountain. Well, I had no idea fighters were such anchorites and, as a matter of fact, I don't think many of them are. But it was one last touch to show that the kid had had no life at all except fighting and suddenly that was gone.

I like these ninety-minute dramas, because, for once, the writers have a little time. The characters can be a little more rounded;

the scenes have more body and color. In short, the viewer gets a chance to know and to care about the people much more, and I rather think we will remember them much longer than the characters of most TV dramas, whose outlines seem pretty dim five minutes after the play is over. Incidentally, this was Ed Wynn's first straight dramatic role in fifty-four years of show business and he was great. ■

■ "My name is Mark Bragg. I'm dead. Ninety-two per cent of the world's population is dead. I was one of the first. I was lucky." You sure were, chum. Because then you missed all the dramas and books on the subject of our extermination, like *Level 7*, a novel about life in the atomic catacombs where a push-button war is conducted. Every one got wiped out, including the button pushers. Before that I'd read Nevil Shute's *On the Beach*. Same thing. To the last man.

Alas, Babylon, by Pat Frank, was dramatized for *Playhouse 90* by David Shaw in 1960. The above grim quote opened the show. It's still very popular among writers to exterminate the human race. It's a fad. It'll pass and the writers will go on to other enthusiasms. Proletarian novels about the life in the next world. "Angels, unite. You have nothing to lose but your feathers!" Cute stories about life in the ruins where boy meets girl and they have *happy* problems.

But that comes later. Now we're still in the extermination phase. And, in *Alas, Babylon*, it was grim, brother, grim. My favorite line in this was when the heroine came back from the window and said, "My God, they got Orlando!" I can remember way back—hell, it wasn't that long ago—when the line read, "My God, they got George!" Now they get whole cities. "My God, they got Chicago!" exclaimed Heloise. (You can have that line. I've decided to give up creative writing.)

As extermination fiction goes, *Alas, Babylon* was a ripsnorter.

The narrative moved like lightning from uneasy peace to total disaster with a sure-footed mounting excitement that had me breathless. The transitions—either the work of adapter Shaw or of the director Robert Stevens—were particularly dramatic. In one of them, for example, the action shifted suddenly, explosively, from a character quoting the "Alas, Babylon" passage from the Bible to jet bombers streaking through the sky; in another from the drunken hero at a supermarket to the quiet orderliness of the underground "push button" headquarters, the ultimate expression of "man's genius or his folly."

Pat Frank is very good at apocalyptic fiction (and it's getting to be a genre like the ashcan school). In the beginning his hero has just lost his wife. He drinks and chases girls. In the end, he doesn't drink so much and he wants to be a good husband. (Ninety-two per cent of the world population has died in order to teach him to stay home nights. You think, Mannie, it's maybe dramatically convex?)

The narrator is a dead man and this device is piquant, to say the least. Lines like: "Those were the last words I ever heard." (Swiftly followed by a black screen and a commercial.) Mr. Frank is not at all sentimental about life in a ruined society. His townspeople—hanging sullenly about the empty supermarket exchanging vicious rumors—act like spoiled apes. They're selfish and empty and, in some cases, vicious.

Kim Hunter played the part of a hysterical mother, and the worst thing I can say is that she did it well. The role of women in end-of-the-world fiction is becoming as well trod and clearly marked as the Lincoln Highway, but it's not a pleasant path at all, girls, and you might as well face it. The women in these things are incessantly wringing their hands and whining about the old days before Orlando disappeared. Women are essentially life-creating types, and end-of-the-world drama doesn't sit well on them.

I've read quite a lot of this sort of fiction, starting clear back with H. G. Wells, whose end-of-the-world romps sound quaint and Victorian in the light of these rude fellows today, and one thread seems to run consistently through all the books. It's always an accident. The country that starts the rockets firing always thinks someone else started it first. Irony lies heavy as lead all over these scripts.

Alas, Babylon had no proper ending; it just sort of petered out into platitudes about enjoying every minute of what little life is left. The note of irony was sounded in the final words: "Who won the war? We did. We clobbered 'em." ■

■ There was only one thing wrong with Phil Silvers' musical comedy *Do Re Mi,* which opened on Broadway in 1961. It wasn't any good. But apart from that.... After all, it had lyrics by Adolph Green and Betty Comden. It had a score by Jules Styne. It had a book by Garson Kanin, who directed it. It had Mr. Silvers and Nancy Walker. It had tons of money spent on it by David Merrick. And in addition to all that, you think it shoulda been good, too? Whaddayou—a Communist or sumpin?

I saw *Do Re Mi* about a week after it opened, and the audience was a mixture of the hip crowd, who call Julie and Betty and Adolph by their first names, and the slobs. The hip crowd wandered around with bright smiles on their faces saying, "Isn't this fun?" with varying degrees of success. The slobs—guys who simply spent $8.60 and expected something in return—looked stunned. My companion encountered a shipboard friend, a lady from New Jersey, a representative of the populace, those fools. "Isn't this awful?" she whispered. But I noticed she whispered. The populace has been thoroughly cowed in regard to shooting off its mouth about Broadway shows. Not so cowed, though, that many of them didn't rush up the aisles and tumble down from the balcony to get out of the theater even before the curtain went down.

Now, there are two kinds of musicals. There are the serious ones with lovely music, story, and characterization, but without a laugh in them—like the Rodgers and Hammerstein musicals.

Then there's the old-fashioned rowdy kind with only rudimentary efforts at character and story but lots of laughs. This was the second kind except it had practically no laughs, either.

Do Re Mi opened with a parody chorus number in a night club which, by an unfunny coincidence, is how *Pal Joey* opened. Almost immediately, Nancy Walker started singing a song, "Waiting, Waiting," which sounded like a bad imitation of "Adelaide's Lament" in *Guys and Dolls.* A few minutes later, the scene was a drugstore with a juke box which came straight out of *West Side Story.* Later, there was an audition scene that came out of *Say, Darling.* Later, the lovers met and fell in love at first glance just like *West Side Story.*

There were innumerable tidbits which didn't remind you of anything that specific but seemed to have been shipped over intact from Cain's warehouse. Years ago, I promulgated a law that said you could tell how bad a musical was by how many times the chorus yelled "Hooray!" This law later fell into discard because hoorays were abandoned. But this quaint custom was revived in *Do Re Mi.* The chorus incessantly yelled hooray.

Then there was a song called "It's Legitimate" in which Mr. Silvers and three other men marched straight up and down, their arms swinging smartly at their sides, great confident smiles on their faces, and yelling so loud that you could swear it must be a marvelous lyric because no one would yell a lyric that confidently unless it were. Except that it wasn't. It was awful.

And finally, there came a time—mercifully, the show was almost over—when Mr. Silvers faced the audience and delivered a *recitative* as the orchestra writhed in agony in the pit. Well, sir, have you ever seen Ted Lewis talk about the heartbreak of old Broadway? Or Sophie Tucker about the pangs of motherhood? It was like that—only mawkish.

There were a few good things about *Do Re Mi.* "Cry Like the Wind" was a lovely song; "Make Someone Happy" was a good song. Once in a while Phil Silvers, who may be the funniest man alive, broke loose, as he did in a number called "The Late, Late Show," which was the only decent show number, again in "V.I.P.," again when he was telling an orchestra how to comport itself.

But these were awfully occasional gleams. In the four years Silvers was on the air as Sergeant Bilko I never saw him do a script anywhere near this bad. And television is free.

Adolph Green and Betty Comden came to public notice making fun of musicals like this one they committed. What really bothers me is that it is almost considered subversive to complain. There, of course, have always been the insiders and the great unwashed, which means the rest of the world. But always before, the inside mob had better taste than the populace, demanded more, and was quicker to complain. Now, it seems to me, it's the other way around. ■

■ For a good many years now, nuns have been hot box office. Just put Audrey Hepburn in a habit and get Gregory Peck as the unbeliever who sees the light in the last few minutes, and you can hardly miss. And going right along with the nun cycle has been the children cycle. Not long ago you could barely enter a Broadway theater without discovering the stage hip deep in childhood. At *Music Man* you found little Paul O'Keefe and at *The Miracle Worker* you found Patty Duke and a passel of blind children and at *Gypsy* the air quivered with the happy cries of the little darlings.

And that brings us to *The Sound of Music,* which has both children and nuns. This is what is known as touching all the bases. Oh, brother, did they ever touch all the bases. Not only have they got children in *Sound of Music,* but children of all ages from six to sixteen, seven of 'em. This is really touching all the bases, all seven bases, And nuns, too. And, when I saw it, they had Mary Martin on top of that.

In *Sound of Music,* Mary Martin was first a nun (or rather a novice, but she's surrounded by the real articles), and then she is the mother of seven children. All I can say is that I'm happy I'm not a theater critic. In the first place, you can't possibly say anything unkind about Mary Martin, ever. You would be considered subversive. But to cast a vote against Mary Martin playing first a nun and then a mother—well, you'd be deported. Naturally. Can't have people like *that* in this country. And to come out against the seven ages of childhood, and motherhood, and nuns—well, you'd probably be hung first and then deported.

But out in the crowd at intermission, I did hear some one mutter, "It's *Little Women* with chocolate marshmallow sauce." But I didn't say it! Somebody else said it! They can't hang that on me!

Actually, I enjoyed *Sound of Music* very much. Cried in all the right places and everything. But then I've been trained in the toughest school of all—television. Anyone who has sat through as many domestic situation comedies as I have can absorb seven little dumplings, twinkling their roguish smiles, romping around in their nighties, being afraid of thunder and all that—and Mary Martin, too.

We've been through it all with Robert Young. Many times. After a few sessions with *Father Knows Best*, a fellow can take *Sound of Music* in his stride.

Hell, I sat up with Desi Arnaz, that symbol of happy family life, when he and Lucy had their first child practically on camera. I was right there, sobbing my eyes out, when Little Beaver ran away from home the first time. I was around, clutching at my heartstrings, when Patty Duke looked up at an actor in *Prince and the Pauper* and cried, "Are you a real king?" I was right there, tearing my hankie to shreds, when the children came pelting out of the forest and scampered back to their mommy's arms in *The Pied Piper of Hamelin.* (I know that's not in the original story, but on television we handle things differently.)

Oh, I've been well trained, all right. But what I want to know, Mannie, is where do we go from here? How do we top *The Sound of Music*? We mustn't despair; we must push forward. Now, how does this sound to you, Mannie—understand, I'm just spitballing—suppose we had a hunchback who rang the bells in the cathedral—if we play our cards right we can get Bing Crosby for the hunchback—and high up in the tower he is hiding this little girl, Patty Duke, who is taking care of her baby brother. We got a brand-new twist there, Mannie—the baby brother. Well, now, get this—little Patty Duke is feeding the baby brother his bottle—rolling her eyes in terror because she's afraid of the dark—and listening to the bells, when she is discovered by the Mother Superior. Helen Hayes, of course.... I can't go on. Already, I'm crying my eyes out. ■

■ I saw a far-out movie, *Last Year at Marienbad,* early in 1962, and I must say I was disappointed. This is the film directed by Alain Resnais, who gave us *Hiroshima, Mon Amour,* which I loved, and my complaint about *Marienbad* is that it isn't far out enough.

Last Year at Marienbad arrived here with a towering reputation for being incomprehensible. The reviews were so puzzling that you had to read them in a mirror, or upside down or sometimes left to right and down. These were the murkiest reviews to come along since the book reviewers tried to explain *Ulysses.*

If there's anything I like, it's a good incomprehensible far-out "moom pitcha" and I went to the Carnegie Hall Cinema with two dollars clutched in my hot little hand and stood in line with the other avant-garde (interesting collection of beards, deep thinkers, and intense young ladies in line there), and waited expectantly.

Last Year at Marienbad starts out very promisingly. A stretch of plain black film with a voice talking. In French yet. It'd be better if it were in Hindustani, of course, but French will do (except in France, of course, where it really ought to be some other language).

The first couple of scenes—a long exploration of the rooms and ceilings of the castle—were pretty good. And the opening sequences with people all sitting around like chess pieces, saying nothing, were marvelously unrevealing and delightfully confusing.

But then the principals, Delphine Seyrig and Giorgio Albertazzi, appeared and things got (I'm about to use a nasty word so get the children out of here) explicit. The hero, in short, is trying to seduce somebody else's wife. So what's so far out about that? This has been the basis of every movie since Rin Tin Tin. Now, if he were trying to make out with a llama . . . or his own wife. . . .

And do you know what the girl says? "Leave me alone!" What's new about that? Even worse, what's incomprehensible about that? If she'd said, "The calla lilies are in bloom." Or "Nevermore the rillera." Or "The heart is a lonely hunter." Or something. But "Leave me alone!" Even the clods can understand that.

So it went for ninety minutes—he pursuing, she saying, "Leave me alone." People started to walk out, not (I bet) because it was too incomprehensible but because it wasn't incomprehensible enough. Of course, there were *some* nice confusing bits. There were also some lovely shots of the castle.

The heroine looks a little like Jacqueline Kennedy, and the whole movie reminded me strongly of Mrs. Kennedy showing off the White House. "This is the Red Room. It's red." That sort of dialogue. When your mind starts wandering to thoughts like that, you're not being sufficiently puzzled.

All of which leads me circuitously to the whole subject of the far-out in the movies, the books, the paintings, the music—where it all started.

We have all been beaten into the acceptance of the weird to the point where we get awfully restive if we find anything at all understandable. Just the other day I saw an old-fashioned movie, *Dinner at Eight.* It had motivation. Remember motivations? People did things because they wanted power, or money, or social position, or sex. You know—all that old-fashioned stuff. Jove, it seemed out-of-date. Slow-footed. Plodding. Explicit!

I saw a Renoir the other day. A painting of a girl with the nose in the right place. Only two eyes. Almost made me sick. They don't even put pictures like that on candy boxes any more.

Our taste has been so corrupted that we may never be able to look at a picture of a pretty girl again. ■

Good neighbors?

■ I love the Peace Corps. The world is so brimful of hate at the moment that a little love and idealism refresh the spirit. The Peace Corps has the bloom of innocence about it in the best sense and in the best American tradition.

If we must send innocents abroad—and we are exporting them in all directions—it's pleasant to send someone with a book and a seed in his hands rather than a gun or a fistful of money. Practically every American who has been seen in the hinterland has had a gun on his shoulder, and the tourists in the cities have had their billfolds. The symbols of violence and corruption—guns and money—form a terrible image of America and not at all an accurate one.

The symbols of the Peace Corps are the hoe and the book; there is an inviolable air of asceticism and high purpose, and we need to reawaken those feelings in our affluent society. Also, I think, we need to unfurl those banners in places where so many less creditable American banners are waving.

"Nobody ever writes about any of the encouraging things that happen to the Peace Corps," complained William Haddad, deputy director of the Peace Corps. "But there are some. We have been received everywhere with tremendous enthusiasm—Colombia, the Philippines, Ghana.

"In Ghana, there was a reception at the airport and the Peace Corps delegation sang a Ghanaian song, which is a sort of 'America the Beautiful' of Ghana in Twi, the native language. Well, sir, the Minister of Education, who'd been rather skeptical of the Peace Corps up to that moment, grabbed the microphone and shouted *hip, hip, hooray*. The song was carried on the Ghanaian radio and by the next day everyone was talking about it. Made the Peace Corps very big in Ghana—knowing their song. No American had ever come to Ghana speaking any Twi at all, and we came singing it."

It is very easy to poke fun at this sort of thing and it is very dangerous and very wrong. Americans abroad are known as rich and rude; a few poor and polite Americans can undo a century or so of bad manners.

"We have a bricklayer going out to Pakistan," said Haddad. "He comes from a long line of bricklayers and he's studying Pakistani soils to see if he can make a better brick than they've been making out there."

That's the spirit of the organization—and, for once, we're making friends with *people.*

In March, 1962, when I was in Lima, Peru, Father Dan McClellan said, "We have made friends with lots of governments, including some good ones. But when the governments fall, where are we? We don't make friends with people."

Father McClellan is the priest who started the Credit Union six years ago in Puno, Peru, an Indian community 14,000 feet high in the Andes. The Credit Union was an effort, and a very successful one, to take the Indians' money out of the mattress, where they usually hide it, and put it to use. In Peru, legal interest rates run as high as 50 per cent, so the poor Indian can't borrow money without putting himself into perpetual bondage to the oligarchy which owns Peru. The only way he can get money is to hoard it.

Father McClellan's Credit Union got the Indians' money out of the mattresses and into their own Credit Union, which now has 275 branches around Peru and $3,500,000 of its own money, all of it belonging to the Indians. Last year the Credit Union got a million-dollar loan from the Alliance for Progress. The

Indian now has a place where at moderate (by Peruvian standards) credit rates he can borrow money to buy a llama or some seed and fertilizer.

The priest is the mortal foe of government-to-government loans, which is our usual practice. Bureaucratic waste eats up something like 80 per cent of these loans before they funnel down to the levels where the money is supposed to go to work. Even if government-to-government loans were made with the utmost efficiency, they generate no great warmth for the lenders from the beneficiaries. Most South American people—and this is especially true of the Indians in Peru—feel their government is their enemy, not their friend. Would you feel particularly friendly toward someone who has loaned your foe some money?

I feel most strongly that American efforts should be increasingly toward projects like Father McClellan's, or the Cornell Vicos project (which I'm coming to in a minute) or the Peace Corps, which deal directly with the people—and less and less with efforts funneled through foreign governments which steal our money and earn us nothing but the enmity of the people.

"We just gave nine million dollars to the Peruvian government to study agrarian reform," said Father McClellan cynically. "Hell—if you'll pardon the expression—we haven't got time to study reform any more. The time for action is now. They hire a bunch of lawyers to do the study and there goes the money. The Indian has been fooled so often he's not going to open his yap until he thinks you're really his friend. The Indian knows we're truly his friend now.

"There are now seventy-five thousand Indians who have their money in the Credit Union. Multiply that by five for the average Indian family and you'll see how many friends we've made. We started with thirty dollars; now we have three and a half million. The Peruvians warned me not to trust the Indians. They said the Indians would never pay. Why, we have a better payment record than Credit Unions in the United States."

Cornell University's Vicos project is one of the great social experiments of our time. In 1951 the university, almost by inadvertence, became feudal overlord to a group of 1,800 Indians in a valley plateau 8,500 feet up in the Andes nestled between a couple of the tallest peaks in the world, and there it began its attempt to move the Indians bodily out of the sixteenth century and into the twentieth.

This unlikely and ambitious enterprise started when the Department of Sociology and Anthropology of Cornell decided to study the impact of European troops scattered all over the world during World War II and set up study areas in Thailand, India, Nova Scotia, among the American Navajos and among the Andes Indians. To study the Indians in Peru, Cornell rented a hacienda of 18,000 acres, acquiring 1,800 doped, pathetic and backward Indians.

Under the local customs which have obtained there for some four hundred years, the *patrón* is entitled to three days' work a week from his resident Indians. The Indian's wife is obliged to cook for the patrón, and a daughter—if he has an attractive one—to provide sex companionship. It's a lovely life if you're a Peruvian overlord and hell if you're an Indian. The Peruvian ruling class, which is what our government deals with almost exclusively, would like to keep conditions that way and has been spreading the word around that Cornell University is a bunch of Communists for doing anything at all for the Indians.

Cornell moved into this medieval community after the harvest in 1951. The Indians were starving, which is normal. They were dressed in the remnants of a sixteenth-century page boy uniform which a Spanish overseer had put them in four hundred years ago and which they wear to this day.

Their ancestors, the Incas, were among the world's great farmers; they domesticated the potato and introduced it to the world. Their descendants had forgotten everything. They scratched the ground with sticks and, if they were lucky, a few sickly tubers came up to feed them and their families for the winter.

The Cornell group taught the Indians again how to plant a potato, in orderly widely spaced rows, and taught them irrigation. Cornell brought in new seed, taught the Indians to dip it in fungicide and to spray the plants for disease. Because of their terrible hunger, the Indians dug up the first crop of potatoes and ate them before they were half grown.

Cornell then went to work on the social structure. First they introduced sharecropping, splitting the crop with the Indians. The margin of survival is so thin in that backward area that the Indians never had enough to eat, much less enough to sell. Gradually, Cornell weaned the Indians from subsistence farming (if you could call it farming) into the money economy, into raising enough to sell in the market.

As the Indians built up their own capital, Cornell taught them the uses of credit to buy seed, and tools to modernize their agriculture. Meanwhile, the university has been teaching the Indians an even more important skill, how to make their own decisions—decisions about pasture of animals, about crops, even about the control of goat rustling which was endemic for a while. That was the real key—the psychological training of the Indians to think of themselves as human beings.

This is the American abroad at his lovely best, being utterly selfless and tremendously capable. The Cornell experiment, however, could all have gone to waste if the Indians had not acquired the land they had learned to cultivate. There was some doubt they would ever get it. The Peruvian rich don't like the Indians to get the idea they're entitled to anything, and even though we were offering to pay about a third more than the land was worth, the sale dragged for months in the courts.

If the hacienda had reverted to its owner, the Indians and the land would have reverted to the Middle Ages and Cornell's brilliant ten-year experiment would have been wasted. But in September, 1962, the Indian community of Vicos finally received title to its own land, and the news spread through the river valleys of the Andes. Perhaps someday more people than the Vicos inhabitants will have reason to be grateful to Cornell. ■

■ Peru is the land of the forty families who practically own the joint. "Except that it's more like five families," an American told me when I was in Lima. When you think of South America as a feudal domain with a few vastly wealthy Spanish families crushing the illiterate Indians under ancient oppressions, Peru is the place you're talking about. And it's all true. (Except it isn't as true as it once was. Only seven years ago the left-wing Apra party was underground and thousands of its members had to live in exile in Bolivia. Today the Apras live right in Peru.)

Lima has doubled in population in the last twenty-two years and it will double again if something is not done to halt the rush of Indians off the Andes to the sea.

"The Indians have just discovered how miserable they are," an American told me. "After four hundred years at fourteen thousand feet they've discovered it gets cold up there and there's nothing to eat."

What kept the Indians on those high plateaus so long? What got them up there in the first place? Well, things were different four hundred years ago. If you dipped into Pedro de Ciezade León's book *The Incas,* which was published in Seville in 1553, you read of "the abundance of food in the fertile land," of the herds of "deer and llamas, and rabbits and partridges and turtledoves and other game," as well as the abundance of crops and the great agricultural skills of the Incas.

The great tragedy is not that the Indian has not entered the twentieth century, but that the all-devouring Spaniards knocked all the sixteenth-century wisdom out of him, too.

The Indians live on the haciendas (or ranches) owned by the absentee landlords, who are carefully protected by a mass of laws designed to give them everything and to keep the Indian in his place. No, it's not slavery; serfdom is the word for it, and in many ways it is worse than slavery.

The Indian is permitted to work sixteen hours a day on his freezing plateau for a wage that keeps him in perpetual bondage. To make him forget his cold and his hunger, the foreman doles out a hatful of coca leaves for him to chew the cocaine out of and keep himself doped and quiescent.

But the word has trickled to the high plateau that it is warm on the coast. And so the sixteenth-century Indians are pouring down the slopes to the sunny coast, where there's no food either, but at least it's warm. An Indian with no skill and frequently no Spanish (the language is Quechua) suddenly enters the money economy for the first time in his life. And what does he do in the money economy? The Peruvian government, one of the most slow-moving bodies in Western civilization, wishes it knew.

The Peruvians themselves have so lost faith in their own country that they are stashing their money away in New York and Switzerland while asking us to provide the capital to modernize their economy. In that way, if the Communists take over the country in three years, which is entirely possible, the Peruvians can skip and leave us holding the bag, as is our wont.

Peru, in short, is a place where you can get awfully angry. The total selfishness and utter absence of a social conscience seem heartless and cruel until you reflect that the social conscience in America is a relatively new thing. How long ago was *The Grapes of Wrath?* ■

■ It's easy to criticize the sins of others. After wandering among the underdeveloped nations of South America early last year, it was nice to be back in a highly developed nation like our own. I mean, one gets tired of the holes in the streets in Buenos Aires. Why, you keep asking yourself, doesn't Buenos Aires keep the streets beautifully repaired the way Mayor Wagner keeps New York's streets? (Great balls of fire, *look* at New York streets! Some of them look like the battle scene from *What Price Glory.*)

I had barely set foot in South America when I was told that practically everyone in Uruguay had two jobs—one for the government, and one for someone else. Coming from a highly developed economy like our own, I was unprepared for the Uruguayan Navy. The Uruguayan Navy had only three ships—two destroyers and one frigate—and was full of Navy officers who held down other jobs, their sole Navy duties being to collect their pay. (What's this about moonlighting in the New York City Fire Department? You mean a New York City fireman can't make ends meet without two jobs?)

Coming from a country with a strong liberal tradition like our own, any American would have been particularly aghast at the sway exercised by the Army, the Navy, and the Air Force on national policy. We, of course, are accustomed to civil control of the military. (When was the last time the United States Senate told the Air Force it couldn't have something it wanted?)

To an American, a real big laugh was the Brazilian aircraft carrier. As a matter of fact, even the Brazilians found it pretty funny because it hadn't any planes on it. The Brazilians called it "Bella Antonio"; that's Brazilian for an effeminate man, which is to say, beautiful but ineffectual. Brazil needed an aircraft carrier—especially one without planes—like we need the B-70. The aircraft carrier was strictly for prestige purposes because Argentina had one. (I got a big yock out of the Brazilian aircraft carrier until I got back and discovered that the B-70 had become a $10-billion boondoggle—lots of pilots sitting around doing nothing, now that the missiles had taken their jobs, and their purpose in life.)

One of the largest American complaints, not only about Brazil but about all South America, is that they waste so much money supporting an enormous and reactionary and largely superfluous military machine while they neglect really vital needs such as education. (Now let's see. Our last military budget was $55 billion. Meanwhile, Kennedy can't get his measly little $4-billion aid-to-education bill even started, can he?)

One of the basic conditions to Alliance for Progress aid is that the South Americans do something about their income tax. Or rather their lack of income tax, which the rich manage so easily to avoid. The rich in South America consider it an outrage that we even mention the subject. (That reminds me, when was the last time you heard anything about eliminating that 27½ per cent oil depreciation tax allowance? Taxing Texas is considered as blasphemous as taxing the rich in South America. It's all very well to talk about tax reform in South America so long as we don't have any of those dirty words here.)

And, if you really want to get angry, just consider how the South Americans treat their Indians. Poor Indians have no rights at all in Peru and no chances. (And how many rights have our Indians? Indians on reservations can't even vote!) The Argentines have no Indian problem at all, because they wiped out their Indians a hundred years ago. (Just as we almost wiped ours out a hundred years ago.)

Oh, it was great to be back in a civilized country and reflect about the sins of others. ■

■ In South America politics is irreconcilable. When you lose an election, the general rule has been: blow the country before you land in jail or get shot. In Uruguay you find hordes of Argentine refugees. Bolivia once had thousands of Peruvian refugees and now Lima has thousands of Bolivian refugees who cannot return home, probably ever. It's as if you lost an election in Rhode Island and had to flee to Texas to live.

I had a talk with a Bolivian exile who would not allow his name to be used because there are still friends and relatives in Bolivia. (Bolivia is a place where they like to hang their politicians on lampposts, and there have been times when every other lamppost in La Paz had a politico dangling from it.)

There are roughly 2,000 Bolivians living in Lima, my refugee estimated, and probably 18,000 Bolivians in exile in all, many of them in Argentina and Chile. Most of those in Lima and Argentina, he said, are from the professions—doctors, lawyers, teachers, journalists—all people whom Bolivia can ill afford to lose. Bolivia, of course, is in desperate financial straits, and one of the principal factors hindering recovery is that so many of its best-educated and best-trained citizens have had to take to their heels.

"You must understand that a great many South Americans are self-exiles," said my refugee. "They didn't have to leave their native countries but because of the situation in their countries, people exile themselves. Whole families exile themselves.

"This is a serious problem as far as Bolivia is concerned. It has a small population [3,462,000], many of them illiterate Indians. For such a little country to lose its elite teachers, technicians, liberal arts professors, engineers, lawyers and doctors is a loss of human capital that is almost irreplaceable. The best doctors and lawyers set up practices elsewhere and then it's hard to get them to come back, as they get deeply rooted. One of the most serious charges against the revolutionary government of Bolivia is that it has depleted the country of its best-qualified men.

"Psychologically, it's pretty hard on all of us. You feel terribly depressed living in exile. You feel everyone is against you. There are terrible frustrations. Then there are the memories of home. You cannot uproot those. Man does not live by bread alone."

Bad as the exile problem is in Bolivia, conditions are even worse in Paraguay, and Bolivia is full of Paraguayan refugees—probably 50,000 of them. ■

■ One night while I was in Buenos Aires, I had dinner with a Communist student. He was lean, hard, bright, and serious to the point of solemnity. He explained very quickly that he was not a Communist but a Marxist-Leninist. Communism is illegal there as it is in the United States.

I asked him what was the difference between a Marxist-Leninist and a Communist, and he explained that the Communists were international in their thinking where the Marxist-Leninists were national. This is very much the party line in Argentina, which is intensely nationalistic on all levels. The Communists have run into intense opposition in promoting a revolution which seems to be directed by Moscow. Consequently, they are soft-pedaling the Moscow line and emphasizing the strictly native origins. Nevertheless, José (which is not his name) is strictly a Communist who talks the pure party line. And if there is ever a Communist uprising in Latin America, José is of the type that will be its backbone.

Many of us in the United States are inclined to think that if revolution comes it will be the lower-class and peasant misery that provides the spark and the fuel. But this was not true in Cuba and it doesn't appear to me to be true in the rest of Latin America, either. Castro's beard obscures the fact that he's a college boy, a graduate of the University of Havana. Che Guevara, his second-in-command and the ideological brain of the Cuban revolution, was graduated from the University of Buenos Aires, where he attended the medical school. The medical school, I'm told, is saturated with Communists. An American newspaperman asked one of them why the Communists were so interested in becoming doctors and he replied, "Because it gets us in touch with the people."

José, who was nineteen when I met him, was to enter the University of Buenos Aires this year to study sociology, another branch of learning which will put him in touch with the people. If the Vice-President of the United States gets eggs or stones thrown at him in the next four years in Buenos Aires, José will undoubtedly be in the crowd throwing.

Students in Argentina are a different breed from our college students, altogether humorless, intense and far more politically aware. I asked José if he supported Castro and he said, "Unreservedly. This is what we are working for in Argentina."

Hundreds of Josés are fanning out from Latin American universities as doctors, as lawyers, as sociologists. They are the greatest source of Communist infection in Latin America, far more dangerous than any peasant leaders or labor leaders. The most effective Communist leaders in Latin America are intellectuals, and the Latin American university is their rallying point, their headquarters.

The University of Buenos Aires is the largest university in our hemisphere. Its ruling council is composed of rectors, faculty, deans, alumni and students, and one of every four council members is a student. However the students, by threats of strikes and demonstrations, exercise far more than 25 per cent control over selection of faculty and university policy.

The University of Buenos Aires used to be one of the best universities in the hemisphere. It is now one of the worst, its standards wrecked largely by student control. Leftist students controlled the council for years but recently they have been tossed out by a surge to the right, something like the surge to the right in our universities.

Shortly before I talked to José, five thousand students at the university had switched from left to right, throwing the pro-Castro students out of the ruling council and putting in their own men. Discontent with Castro had started with his tractor-for-prisoner deal and got much stronger when he admitted he was a Communist. At the same time, anti-Communist students were taking over control of the Student Federation of Ecuador, which had been under Communist control for seventeen years. In both cases the intense nationalism of the students had a good deal to do with the revulsion against communism. That's why the new party line is Marxist-Leninist, which, it is claimed, is strictly Argentine in Argentina, Ecuadorian in Ecuador. But it sounds just like communism to our ear. ■

■ A part of the Argentine's intense nationalism springs from his personality, which has been shaped—according to Raúl Scalabrini Ortiz y Gassett—by the pampa. "The pampa promises . . . promises . . . promises . . . ," says Gassett. "The Argentine lives what I would call his individual concrete future. This is not the shared future of a common ideal, of a collective utopia. Each individual lives his own illusions as if they had already come true."

The Argentine—both as an individual and as a nation—is a loner, and this goes far to explain what happened at Punta del Este in February, 1962, where Argentina stubbornly went its own way. Following the lead of the United States down there is like voting for civil rights in our own South—it's political suicide. If Brazil, Mexico, and Chile had gone along (particularly Brazil), Argentina would have voted to toss out Cuba too, because that would have meant that Argentina was not allying itself with the United States but allying itself with the hemisphere as a whole.

A great many diplomats and newspapermen are very bitter and deeply resentful at our State Department over the actions taken at the American Foreign Ministers' Conference at Punta del Este. (The Argentines are deeply split over this.) Many feel the conference should never have been held, that it gave Castro a matchless platform to play martyr for his potent left-wing sympathizers all over Latin America. They say it split the hemisphere and stirred up both the right and left wings all over South America, presenting not only Argentina but also Brazil with first-class political crises.

They also believe that if we had not been so insistent on voting Cuba out at the time of the conference, if we had been willing to wait a couple of weeks for a meeting of the Council of American States, a formula could have been found on which Argentina, Brazil and Mexico could agree. But these arguments fail to take into consideration the North American temperament. We don't understand or sympathize with their temperament, and this does no good for the Alliance of Progress. We believe in doing, the Argentine in being. Argentina is one of the richest countries in natural resources on earth and the Americans who live there are eternally exasperated at the Argentine for not developing his beautiful country. But the Argentines simply aren't that interested in hard work.

The Argentines feel their country is destined for the most exalted destiny, but—and this is the part Americans can't understand—they don't have to do anything to bring this about. The promised future will come not by their own effort but by magic or divine grace. Eduardo Mallea, in his book *Historia de Una Pasión Argentina,* says the Argentine motto is "God will provide." The Argentines firmly believe and frequently say "God is Argentine"—so why do they need the Alliance for Progress? ■

■ Right after Punta del Este it was fashionable in Rio de Janeiro for the politicians to explode into print with the cry that "Brazil is sitting on a powder keg." The powder keg metaphor was very popular there, but one couldn't help feeling that no one could sit on a powder keg more lightheartedly than a Brazilian. In fact, he probably wouldn't sit on it; he'd stand to bang out rhythms on it and the children would start dancing in the streets.

I had lunch with a Brazilian who came from the northeast sector of the country where 22,000,000 people were living in the most appalling poverty. "What do they do in the northeast?" I asked. "They starve," he replied cheerfully.

Last year the northeast section, centering around Recife, began to receive publicity in the United States from Adlai Stevenson's visit, talk of shipping United States wheat and flour to the area, and from the SUDENE plan (Superintendency for the Development of the Northeast). The plan, put together by the Brazilian economist Celso Furtado, had attracted the attention of the Washington administration right up to President Kennedy.

The SUDENE plan is an immensely ambitious scheme to industrialize the area and resettle its population, comparable in scale to our Tennessee Valley Authority. Success or failure of the plan, some people say, will mean the difference between whether Brazil falls into the hands of the Communists or not. Others tell you cynically that the northeast and its starvation have simply been getting an inordinate amount of belated recognition in the United States press.

A Hindu philosopher passed through Rio de Janeiro not long ago and wrote back to his people, in gentle wonder, that Brazil was "the only working anarchy in the world." Barry Goldwater, who feels that the best government is the least government, would be absolutely enchanted with the place.

The Brazilians do not have any government—well, almost none. After Janio Quadros left the Presidency—and the country—in a huff, the Brazilians were saddled with João Goulart. They didn't trust Goulart so they stripped the Presidency of most of its powers and scattered them among the Parliament, a Prime Minister and the Cabinet so that no one could really get anything done.

The situation is further complicated by the intense unpopularity of the new capital, Brasilia. Legislators loathe the place so intensely that they do what they can to stay away from there. Consequently, it's almost impossible to get a quorum to pass a bill. The Parliament was in special session when I was there last year, and it took a week before a quorum got together.

I asked Carlos Lacerda, the witty, conservative Governor of the state of Guanabara, what he thought of the Alliance for Progress, and I got a bright lecture about the American idea that American dollars will solve any problem.

"Democracy can be saved only by those who believe in it," he said. "I don't despise money but if we stay in the field of economics, we'll never save this country from the Communists. The danger of communism here is that it is spreading out—not only in the poorer sections but among the most prosperous sections. It is infiltrating respectable elements of the press and labor." A popular conception, he said, is that "if you feed the people that's enough. But this is a battle of ideas. This is a battle for the minds of men."

Lacerda, like many Latin Americans, thinks we North Americans are too materialistic in our preoccupations. ■

■ "The Brazilian is the most political animal on earth," a diplomat in Brasilia told me.

I had lunch with a lady who teaches law at a Brazilian university and had the temerity to mention Governor Brizola's land expropriations in Rio Grande do Sul. Instantly the air was blue with politics of a complexity, sophistication and humor that could hardly be found anywhere outside of France.

But does this sophistication, this comprehension of issues, this political volubility lead to political stability? Don't be silly. The Brazilian political situation is about as stable as that of the French, with whom, incidentally, there are close analogies. You may set it down as one of Crosby's Laws that the more politically conscious the people are, the more chaotic the politics.

The Brazilians are marvelous at political jokes, and the best political jokes have more than a germ of truth in them. The Brazilians, for example, came up with the best joke at Punta del Este, which went: "U.S. Ambassador Morrison has just handed in his expense account: breakfast, thirty pesos; haircut, fifty pesos; newspaper, two pesos; lunch with the Haitian Foreign Minister, fifty million dollars."

One of the political jokes going the rounds was about Janio Quadros, that extremely able, enormously popular, but emotionally unstable President who astounded Brazil (and many say himself) by resigning and storming out of the country. According to a popular joke, Janio was so bewildered by his own actions that he went to a psychiatrist and asked, "Am I crazy?" The psychiatrist put him through a series of tests and then told him, "No, you're not crazy, but those six million people who voted for you are."

Again, there's a germ of truth there. Janio Quadros was one of the most popular Presidents ever elected. But he was also impatient with the democratic process and he resigned in a fit of petulance. Instantly his popularity plummeted. "He couldn't," people would tell you, "have been elected dogcatcher."

Brazilians are marvelous at paper revolutions in which power changes hands without anyone so much as getting his arm twisted. They even got rid of slavery without a shot being fired, which, God knows, is more than we did. They have the world's most civilized revolutions. ■

■ One of the hallmarks of an underdeveloped country is the ability to absorb vast quantities of oratory. Street crowds have listened to Fidel Castro's harangues for as long as five hours. Khrushchev's massive monologue to the Communists' twenty-second congress ran for seven hours in two installments, and the faithful listened. You and I would go out of our minds. But our forebears used to travel miles by horse and buggy to listen to spellbinders declaim up to four hours and love it.

What's happened to us anyway? Are we sissies or something? It's commonly held that the radio killed the two-hour political oration. Roosevelt's fireside addresses ran barely thirty minutes. And then television came along and cut our attention span even further.

Anyhow, I decided to test my stamina at the Punta del Este conference by listening to every blessed word uttered by Osvaldo Dorticós, President of Cuba, and head of its delegation, a hard-shell Communist but definitely in the third echelon of Cuba's top orators. I'd been warned his speech would run two hours. Actually, it ran almost three.

At the end of the first hour, former U.S. Deputy Assistant Secretary of State Richard Goodwin walked out muttering, "I heard this speech last August." At the end of the second hour, Dorticós was still going strong—but the audience was tiring fast. Pretty blondes in the audience were beginning to let their eyes wander from the speaker to younger males. Some of them walked out. When the speech had run for two and a half hours I counted the people around me who were sound asleep. There were six, including Presidential Assistant Arthur Schlesinger, a great speech writer in his own right. (He can dish it out but he can't take it, I thought.)

"We are all ready in Cuba to work every day and to die on exceptional days," shouted Dorticós, but by this time he had lost the attention of about half of those soft imperialists who were his audience.

The speech started at 10:30 P.M. and ended about 1:20 A.M. I went the route, every last word of it, but I'm soft as putty. If I had it to do all over again, I wouldn't do it all over again. ■

■ There was a saying at Punta del Este that "Latin America is just a bunch of nations united by a common distrust of the United States." The avowed aim of Secretary of State Rusk and his

American colleagues at the American Foreign Ministers' Conference was to change this to read: "Latin America is just a bunch of nations united by a common distrust of Cuba." This, by a squeaky two-thirds majority of fourteen to one with all the big nations—Mexico, Argentina and Brazil—abstaining, was done. Cuba was not tossed out of the club; it only had its keys to the men's washroom taken away from it.

The Alliance for Progress is the new-style dollar diplomacy as opposed to the old style or Coca-Cola–United-Fruit-style dollars. They are the same dollars, but liberals can comfort themselves that dollars spent to spread social welfare are a good thing, whereas dollars which enrich the United Fruit Company are not. Still, this kind of tough diplomacy will leave scars all over Latin America that will take a while to heal.

Senators Bourke Hickenlooper and Wayne Morse and Representatives Armistead Selden and Chester Merrow, who were not part of the hard bargaining teams which hammered out the eventual agreement at the conference, helped out (if that's the word for it) by collaring hapless Latin American delegates and (as they said) "letting our views be known." The views were quite simple: If you're not with us, you're against us. If you're against us, Congress is going to take a very cold view of any foreign aid toward your country.

The big Latin American countries achieved their peace with popular opinion at home by splitting their vote on the issue of communism in the hemisphere. They were against it, thus placating the right wing; on the other hand they did not vote for the expulsion of Cuba, thus placating (they hoped) the very potent left wing in their countries. No Anglo-Saxon could divide his sympathies so skillfully.

Every conference produces one word that everyone falls on as the solution to all their problems, meaning what you want it to mean and also meaning what the other guy wants it to mean. The big word to come out of the Punta del Este conference was "incompatibility," a word hitherto consigned mostly to the divorce courts, but destined after this conference to bigger things.

Both the Argentines and the Mexicans claimed they brought

"incompatibility" (in Spanish it's *incompatibilidad*) to the conferees. The Argentines thought up "suspension" in place of "expulsion" and the Colombians dragged in an even lovelier word for it—"deprived" (*deprivado*). Everyone, it seemed, contributed a nice shiny word to the conference except us. We only brought money. ■

■ The breakup of the American Foreign Ministers' Conference had this flavor: a little sour, bittersweet. The conferees had met two weeks earlier as friends or foes or strangers. New friendships (and new hostilities) were created between conferees and press. There were great acts of friendship and massive betrayals, but whether the one or the other, the cast were no longer strangers.

The *Figaro* correspondent treated the whole conference as a delicious Gallic joke. The jolly *Tanjug* correspondent from Yugoslavia gibed at his friends (he had many), "The United States got two-thirds of the votes and lost two-thirds of the people. You got the votes you need but not the votes you want. Ha-ha."

"We got to watch those Communists," growled an American correspondent. "They're developing a sense of humor. Our side used to have a monopoly on the stuff." Said another one: "Like the bomb. They're stealing the jokes like they stole the bomb. They got spies everywhere—putting jokes on microfilm."

The breeze blew through the lobby from the inviting sea—which to the Americans, headed back to the frozen North, would soon be a tantalizing memory. In the corner of the lobby was the Great Lover of the American diplomatic corps. Brown as a nut in spite of all those hours he spent on the dance floor, he was saying good-by to three of his girl friends.

"All three of them together," marveled a Polish correspondent. "That's his greatest act of diplomacy in this conference."

"It's his only one," muttered somebody else.

Foreign ministers' conferences have their own rhythms, alternating between hope and despair. Like breathing out and breathing in. Dictated by the great wire services. Pumping out hope to the afternoon papers, despair to the morning ones (usually). "Hope rises," "hopes plummet." Even the most independent members of the press are influenced by the great pulse of the wire services, and the diplomats themselves, despite their inner knowledge, are swayed far more than they realize by the great pulse. It's this tension that holds the conference together. The tension of opposites. The sense of what will happen now, who will win, who will lose. But when it's over, it's over. The great pulse has stopped, and a great languor takes possession of everyone.

At the back of the hotel the flags of twenty-one nations whipped in the breeze. The Uruguayan cadets in their dress uniforms were drawn up in rows of two (well, it's a small country), the cockades blowing in the wind, their white-crossed bandoliers gleaming in the soft dusk. The commander right-faced them and marched them off, their arms swinging like the English. They looked, in their tall hats and swords and round buttons, like something out of *Babes in Toyland.*

Overheard from those saying good-by: "You going to Buenos Aires? Where you going to stay? I'll be at the City Hotel." "If you get to Lima I'm in the book." There was a tremendous scribbling of names and exchanging of phone numbers and addresses, 97 per cent of which would never lead to anything. Simply a symbol of a shared experience. A shared fellowship.

Down in the pressroom bar the hard-core drinkers were having a last belt before the bar closed and the gambling wheels came back. The slender brown barboy was telling the American reporters he was going to America.

"We have bought a Reo," he explained in his careful school English. "Nineteen twenty-six but in very good condition." He carefully took down all the American addresses and telephone numbers because he wanted to call and say hello when he got there.

Outside it had grown quite dark. At the back of the hotel they were taking down the twenty-one flags, still whipping strongly in the warm wind from the salt sea. ■

■ In Latin America, whether they love us or hate us, there are signs of our U.S. culture, not necessarily the examples we're proudest of.

In Europe the signs are all over the place: Europe is in the grip of our mass culture. While Europeans are wallowing in prosperity, there are drastic changes in consumer attitudes over there. In London, the middle classes are buying suits off the rack and shirts and ties over the counter, rather than having them made as they have always done. The class structure is leveling. Three times as many cars are on the roads and half the homes will have refrigerators by 1970 in place of one in ten homes now. As Americans are showing signs of being as individualistic as the French (at least in consumer attitudes), the French are taking over our old bad conformist consumer attitudes.

Europe, furthermore, now looks to New York at the center of the arts—a statement that will lead to some outraged howls.

It's a feeling you get whether you are talking to Frenchmen in the arts or to Americans living abroad. The center of their universe is New York, which is the headquarters of the world theater, the world's music, much of the world's literature, and increasingly of its art. I don't mean to say necessarily that the writers and the artists are all collected in New York or even that they are Americans, because they aren't.

What I mean is that New York is the headquarters. That's where you go for acceptance of your play or your book or (in a lesser sense) your picture. That's where the decisions are made so that your book or your play or your music is called great (or not so great). If you open big in New York, the play is likely to expand outward to London, Paris, Madrid. (You find even a lightweight piece of malarkey like *Tunnel of Love* in Madrid, which hasn't much theater.) New York's the place—whether you like it or not—which blows the whistle on you.

In ancient times, Romans used to get away from it all, too—the crowds, the pressures of Rome—and build pleasant villas in Spain (whose ruins are still evident). But, of course, they had to go back to Rome to get promoted.

It's wonderful to live in the lovely city of Paris. "But what do they think of my pilot film on Madison Avenue?" (Or in Beverly Hills?) "The book'll be published in October. Then back to New York," says the expatriate author. Or you'll hear, "That lousy foreign editor cut my Khrushchev analysis down to three paragraphs and stuck it back with ship news. Doesn't that idiot realize that was the most important interpretive piece I've written all year?"

Idiot or otherwise, the foreign editor is in New York and he's the boss. And so is the book publisher. So is CBS, upon which the little package-producer who has the nice apartment in Montparnasse and the French wife is so hopelessly dependent. And so is Radio City Music Hall, the ultimate destination of the movies being shot all over Europe. Even where the box offices are in Europe, the bankers and Twentieth Century-Fox are in America.

All these things add up to this strong feeling that Paris and Rome and Madrid are the outer ramparts, the colonies (though that will be ferociously resented). Julius Caesar deep in Gaul, wondering what sort of shenanigans were going on back in the Roman Senate, which was trying to cut his throat, went through mental processes not much different from those of the TV producer who heard somebody had been unseated at CBS—and wondered what this meant to the adventure series he was shooting in Europe. ■

■ Differences in national cultures and national attitudes were shown back in 1954, when eight countries—England, France, Italy, Switzerland, Germany, Denmark, Holland, Belgium—were linked together in a television network for the month of June.

To Americans, the programs offered would have seemed impossibly dull: a stroll down the Rhein at Bad Godesberg; an inspection of the pictures at the Vatican; a fête for the children of displaced persons in Holland; a promenade in London at night; the illumination at Versailles. (Since this was written, Telstar has spanned the ocean. The Americans weren't exactly overjoyed.)

But Europeans are interested in much different things than we are. They like to travel; these little glimpses of not-so-far-away places gave them a vicarious satisfaction. In addition, they have a deep interest in one another's culture.

It was interesting to note that one French show broadcast to all eight countries concerned a new visitor to Paris—his first impression of the restaurants, the shops, the streets, the girls. And from Britain came a show of Queen Elizabeth reviewing detachments of the Royal Navy in London.

Every nation tried to put forth its best foot and in so doing revealed a little bit of its own temperament, its own prejudices, its own self. The Germans, for example, broadcast some sort of youth encampment where the German youths were imbibing fresh air and emitting German songs—as they seem to have been doing for some centuries now. (It was pretty dull, too.) The Swiss, who have always been exquisitely noncommittal and expertly nonpartisan, broadcast a flower show, than which there is nothing more noncommittal or nonpartisan. And yet each of these things—ordinary in itself—provided an extraordinary glimpse from one country to another. ■

■ The subject of international cultural exchanges brings me to an observation I made at the second International Television Festival in Monte Carlo in January of last year. I had sat as a judge and writhed through an American entry, a fifth-rate production of *The Affairs of Anatol,* the sort of TV show I wouldn't sit through on a dull Tuesday night in Los Angeles. This was followed by a Russian entry called *The Music of Verdi,* which was also pretty bad. The Russian member of the jury, Konstantin Kousacov, turned to me and asked, "Did you like that?"

"Well . . . ," I began, diplomatically.

"I didn't like it," he said emphatically.

Which led me to my observation about international festivals: you always hate the stuff from your own country worse than that from anyone else's country because you feel vaguely responsible. Or maybe guilty is the word I'm groping for. ■

Money

■ Money is important. My mother said that, and, by George, no one ever boiled it right down to the kernel so succinctly.

Money is, furthermore, a most serious and tantalizing subject. One night I was watching a half-hour TV dramatic show called *The Doctor.* Some little tale about a farmer who went berserk trying to find some buried money on his place. A little while later, an old British film came on—a little less than a masterpiece named *Hard Steel*—and this, too, displayed the disintegrating effect of success and money on a man's character.

My own feelings in the matter were summed up succinctly by the late George Kaufman one night on *This Is Show Business.* Martha Wright asked the panel to supply her with a formula for happiness, a tall order. "Well," observed Tanglethatch sourly, "we all know money doesn't bring happiness, so just give your money away. Give it to me."

Clearly, Mr. Kaufman was not afraid of the corroding effects on him of cold cash. Neither am I. The destructive effect of gold on our souls has been a rather persistent refrain in our literature for a long time. Well, it's a valid enough theme, but I should like to register a small dissent. It doesn't *have* to happen that way.

I once knew a guy, a terribly cantankerous and generally neurotic fellow, who inherited a bundle of money. He had been a conspicuously unsuccessful collection of traumas—until he could pay his bills. Then he blossomed out into a benevolent, though dull, chap. He was good to his mother; he lowered the volume of his radio in deference to his neighbors; he contributed generously to Cerebral Palsy. His character didn't deteriorate at all under the impact of money. It improved.

I don't know that money really makes such monsters of us as the books say. The people I've found most passionately indignant at the condition of the poor are the very rich who have a lot of time on their hands for indignation. The rest of us are too busy earning a living. I've met some awfully nice folks who were successful and some awful crumbs who weren't. I should even like to make the faintly subversive suggestion that the nice folks were nice *because* they were successful and had a little cash in the bank, that the crumbs were that way because they weren't and hadn't.

Just about the time I'd gotten this conclusion weighed and found valid and filed away with other pieces of realization, my son announced triumphantly, "It is easier to get rich in the United States today than ever before."

"Now, where did you get such a silly idea?" I inquired.

"It says so right here in *Look* magazine." And he showed me. Sure enough, there it was in black and white. An article called "Money," by Leonard Gross. It opened with "It's easier to get rich in the United States today than ever before."

"If it's that easy to get rich, Daddy, why is it that you . . ."

"Why aren't you in school?" I snarled.

"There isn't any school. The Mayor closed all the schools because of the snow. Daddy, if it's so easy to get rich, how come you aren't . . ."

"Go play in the snow! Very good for you!"

"Practically everybody is rich except us, Daddy. It says right here this man Jameson started an electronics company with three thousand dollars and four years later he had one million eight hundred thousand. Why don't you do something like that?"

"Because I'm yat-a-tat-tat-ing with you all day long! That's why," I snapped.

Why was *Look* magazine putting ideas like that in the heads of innocent children?

I picked up the magazine, which had a gold cover that week. "All About Money," it said on the cover. "How It's Made," "How It Grows," "How It's Spent," "Can We Afford to Be Rich?"

Can we afford to be rich?

How would I know? I know I can't afford to be poor, because my creditors keep nipping at my heels. But if I can't afford to be rich either, what can I afford?

I opened *Look*. "Frank Jameson," it said in black type easily accessible to all small children, "is living proof that in our society today a man who wants to can still get rich. Jameson had no advanced degrees and no unusual talents. He is bright but not ingenious. . . ."

Hmm! Fine lot of malarkey to put into naïve young heads. I turned the page: "How to pick a stockbroker. A real pro can make you a fortune. Here are some inside tips." Good Lord, how am I going to explain that to the children? Everybody but me is doing it. I turned another page. "Self-Made Woman." "She started with $250. Fifteen years later, she had her first million."

It could ruin your whole day, a magazine like that. ■

■ According to the announcer who used to sell Chevrolets on the old Dinah Shore show, a new form of capitalist slavery was "one-car captivity"—a lovely phrase.

You're chained to the land like serfs in the Middle Ages, you peasants who own only one car. That's one of the current brand marks of the underprivileged—one car.

Lord, I remember way back when Will Rogers was making Depression jokes about riding to the poorhouse in an automobile. The next Depression we'll be riding to it in two automobiles—

one for the teen-agers in the family. What still scares me about that Chevrolet battle cry—two cars in every garage—is that it sounds so much like two chickens in every pot, which has a Depression smell to it.

There have been some other harbingers from the automobile world that had the ring of disaster about them. One of the Hollywood columns harbored an item that Mary Benny, Jack Benny's wife, was halfway home from Chasen's one day before she noticed she was driving the wrong Rolls-Royce. So many Rollses in the back lot that it was getting difficult to parcel them into the right hands.

Years ago, I went to Chasen's with a rich Hollywood writer who turned his Cadillac over to the doorman with the remark: "I don't need a check, do I?" And the doorman said, "You better take a check. We got nothing back there but Cadillacs." I remember being terribly impressed at the time. Not any more. The social prestige of the Cadillac has taken an awful dip. The only really upper-class car now is the Rolls-Royce, and already in chic circles in New York there are mutterings against the *standard* Rolls-Royce: "My dear fellow, you're not going to buy your Rolls right off the rack, are you?" If it isn't a custom-built Rolls, you're awfully non-U.

I don't know about the rest of you clods, but I find this automotive snobbery exhilarating. The frank fact of the matter is that I don't even own one car. You suppose the Chevvy people have a phrase for non-car people? If a one-car guy is a captive, a non-car man is just barely breathing. He's hardly on the threshold of consciousness. Car ownership is getting to be a premise of existence. We'll have to rewrite Descartes to read: "I own a Chevrolet; therefore I am."

Sam Levenson has pointed out that this spoiled generation of teen-agers has appropriated the family car as if it were one of their constitutional privileges. Kids have been running away from home since the dawn of time, Levenson points out, but this current crop announces to Mother and Pop, "I'm running away from home. Call me a cab." ■

■ *Commander Jet 1121,* the full-page ad read. "The Aero Commander Jet 1121 heralds a breakthrough in executive transportation! A 500-plus-m.p.h. aircraft, this great, new multiplier of management productivity will operate from short fields with ease and safety . . . will seat four to six. . . . An economic breakthrough, too, the Aero Commander Jet 1121 is priced at less than $600,000 fully equipped. . . . It's for sale now. You can order yours today."

Sounded just like what I'd been looking for. I had just a few questions. How short a field? I was thinking of using it for going home to Oconomowoc for weekends, but that back lot is pretty brief. Priced at *less* than $600,000? How much less? $599,999.95? I'd seen that priced-at-less jazz before and it wasn't much less.

Aah, the affluent age! Just when the Kennedy administration was cracking down on expense accounts and yachts for executives, Aero Commander was introducing its little old jet runabout for 600,000 clams. Listen, fellows, I said, if it's not deductible, I can't afford it. A fellow can't even take a safari any more without the Feds breathing down his neck. There is no reason to expect they will let you get away with a jet plane.

I could just hear the Internal Revenue fellow asking me, "Listen, do you *have* to get there at five hundred miles an hour? What did you accomplish that you couldn't have done at three hundred and fifty miles an hour? Or maybe on the telephone?"

The ad appeared the day we finally got our first man into space. You might say the Commander Jet 1121 for executive travel was already obsolescent. Your really status-conscious executive was dreaming of the Commander Rocket which would get him to Los Angeles in five minutes at a mere cost of $100 million. (Well, maybe they'll mass-produce these rockets for a lot less—like $25 million. A real economic breakthrough. To rearrange Pyrrhus a little bit, another economic breakthrough like that and we're undone.) ■

■ Wars used to be won by patriotism and 10 per cent. Now it's patriotism and 44 per cent. At least that's the profit the government charged Douglas Aircraft made in developing the Nike missile and one that Donald Douglas claimed was fair.

The normal cost-plus offered by the government, Douglas explained, didn't cover all the "dirty little details" of managing a complex weapons system. The government complained Douglas made $63.9 million, rather a nice profit, developing the Nike missile, which was largely produced by subcontractors. Douglas protested that his company only—I love that *only*—made $29.8 million. He asked for ten days to be able to prove the company had made $33 million less than the government said it did.

This is another new trend—boasting about how *little* you made. I'm particularly entranced by the new drift in magazine advertising. The *Saturday Evening Post* in an ad last year said, "There is a dinosaur aura about some of America's larger magazines these days. An overconcern for bigness and a dim-eyed disregard of the mental level of the content . . . an urge to say 'I'm bigger than you are.' We have stabilized our circulation base at 6,500,000. There will be no increase in the base in 1962."

Well!

Next thing you know the magazines will be taking full-page ads boasting, "Our circulation is smaller than your circulation." I can see it now: "In the last quarter—*Crumb* (The Magazine for Tired Intellectuals) lost 20,000 circulation. No other magazine can make this claim." Followed by one of those charts showing the relative circulation losses of *Life, Look, Saturday Evening Post,* and *Crumb.*

And all the other magazines will leap to their own defense with full-page ads, boasting that, where *Crumb* may have had the largest overall loss, *Badger* (The Magazine for the Woman with Everything) lost in the really key areas. Naturally, that's what really counts. "Our losses on the newsstands cannot be matched by any other magazine!" screams *Badger.*

"Aha," screams *Trumpet* (The Magazine of Upper Class Right-Wing Orthodox Opinion) in a full-page ad in color. "No other magazine can top our losses in home subscription. We have none at all! We defy any other magazine to make this claim."

Well, it'll be interesting.

Last year was a great one for the reverse record, the "Nobody did worse than we did" claim. Leading the parade of reverse records was General Dynamics, which lost $143 million in 1961. This was believed to be an all-time record for one corporation in one year. (Congratulations, G.D.! I knew you could do it.) General Dynamics lost a total of $425 million in developing its 880 jet airplane and *that* was a new record, too, by cracky. The old record, held by Ford Motor Company, was $260 million lost in developing the Edsel.

I think I can say without fear of successful corroboration that we can look forward to great new reverse records in all fields. It's altogether possible that *Cleopatra* and *Mutiny on the Bounty* will lose more dough than any pictures yet made or contemplated, and that the Alliance for Progress will have even less to show for the hundreds of millions it proposes to spend in South America than it did last year. ■

Lunacy

■ Sometimes a man wonders whether the women of this fair land are people or whether some other designation ought to be given them—say, *plips*—to distinguish them from the rest of us.

The things women have gone nuts over resist rational interpretation, and way up on the head of the list—strenuously resisting any form of explanation—was Liberace. The Liberace cult flourished around 1954. His audience was two-thirds female. I don't know how the one-third males got in there. Dragged, I expect. You notice it took two gals to drag each man in.

If women voted for Liberace as a piano player—and they sure did—it raises grave questions about their competence to vote for anything. I'm not suggesting that we repeal the Nineteenth Amendment, exactly, just that maybe we think about it a little bit.

At the apex of the craze, Liberace—his dimples, his flashing teeth, and (only incidentally) his piano—was displayed on 217 TV stations in this country, including one in every state of the Union, and on every single station in Canada. They were being seen in Alaska and Hawaii (then not states; taste had nothing to do with statehood), Cuba (aah) and Venezuela. In New York City he was on TV twice a day five days a week and on radio five half-hours a week—delighting heaven knows how many elderly and teen-age plips and infuriating God knows how many men.

The program used to open with Liberace banging away on his piano in almost total darkness; then the lights came up gradually and there was Liberace, bathed in illumination like a minor revelation. He played the piano just as well in the dark as he did in the daylight, which is to say not very well.

The Liberace repertoire deserves special mention of its own. It isn't true, as an embittered friend of mine once said, that Liberace just played "Lady of Spain" over and over again in different keys. He had lots of other numbers, most of them Rachmaninoff's "Prelude in C Sharp Minor." He played them heavily with little theatrical flourishes and trills and usually ending with one finger scampering the length of the keyboard.

While he was playing, other dim figures used to float around him—a girl with a tambourine, or men with violins, or what have you. Liberace's counterpoint to an electric guitar reminded me of a statement Joseph Conrad made about another piano player in *Victory* who, he said, rained notes like hard round pebbles on the defenseless skulls of the onlookers.

Once in a while, Liberace would raise his lungs—he had a voice like an unsuccessful contestant on the amateur hour—in song, and on these occasions you were thankful that Rachmaninoff didn't write words to his "Prelude in C Sharp Minor." He did comedy numbers, too, horrible enough to drive Victor Borge right back to serious music. Still, millions of plips swooned from New York to Amarillo.

One night we were all in luck. On his filmed TV show, Liberace invited us all in to see that celebrated house he built for himself and Mom out in the San Fernando Valley—you know, the one with the swimming pool shaped like a piano in the backyard.

"I'm real happy to see all you folks," he declared at the opening of the show, twinkling and dimpling like the angel that he is. "If I knew you were coming I'd have baked a cake." Forthwith, he sat down at the piano and played guess what while a bunch of jokers in chefs' hats accompanied him on fiddles in the background. Liberace once told a *Look* interviewer that when he was singing in what he calls his "breathy voice" he got "all tingly," and I'm sure he was frightfully tingly at this moment.

A moment later, there were films of Liberace at the door of the celebrated house: "C'mon in," he invited, twinkling and dimpling. "You like it? I want you to see my c'llection of miniature pianos." Liberace had a way of making his consonants sound like vowels and eliminating the vowels altogether.

"Well, ladies and gen'lemen, do you like my home? Mother 'n' I 'n' the poodle live here. 'N' there's someone else who dwells with us 'n' it's to heaven I speak."

Straightaway, he sat at the piano and, all a-tingle, sang "God Bless Our Home" in which he blessed the walls, the roof, and everything else except the bank vault.

"Bless the folks who live within. Keep them pure and free from sin," he intoned as millions tingled.

"Well, there's something else about my home that I think is quite different—George, have you got some backyard music?" Well, I thought, here's what we've all been waiting for—that swimming pool. He swung into the strains of "Back in Your Own Backyard," playing in a style the like of which I haven't heard since they took the player piano out of Red Circle Inn roughly thirty years ago.

Then, through the magic of film, we were transported to the edge of that famous swimming pool in the backyard. There was Liberace in a bathing suit and bless me if he wasn't dancing on the black and white keys, which had been painted on the edge of the piano-shaped pool, to the strains of "Back in Your Own Backyard." Hands on hips, he pranced roguishly from black key to black key, the length of the pool.

" 'N' now, I'll do it the hard way—backwards," he declared, liltingly. And backward he came, leaping from painted black key to key, his plump posterior waggling at the cameras as gracefully as a rogue elephant.

There was thunderous applause—heaven knows where that came from. "Than' kyew. Than' kyew," said Liberace, exposing those miraculous teeth, one of the wonders of the dental world. "Didya like it?"

An instant later, he was back on the stage again in white tie and tails—wafted there, I expect, by little flights of angels. "I hope you liked my house 'n' I hope you noticed it's on the sunny side of the street." A song cue, if ever I heard one. And he went into "Sunny Side of the Street." ■

■ You can't discuss lunacy without a bow in the direction of our most celebrated lunatic, Oscar Levant, a marvelous pianist, an inspired wit and a complete nut. On a local Los Angeles show called *Words about Music,* a radio panel show with Frank de Vol as moderator and Levant and Elsa Lanchester as permanent panelists with a couple of local celebrities each week as visiting firemen, Oscar Levant once delighted and outraged a lot of Hollywood denizens. Theoretically—but just theoretically—the panel was supposed to discuss old and new songs by composers who visited the show each week.

Levant, of course, was never reticent about the fact that he was a psychiatric problem of Herculean proportions, a sort of classic case of self-inflicted misery which psychiatrists may profitably study for years to come.

On the very first of the *Words about Music* shows, de Vol asked Levant how come he hadn't been seen on TV for so long. "I've been sick and in retirement," said Oscar. "The retirement took."

"What do you think of this show?"

"If it's bad enough," retorted Oscar, "NBC will probably grab it and put it opposite Ed Sullivan."

"How do you feel about being on it?"

"I feel utterly degraded."

"Where have you been all these years?" asked de Vol.

"I've been escaping reality."

"Now, come on, Oscar," said de Vol. "No one can escape reality."

"I can. I have character. I also have a drugstore."

Well, that's a fair sample of Mr. Levant's running stream of comment. It is, to say the least, uninhibited—not only about himself but about everyone else.

Here are a few of his other comments:

Regarding Bing Crosby's *High Tor:* "It was a Sleepy Hollow sort of thing—quite sleepy and very hollow."

To Zsa Zsa Gabor: "You have discovered the secret of perpetual middle age."

Concerning Judy Garland: "She's three nervous breakdowns up on me but I'm two suicide attempts up on her. We sit around discussing sanitariums. When I like her, I think she's the greatest singing artist in the world. When I don't like her I think the same thing—but begrudgingly."

Of Paul Coates, columnist and TV reporter: "I was wrong when I said Coates wears a toupee. As he pointed out, that greasy little patch of hair is all his own."

Or: "I was surprised at Ike's endorsement of Nixon as his running mate—but not as surprised as Eisenhower."

Sammy Cahn was the composer on the first show, which gave them an opportunity to play some of his hits and also a new song of his called "Kiss and Dream."

Said Levant: "I think that title "Kiss and Dream" is a psychiatric problem. I have a pill that induces nightmares and reduces blood pressure. Now I have nothing but nightmares; I have no blood pressure left."

The other panelists tried to get a word in edgewise now and then. They rarely succeeded. ■

■ And then there was Elvis, who exploded on the scene in the fifties.

The best description of Presley's first major television performance (on the Milton Berle show in mid-1956) came from the chairman of the music department of Bryant High School, Harry

A. Feldman, who wrote Berle: "The guest performer, Elvis Presley, presented a demonstration which was in execrable taste, bordering on obscenity. The gyrations of this young man were such an assault to the senses as to repel even the most tolerant observer.

"When television entrepreneurs present such performers to millions of viewers and pronounce them great, when such deplorable taste is displayed in the presentation of primitive, shoddy and offensive material, one begins to understand the present-day attitude of our youth. We in the classroom can do very little to offset the force and impact of these displays in our efforts to stem the tide toward a cultural debacle."

About the only guy who ever summed up Elvis "the Pelvis" any better than that was the California policeman who, after watching him writhe around a stage, commented, "If he did that on the street, we'd arrest him."

One appearance of this unspeakably untalented and vulgar young entertainer brought forth a huge storm of complaints from both press and public. Even gentle old Ben Gross of the *Daily News* of New York blew his top. I doubt that in the thirty-odd years he's been writing that column Ben has ever gotten quite so angry.

A lot of other people felt the same way—including parents, teachers, and sociologists. And just about eight years later, all of these same people were doing the twist.

Elvis the Pelvis must certainly get some credit for starting that craze. He did it first or, if not first, at least most publicly. As for me, I still think the twist looks better on girls than on boys. ■

■ I was among the fortunate few who were at their radios when Milton Berle did the balcony scene from *Romeo and Juliet* and, by yonder blessed moon, it was an experience I shall not soon forget.

Then, some years later, it was my privilege to witness Eddie Fisher playing Romeo opposite—oh, brother, that *was* a night—Margaret O'Brien's Juliet. Mr. Fisher played Romeo sheepishly, with a sort of half-grin on his face, as if any moment he expected Milton Berle to elbow him aside and take over. Even then I found him less distracting than Margaret O'Brien. Miss O'Brien was the only Juliet in my experience who looked much too young for the part. There have been a good many complaints in the past about great ladies of the stage, well into their forties, trying to impersonate this slip of a fourteen-year-old girl.

Well, Miss O'Brien looked age twelve and sounded age ten. She whispered away, in her little-girl manner, about high passion and ancient feuds as if she didn't really understand the words but was terribly proud of being able to pronounce them.

I'm waiting for Red Buttons to tackle Romeo and, the way things have been going, sooner or later he will. ■

■ I was in the shower one day singing "Twixt Forty-Five and Fifty," the theme song of the Forgotten People (which is anyone over the age of fourteen), and feeling sorry for myself. The world, I reflected, is not run for us ancients. We are just here to pay the bills. (This is not a brand-new thought, I realize, but even if it's old hat, there is a certain bitter truth in it, and this particular bitter truth needs constant reassertion if we are not to be overwhelmed by the Little People.)

It's not that I'm opposed to youth. Youth was great when I was a youth, but, by George, they broke the mold right after me. At least the mold I came out of could not have been the same one that produced Fabian, whom I saw on the Ed Sullivan Show one night, caterwauling or whatever he was doing. Fabian, I had been informed, was one of the newer enthusiasms of our young set and one of the more presentable young singers.

Singers?

Presentable?

He was wearing a slipover over an old T-shirt. The hair looked like something Medusa had sent back to the store as unworthy of her. Although, I was told, he was applauded as one of the more stationary and therefore admirable young entertainers (a word that has been thoroughly debased in my lifetime), he revolved like a top, snapping his fingers and jerking his eyeballs.

As for his voice . . . well, of course, singers gave up singing years ago in favor of shouting—but this one couldn't even shout. The song he was mouthing was enormously improved by total unintelligibility. Just in case you could make out a word here and there—God forbid—they turned up the electric guitar (or whatever it was that made that awful racket in the background) and just to be doubly sure that that horrible song and the dreadful voice of young Fabian were totally drowned out, the young audience was encouraged to shriek, whistle, stomp, and, if necessary, set fire to Ed Sullivan.

And that, fellers, is how a sweet chile becomes a teen-age idol in our wonderfully advanced civilization in this here twentieth century. Oh, there's one other requisite to becoming a popular singer these days: you got to be utterly loathsome to adults—and that ingredient this little fellow has in generous quantities. God bless his little growing bank account.

I suppose we were revolting against our parents, too, when we were little spratlings, but the singers we liked—Bing Crosby, for example—could really sing. And you know why? Because he had to please not only us but our fathers and uncles, because our fathers and uncles owned and operated the record companies and the radio networks, and they didn't pay all that attention to the likes and dislikes of us little shavers. (In fact, I can't recall anyone paying any attention at all to me when I was thirteen.)

Today the revolt is not so much against adults. It's against singing itself. It's against song itself. It's against—considering the quality of the lyrics—language itself.

Why do we put up with it? Record executives, who no longer

pretend this junk is anything but horrible, plead that they have to cater to young tastes. But why? It's our house, and our TV set. ■

■ Gardner McKay, a muscled and wildly beautiful young man, was selected by *Life* magazine in 1959 as the successor to Tyrone Power in the dreams of the nation's women, an accolade something like that golden apple Paris gave to Aphrodite, only more lucrative, of course. If Aphrodite had had a modern press agent she could have parlayed it into a TV film series with residuals and goodness knows what else.

McKay had a press agent (or rather ABC had) who wrote prose almost as wildly beautiful as McKay's storied countenance. "McKay," wrote this latter-day Homer, "leader of Hollywood's hearty young men, a new and fast growing group of outdoor-minded actors who lead the rugged active life . . . in addition to being an active physical giant (six foot five), McKay is a man of deep inner dimensions. His intellectual curiosities run full range. For every hour he spends in physical action, he devotes two to mental stimulation. Among his intellectual diversions are chess, voracious reading and conversation in four languages. His mountain cottage is stacked with books (Chekhov to D. H. Lawrence) . . ." and so on.

McKay had been cast as hero of an ABC-TV series called *Adventures in Paradise* (a title Milton was groping for but missed), which was "by James Michener," the Homer of the Pacific islands, and produced "by Martin Manulis," one of TV's best producers. (In case you want to know why I put those two things in quotes, it's because *by* in television doesn't mean written by or produced by in the sense you and I are accustomed in the word.)

Mr. Michener, who has more or less appropriated the Pacific Ocean as his special literary possession, originated—a word that has very elastic connotations in this business—this series. (The actual scripting is done by some twenty-five other writers.) "I drafted the original outline in quite extensive detail—biographies of the principal characters, various settings, what we are after and so forth," said Mr. Michener, who lives in Hawaii. "I have done two of the stories—not the actual shooting scripts, of course—and I have two more in progress. . . . I'd been approached by quite a few television people to do a television series. One of the principles I laid down was that the series was not to be shot on location by enthusiastic amateurs."

McKay, who had not been seen on the world's screens (except for a bit part in one picture), was already getting astronomical fan mail on the basis of the cover story in *Life*. Or to sum it all up, the author of *Adventures in Paradise* wasn't actually writing it. The islands of the Pacific were the setting, except you would never see them. The star was getting fan mail from a lot of people who had never seen him act.

Like the man said, there's no business like show business. ■

■ Back in 1960, in one of his curiously well-publicized personal appearances on this side of the Atlantic, Soviet Premier Nikita Khrushchev joined entrepreneur David Susskind on the latter's Sunday-evening session called, with some accuracy, *Open End*.

It wasn't so much an interview as a summit conference between the head of Talent Associates and the head of the Soviet Union. (I'm giving the billing there more or less in the order of their importance.) However, fears that David Susskind might sign a separate peace were quickly dispelled. He's with the free world all the way, is Mr. Susskind.

Nevertheless, I got the feeling that David had some kind of document in his back pocket there, and that if he could just straighten Mr. Khrushchev out on a few small matters—the U-2 (forget it), the Congo (get out and stay out), the RB-47 (submit it to arbitration)—Susskind and Nikita could sign a world peace treaty right there and it would be another first for WNTA-TV, otherwise known as Channel 13 (which, with absolutely no cause-and-effect relationship, two years later became an educational-television station).

What Henry Shapiro of United Press International later called a "monstrous exercise in futility," and others called a monstrous exercise in ego (mostly Susskind's, though there were a *couple* of egos on view there), I feel was really a monstrous exercise in naïveté. Take your pick. They're all lovely words. I think Susskind was monstrously naïve in thinking he could cope with this Russian bear, who is a very tough baby intellectually as well as every other way. But also I think Khrushchev was pretty naïve in showing up at all.

After about the first hour, I think Khrushchev got the idea that this wasn't an interview and it wasn't even a platform or, if it was a platform, he was sharing it with Mr. Susskind, and he hadn't intended to do any such thing. Anyway, he got up to go and then there was another twenty-five minutes of futility or ego or naïveté on foot. Perry Como used to have the world's record for length of time in saying good-by to his guests on television, but it's been shattered by Susskind.

Anyhow, Khrushchev finally got off (and I bet somebody at the Russian Embassy caught hell for letting him get into this) and then the telecast shifted to a group of experts in the back room of the United Nations. They included *The New York Times'* Harry Schwartz and the New York *Herald Tribune*'s Joe Newman and Marguerite Higgins, and I thought they were all wonderfully kind to Mr. Susskind. Apart from Mr. Shapiro's murmuring "unprofessional," there was little comment on the quality of Mr. Susskind's interviewing, which is—well—astonishing.

Susskind doesn't ask questions, really. First, he issues an editorial saying how foolish is the opinion his interviewer holds on the question he is about to ask. Then he asks the question, gets the opinion he has earlier deplored, and promptly disagrees with it. Susskind has done this not only with Khrushchev, but also with Richard Nixon. What ensues is not an interview, but an argument.

As in most arguments, no one really wins, and far from changing the other guy's opinion, you wind up strengthening it.

Anyhow, it was an historic occasion. There has not been any more unlikely confrontation since H. L. Mencken interviewed Rudolph Valentino, another towering eminence, back in the twenties. ■

■ Every man used to have two families—his own and Dorothy and Dick's. (Dorothy Kilgallen and Dick Kollmar, as if you didn't know.) Man led his own grubby little life with his own family, but every morning he tuned in to get a little glamour to help get down the oatmeal. Made existence palatable.

Well, sir, I remember when Dorothy and Dick were invited to lunch at the Duke and Duchess of Windsor's outside Paris, and for weeks we listened, starry-eyed, to their adventures—the oatmeal forgotten. I once had an aunt who could spin out a single luncheon into twenty years of reminiscence, and I won't pretend that Dorothy and Dick could even lay a hand on the old girl in this field. But still they did mighty well: a couple of weeks, not only on their morning show but on their late afternoon show—all over a single lunch. We heard just what they ate, what everyone wore, what everyone said.

Of course, some of it was a little maddening because there wasn't time, you understand. Dorothy (or Dick) would get to talking about that fascinating conversation after lunch in which the wit and glamour reached a pinnacle not achieved since the days of Madame Récamier's salon—but, unfortunately, we're running out of time now. Tune in again tonight.

Gads, it was frustrating. What *did* the Duchess say to the Duke? What *did* the Countess Bismarck say to Dick? Well, you just had to wait until 6:15, biting your nails.

Then, of course, there was the description of the house—room by room. Here again we were always cut off just when it got interesting. Time and again, it seemed to me, we were just on the threshold of the Duke's room. Well, that's all for today; we'll continue this tomorrow. I practically had one foot in the room—and, wham, they slammed the door on it.

(When they finally got to the Duke's room, they both had a good laugh. It was so much smaller than the Duchess's. This led to a philosophic discussion, punctuated with laughter, that all wives wound up with more sleeping space than their spouses—a situation that I imagine Madame Récamier and her bunch kicked around from time to time, too.)

Then there was the matter of clothes. Dorothy didn't know what to wear and was still pretty nervous about it when she showed up wearing something frightfully simple. But it so happened that the Duchess was wearing something frightfully simple, too, and asked Dorothy where on earth she got that dress. And Dorothy told her. The Countess Bismarck, who was once Mrs. Harrison Williams, asked her where she got the dress, too. And she learned. And so did we.

Well, you have to grow up with the times. Years ago it was the man who came to dinner—and broke his hip and stayed for six weeks. Then it was the couple who went to lunch—and then talked about it for two weeks on the radio. What now? ■

■ A few years ago there was a story in the paper about a Canadian farmer—Russell Fleming of Whitby, which is about twenty-five miles east of Toronto—who had installed a television set in his barn. Originally he'd put it there to help divert the hired hands. But the cows took to looking at it too. Fleming said milk production was up fifteen gallons daily.

I'm not sure I believe this (Whitby, among other things, is the site of Ontario's largest mental hospital), but the story was accompanied by a picture of a cow staring moodily at the set, straight into the eyes of Kate Smith who was smiling prettily.

It was a gruesome sight. The cow bore an expression not much different from any television viewer—docile, passive, uncomplaining. A depressing study in uncritical acceptance.

I prefer the cat that insisted on listening to John Gambling every morning and howled with displeasure when he was turned off. Or the other cat, which pounced on the TV set and turned it off rather than watch the Westminster Kennel Club show. These were animals with minds of their own. I don't think cows are ready for television yet. ■

■ When the accumulated idiocies of our age are weighed by future generations (There's a large body of opinion on my block says there won't be any future generations; this is a pessimistic block.), the sociologists may lead the whole pack.

Then, again, they may not. There's a lot of competition in the field of contemporary lunacy, a lot of professions trying to elbow their way ahead of the mob. There is Madison Avenue, for example, which keeps reading ratings as if they were Holy Writ. Then, there are the statisticians who feed Madison Avenue the numbers it craves as a dope addict craves heroin. "Statistics are a science," these idiots say, feeding numbers into those huge machines during the elections which instantly returned the news that Nixon was the winner. (Later, the machines said it was Kennedy by a landslide and that was just as wrong.)

I'm indebted to Charles J. Rolo in *The Atlantic* for some information on what the sociologists are up to. Rolo waded through a 444-page document entitled *Americans View Their Mental Health*, and the part that interested me most was where a bunch of sociologists sampled happiness. That is, these sociologists punched a bunch of scientifically sampled doorbells and asked the respondents to rate their own happiness.

And this scientifically selected sample (Ooh, I love that phrase) of 2,450 adult Americans rated themselves "very happy" (25 per cent), "pretty happy" (54 per cent) and "not too happy" (11 per cent). What I want to know is, at what time of day did they ask the question? You ask me how I rate my happiness at 11 A.M. —I'm a morning-type guy—and you're going to get a much different, more radiant answer than if you ask me that question at 3 P.M., when my world begins to dim and darken. Along about five o'clock I'm usually downright miserable, so if these sociologists had come punching my doorbell at that hour I'd have thrown the whole scientific sample askew.

Not only is time of day important but conditions must be weighed. You ask a mother to rate her happiness just after she gets back from the supermarket, broke and exhausted, and you're going to get an awful "not too happy." (As far as I can see, that's as unhappy as the scientific sample ever got, which only goes to confirm my suspicion that there is almost nothing more unscientific than a scientific sample.)

I'm incessantly touched by the trusting nature of scientific samplers anyway. I love their assumption that when you ask someone what television program he's looking at (or what book he's reading), he'll tell you the truth. Not bloody likely! On the subject of happiness the degree of prevarication is likely to rise alarmingly.

These scientific samplers should try asking some of the beatniks down the block to rate their happiness. "Wretched, man, wretched!" they'll tell, wreathed in great big smiles. Bloody liars! But in that set, misery is fashionable just as in the suburbs happiness is *de rigueur*. Frankly, if you want the Crosby prediction for the happiness quotient of tomorrow, misery is the coming thing. The beats around here are a pretty avant-garde group. What they liked in music last year is just getting to be hot stuff in Scarsdale. So if misery is the last word here in Greenwich Village, it's going to be the last word in Scarsdale in 1965 is what I read in the tea leaves, men.

But by the time the sociologists get around to writing a 444-page book about it (of the total sample, 44 per cent of Americans said they were in total misery, 37 per cent in abject despair, 11 per cent utterly wretched and the rest didn't know) the fashions will have changed again. But, what the hell, it keeps the scientific samplers out of mischief—ringing doorbells and asking silly questions. If they didn't do that, they might start asking themselves how happy they were or weren't, and frankly, I'd rather not know. ■

■ There's that other nonsense about the strumpet with the heart of gold—and we've had a number of specimens on Broadway lately.

David Merrick, who produced *Irma La Douce*, has been quoted as saying the rumors that *Irma* was dirty would give it a three-year run. The *Herald Trib*'s critic, Walter Kerr, had spread the rumor that *Irma* was *not* dirty, a perfectly awful thing to say about a play. If I'd been Merrick, I'd have sued him for libel. Merrick, it will be remembered, also produced *Suzie Wong* on Broadway, as well as *The Good Soup*, another play about a prostitute. In fact, Merrick has made more money out of prostitution than Polly Adler. Like Polly, he has had his ups and downs with it. *The Good Soup* was shot down by the critics in record time.

However, I forgave Merrick for inflicting *Suzie Wong* on us because he gave us *Irma La Douce*, which I loved. I found *Irma* delicious, cool and cerebral. (Cerebral! Oh, brother, Merrick *will* sue now.) Of all the ladies playing golden-hearted streetwalkers, Elizabeth Seal, who starred in *Irma*, was easily the most adorable as well as the most talented.

That's a sweeping statement, too, because there were scores of actresses playing harlots on Broadway, or in London, or Paris, where *Irma La Douce* was also a big hit. All nineteen-year-old actresses (you may quote this as one of Crosby's Laws) yearn to play streetwalkers, and after they turn thirty, they want to play nuns. It sometimes seems they always achieve both ambitions.

Of all the girls I've seen recently playing prostitutes, the most convincing—if that's a compliment, and I rather doubt it—is Melina Mercouri in *Never on Sunday*. Miss Mercouri is a sort of Greek Lauren Bacall, full of large gestures, tremendous bounce, exuberance and vitality. *Never on Sunday* isn't much but Greek gaiety and glimpses of Greek low life, and it's Miss Mercouri who makes it worth your time.

The golden-hearted strumpet has been around a long, long time. She's always been good theater. But does she exist?

I hate to cast doubt on this ancient image, but are harlots really that good-natured? Right after the war, they were. Aaah, the streetwalkers in London and Paris and Rome! What gay and charming and merry and, above all, hungry girls! Hunger produces great prizefighters, excellent second basemen and marvelous streetwalkers. Prosperity ruins all those professions. All the insouciant and lovely semipros have long since married and settled down.

The streets have been taken over by the full-time professional, the veteran. Good-hearted? Golden dispositions? Come off it! Without exception, your veteran pro has the disposition of a cobra and the belligerence of a Miura bull.

There used to be a Spanish gypsy girl who worked the saloons of Paris. She had fingernails an inch long, and when that paper-thin temper exploded—as it did every hour on the hour—the fingernails would go straight for the eyeballs. Failing that, she'd aim at the cheek, which she could lay open to the bone. Beautiful girl! But the managements of several bistros asked her not to come back because the bloodshed was ruining the tablecloths.

What a gutsy character *she'd* make in a play! And—at the risk of upsetting an ancient dramatic convention—she'd be a lot more representative of her profession than those milksop streetwalkers who smile like angels and are kind to their grandmothers. Kind to grandmothers indeed! I think that gypsy girl ate her grandmother. For breakfast. ■

■ Our publications do once in a while find themselves with the strangest—I guess I'd better say *companions*—here. What I mean is *Time* and the *Times* on the same side of the bundling board.

"It is time to speak openly and candidly of the increasing incidence and influence of homosexuality on New York's stage—and indeed in the other arts as well," wrote Howard Taubman in *The New York Times.* This stunning intelligence, which may have been only fifteen or twenty years late, was such a startling revelation for the *Times* that *Time* magazine gave voice, too, thereby finishing that trend.

Any time the *Times* and *Time* catch up to a trend, it's well on the way out and down. Homosexuality is getting pretty square as far as the dramatic arts are concerned. The big new thing in the sex field is narcissism. Everybody is making love to himself or herself in the mirror.

It's always hard to pin down an exact moment when any new trend starts, but I rather suspect this one had its beginning when Carol Lawrence started singing "I Feel Pretty" to herself in the mirror in the stage version of *West Side Story*. Meanwhile, at Radio City Music Hall, Nancy Kwan, an Oriental sweetmeat in *Flower Drum Song,* sang "I Enjoy Being a Girl" to not one but three of her own images, all delectable, in three different mirrors. I mean there was plenty to fall in love with, all right, all right, but I don't think it's meet that Nancy Kwan should fall in love with that image but, maybe, me.

And that's by no means all. The biggest Broadway hit is *How to Succeed in Business without Really Trying*. The best song number in it is Bobby Morse singing "I Believe in You." To whom? To himself, of course, in the mirror. As a matter of fact, if we're going to get Freudian (and we're not, because I'm temperamentally a mythologist), Morse's whole role is a classic case study of narcissism, a love affair with himself of such flamboyance that Morse is probably the only actor who can make it palatable. (Very funny show, just the same.)

Actually (a word which is to an essayist what a revolver is to Warner Brothers) the French have taken this narcissistic thing much farther than we have. In *Purple Noon,* a very interesting, very unusual and quite beautiful French thriller, hero Alain Delon brushes his hair, staring soulfully at himself, and winds up kissing himself in the mirror, probably the sickest scene in the movies since Frederic March turned into Mr. Hyde out of sheer lust for Miriam Hopkins when I was a wee child.

In *Breathless,* another French movie which I found absolutely fascinating (but don't take the children), Jean Paul Belmondo and Jean Seberg hardly ever tore themselves away from their own images in the mirrors, gazing away, brushing away, with wholehearted absorption. If you want to push this thing, you might summon a pretty good argument to support the idea that the twist, the dance craze that has gone all the way from the Peppermint Lounge to the White House, is a fairly narcissistic operation. When doing the twist you're not supposed to touch your partner and, in fact, you don't really need one; you can—and many do—just wiggle away by yourself in an orgy of self-appreciation.

In fact, Mannie, if we're going to get on top of this trend before it gets stale (which is to say before Taubman, *The Times* and *Time* find out about it), we will have to move fast. How's this for starters—I'm just breathing in and out, mind you—suppose we have for a hero this beautiful boy, Narcissus; he's the son—I'm just talking off the top of my head here, Mannie—of the rain god Cephissus and the nymph Leiriore. He's madly in love with his twin sister—brother, will that sell tickets—and when she gets killed he is inconsolable. He rejects this nymph Echo who is in love with him and also his lover Ameinias (might as well get a little old-fashioned homosexuality in here, Mannie, for the bald-headed crowd) and falls to staring at himself in a pool.

Great song cue, there, leading into "I'm in Love with You." . . . ■

■ "Patriotism is the last refuge of a scoundrel," Samuel Johnson, the closest thing the eighteenth century had to Bob Hope, declared in one of his more acid moments. If he were around today, Johnson probably would reword it a little: anti-communism is the last refuge of a scoundrel.

Anti-communism has certainly amassed to its torn banners the prettiest collection of thieves, varlets, liars, con men and idiots since the Know-Nothing Party campaigned for the proscription of the foreign-born. The more virulent the anti-communism, the harder you had better clutch your wallet and your wits. Early in 1962 this lunacy looked as if it might be on the wane; the United Presbyterian Church joined the Roman Catholic Bishops in denouncing the Right Wing extremists. Up till then it was felt that you couldn't be too far to the Right.

But, at long last, Presbyterians and Catholics discovered that hell is paved with good intentions. (Another of Sam Johnson's wisecracks.) There have certainly been some well-intentioned people among the anti-Communists, but the Presbyterian General Council advised their 3.25 million members to combat communism by love of their fellow man rather than hatred. Old Tail Gunner Joe McCarthy must have spun in his grave. Love of one's fellow man, Senator McCarthy would have been the first to proclaim, is clearly subversive.

All the extreme anti-Communist movements in this country have started in areas like the Middle West or the Far West among people most removed from national or world affairs who know the least about politics, or about subversion or about anything except maybe production of candy bars. Or, to rewrite Samuel Johnson a little more extensively: anti-communism seems to be the last refuge of the paranoiacs. ■

■ Civil defense has grown into one of the great boondoggles of our whole history, and we've had some honeys.

Civil defense since World War II has been fairly hilarious. Remember when we were going to build all those blast shelters? Then a hydrogen bomb blew an island out of the Pacific and the blast shelters were dropped as impractical. Then we were going to evacuate our cities—one of the dizziest suggestions ever contemplated. A civil defense director commented hopelessly, "We can't even get people out of San Francisco after a football game." Gradually, that lunacy subsided.

Then fallout shelters. I rather think this idiocy will continue for a while because I suspect many people are making loads of money out of it. The world's first "Survival Supermarket" opened in Los Angeles, where they are consistently first in loony ideas. The "Survival Supermarket" featured prepackaged food, the daily pack (five dollars per person) or the all-family weekly carton (forty dollars), plastic blood containers (ten dollars for individuals or fifty for the family size), four models of shelters on sale (priced from four to forty thousand) and dental chairs guaranteed convertible to operating tables, air purifiers, generators, and a family barbecue unit guaranteed usable inside the shelter, tra-la (15).

As a matter of fact, my Hollywood spies told me some time ago that the fallout shelter had replaced the barbecue pit as a status symbol of the film colony; some of the world's handsomest barbecue pits were out there, and now the fallout shelters were already beginning to stagger the sensibilities. Jane Powell, the thrush, rushed into print with details about the ducky retreat she had under the driveway. "I've got an interior decorator coming in and we'll furnish it with couches, rollaway beds and a TV set. I'm planning to decorate it with three-dimensional paper to make the room look bigger."

One of the most trenchant and witty sermons to come to my attention on this subject was delivered at the Signal Hill Methodist Church in East St. Louis, Illinois, by the Rev. Robert Gordon, who said, "*The Wall Street Journal* said recently that fallout shelter builders strive hard to guarantee buyers secrecy. You see, you don't want the neighbors to know if you are building one.... They'll come at night if asked. A Milwaukee builder advertises that he will come in an unmarked truck, and that if nosy neighbors inquire as to what they are doing, they will say they are TV repairmen.

"Four hundred Nevada businessmen were told recently by a civil defense officer that what Nevada needed was a trained militia of five thousand men to ward off the invasion of Californians who would be coming to their state for refuge from their holocaust.... It used to be that you could depend on a war to unite the nation. Now we find that while we're boiling and frying another people, we'll be hard at civil war ourselves, fighting and scrambling for survival."

All this does raise some protocol questions. How to behave in the fallout-shelter age? As the King of Siam used to say, it's a puzzlement. The accepted thing now is that one shoots down the neighbor who comes pounding on your shelter door. Why didn't the lazy drone build his own shelter? All summer long, when you paused in the digging, you found him putting. Or pruning the rose bushes. Maybe even reading. All highly unprofitable operations. So, have no hesitation. Right between his eyes. (Remember —squeeze, don't jerk, the trigger.)

However, some small points of etiquette have arisen. One reader queries, "Suppose the attack comes at a dinner party. You had invited the guests for drinks and dinner. But not for participation in the fallout shelter. The bomb falls, let us say, after dessert and during the brandy. But then, just how do you go about getting them out into the radioactive air? I mean without hurting their feelings? Just how do you put that into words or, as they say now, how do you verbalize that one, big boy?"

Well, frankly, I think the jovial approach is neat. "Well, here's your hat and there's the door." Something like that. "Pardon me for not showing you to the gate but my doctor told me radioactive dust isn't good for my sinus. Ha-ha." You ought to get a big laugh easy there. Nothing like danger to bring on a fit of the giggles.

Of course, there's a school of thought among the etiquette crowd that says it might be kinder to shoot the guests right there at the dinner table. Quicker that way. Neater. More merciful. I can't go along with this. I think it's rude to shoot people at the dinner table even with the kindest of motives.

While we're on the subject, we might as well press on the matter of engraved invitations. "Mr. and Mrs. John Doe request the pleasure of the company of Mr. Richard Roe at cocktails and dinner Thursday the twenty-ninth of June at 6 o'clock. R.S.V.P." Then at the lower right, I think, very unobtrusively: "The fallout shelter is unfortunately *not* included in this invitation. In the event of emergency, the host and hostess extend their best wishes and the devout hope that they will see you again. Sometime. Somewhere."

Then there's another school of thought harbors the old-fashioned notion that fallout shelters aren't funny. Oh, they are, too. If there's anything funnier than a back-yard fallout shelter trying to provide protection against a twenty-megaton hydrogen bomb, I can't think what it is. A fifteen-megaton bomb dropped by the U.S. Air Force in the Marshall Islands in 1952 vaporized a twelve-mile island, leaving in its place a hole in the ocean floor a mile long and 175 feet wide.

So, what I say is, drones, let the other fellows dig in the hard ground. Work on your putting. Mow the lawn. It's more useful. ■

■ The John Birch Society plans to get around to getting the United States out of the UN the moment it succeeds in impeaching Earl Warren (which may take some time). The Daughters of the American Revolution, those adorable little reactionaries from Constitution Hall, have complained bitterly about UNICEF, an organ of the United Nations, feeding Communist children who will then grow up to be Communist adults, rather than starving the little beasts as every loyal red-blooded American would do. The Christian Anti-Communist Crusade, Fred C. Schwarz's group of extreme right-wingers, has campaigned not only for getting the United States out of the UN but getting the UN out of the United States.

My spies on the lecture circuit report that the United Nations, out in the grass-roots country, are fighting words. The UN is "a nest of spies"; it's "Communist-dominated"; it's "embroiling us in the Congo and draining us of money." That is the sort of opinion held by people who are both uninformed and fearful. Simple distrust has been fanned into open hostility verging on out-and-out hatred by a series of events—the Berlin crisis, the death of Hammarskjöld and the admission of large numbers of African nations viewed with alarm by the white supremacists of the South. And this is the most dangerous lunacy of all.

Most of the extreme Right Wing criticism of the United Nations is compounded almost wholly of fear and ignorance of what the United Nations is and what it does. For one thing, it's *not* Communist-dominated. In fact, the Soviet Union complains frequently that it is U.S.-dominated. During the Korean War it certainly was, and the Korean War should provide us a useful free lesson in why we should not walk out of the United Nations. The Russians walked out—them and their veto—leaving us a free hand. We would otherwise have had to fight the Korean War single-handed, but without the Russians around we got United Nations support to thwart Communist aims in Korea. The Russians have not walked out since.

If the United States walked out now, the Russians would take over, and even if we took our allies with us (and both the British and French are showing disenchantment with the UN), there would be plenty to take over. Practically all of Africa, Asia and much of Latin America—the underdeveloped world over which the Cold War is being fought. The Russians would like very much to rush into those areas from which the European colonial powers have been departing, and it is the United Nations which is keeping them out. If the United Nations didn't keep Russia out, the United States would have to do it alone—and that is the clash we are all trying to avoid. ■

The arts—fine and not so fine

■ The arts have been in a state of ferment almost as confusing and explosive as the internal affairs of the Congo. The Metropolitan Museum, we all know, had just shelled out $2,300,000 for a Rembrandt called "Aristotle Contemplating the Bust of Homer" when the rumors started flying that it wasn't Aristotle. It was maybe Virgil or maybe not even him. Was Virgil worth two million three? Or was Aristotle, for that matter? Was it really Homer? Or Rembrandt?

It was enough to shatter one's faith in the management of our greatest museum (or junk shop, depending on how you feel about old armor and fake Etruscan statues) if your faith hadn't already been slightly shaken by that price and the lingering suspicion that Mr. James Rorimer, director of the Metropolitan, had been felled by auction fever rather than simply gripped by bad judgment.

Right on top of that, a lady stepped up to a guard at the Museum of Modern Art and said coldly, "Sir, your Matisse is upside down." Surely, this is an historic utterance, deserving to be ranked with "*Après moi le deluge*" or "Let 'em eat cake" or maybe even "A black frog cannot be whitewashed" (Khrushchev) or "I'll stick to my camel" (that Pakistani camel driver after being driven in a Cadillac from Herald Square to Radio City in the noontime traffic). It has always been my feeling that the most shattering thing you can say to a man is "Sir, your fly is open," but perhaps "Sir, your Matisse is upside down" is more civilized, though, of course, you can't use it just everywhere.

The fact that a Matisse hung upside down for forty-seven days before anyone discovered it is a significant and rather depressing commentary on the upside-downness and way-outness of art in general. (A Braque was put in the catalogue of the Louvre upside down, too.) There have been other signs that the art world is either decadent or loony or both. A chimpanzee named Beauty, who had been fingerpainting for six months, had her first exhibition of abstracts at the Bianchini Gallery and sold eighty paintings, which ranged in price from twenty-five to ninety-five dollars.

I saw a good many of Beauty's paintings and the thought struck me that Beauty was far closer to Jackson Pollock than she was to Michelangelo. In fact, there were some of us who thought she had already overtaken Pollock and, when you think it took the human race 405 years to progress from the Sistine Chapel to Jackson Pollock and that the apes got there in a single bound, it makes you wonder. At least it makes me wonder whether the apes have been making enormous strides forward to the people world—or whether people have been making enormous strides backward to the ape world.

Meanwhile the general dizziness has not exactly avoided the world of music. Carnegie Recital Hall one day was the setting for a concert of the works of Yoke One. Against a taped background of mumbled words and wild laughter, a girl spoke earnestly about peeling a grapefruit, squeezing lemons and counting the hairs on a dead child. The instruments went *squeep, squawp.* The hall was packed. (Well, what can a composer do when all the best violinists are in the Air Force playing at White House parties?) ■

■ I write about music all the time in spite of a tin ear and a great supply of what the Catholics call invincible ignorance. I saw *The Gay Divorcee* when it opened in New Haven and I found a song called "Night and Day" very dull and ordinary. (It was Cole Porter, Lord love him, who said, "I wish the critics would stop writing about music. There isn't a single one of them would recognize 'The Star Spangled Banner' unless the people around them stood up.") But what I say, Mannie, is that today's popular music is, in a word, terrible.

Where did the degeneration of popular music start? You'd probably get a dozen different answers from a dozen different people. My own theory is that it started just before the war when the radio networks battled ASCAP over the price they were asked to pay for the use of songs. ASCAP pulled its music off the air, and since every composer of note was a member, music on the air consisted of either stuff in the public domain or perfectly dreadful new music.

Everyone and his Aunt Agatha thinks he can write songs, and during that deplorable period they all trotted them out. Songs that ordinarily would not have got past the receptionist at any reputable music publisher were not only published but played on the air. The public, particularly the teen-age public, got a taste for bad music that it hasn't lost to this day.

I remember one evening when Goodman Ace, on the Perry Como show, wrote a very nice piece for his announcer. He enunciated a rock 'n' roll lyric—than which there is nothing more inane—without benefit of music (if that's what it is) in the style of a commencement address. It went something like this:

Digga boom.
Digga boom.
Digga
Boom.

The Unsinkable Molly Brown contained a song whose lyric went—I'm quoting from memory but I think I'm right—"*Ta ta ta ta ta ta ta ta ta.*" Great lyric, to be enshrined along with that historic and now-standard rock 'n' roll lyric of "Witch Doctor" which goes *"Oo-ee-oo-ah-ah-ting-tang-walla-walla-bing-bang."* Of course *ta ta ta ta ta* is not as complex a lyric—hasn't the poetry, the feeling for syllables, of *oo-ee-oo* and so forth. A man can't get his teeth into that lyric in the shower, which is the true test of a lyric.

However, it is not the lyric that bothers me about that song. It is the melody. The melody goes—you must have heard Dinah Shore singing it—*boom boom boom boom boom.* If you find that description is a bit dull, then you have caught the spirit of the melody precisely. Musically, I should say, it's about on a par with "March, march on down the field, fighting for Eli," which we used to sing in the Yale Bowl because we were young and didn't know any better.

What we are doing in our musical theater is rediscovering the spirit of John Philip Sousa. If I were asked the precise moment in world history when this deplorable trend ignited, it would be the split second that "Seventy-six Trombones" hit the first-night audience and set its pulse to tingling to a mood and a beat that had not been heard on Broadway since George M. Cohan's "Over There."

Practically every curtain in *The Unsinkable Molly Brown,* whose music was perpetrated by Meredith Willson, who also committed *The Music Man,* came down on what sounded like a military band number. *Ooompah oompah oompah.* Trombones and the blare of trumpets.

I hasten to say that my blood tingles just as readily as the next man's at this *oompah oompah* stuff. I get all over goose pimples (on account of I'm emotionally immature) when a military band starts up. But candor and common sense compel me to recognize that musically this is pretty tinny stuff. Musically, in fact, that *ta ta ta ta* from *Unsinkable* is the equivalent of the late Gary Cooper wringing his cowboy hat in his hand and saying, "I realize, ma'am, I ain't fitten to touch the hem of youah garment. I done some pretty bad things in my life—killings and all—but I just want you to know, ma'am, that since I've met you, I've tried to be good." Or to put it another way, it's corn, men, corn.

The heavy beat—more suitable to marching feet than to dancing feet—is conspicuous in all sorts of forms of popular music today.

It's very evident in the arrangement of Bobby Darin's songs. Ahead of Darin, Frank Sinatra was not above using the military blare of trumpets in his arrangements.

On a different and lower level of popular culture there is the revival of Dixieland jazz. Not the best of it, which is wonderful, but the most commercial and assimilable aspects of it. The theme song of the squares now is "When the Saints Go Marching In," which started as a funeral march and is still very much a march. It's the Dixieland equivalent of "The Stars and Stripes Forever."

On the Broadway stage, Richard Rodgers first used (in modern times) this processional with enormous effectiveness with "The March of the Siamese Children" in *The King and I. Camelot,* the Lerner and Loewe musical, has some lovely processionals and lovely processional music. (My only complaint is that there are too many processionals in *Camelot.*)

In general, though, this invasion of Broadway by marching music, some of it on a level not much higher than that played at chowder-and-marching-society picnics in my grandfather's time, represents a crumbling of musical standards. Where are the marvelous musical complexities of George Gershwin in *Of Thee I Sing,* or Jerome Kern's lovely *The Cat and the Fiddle,* or Rodgers in *Pal Joey* or in anything?

Musically, our theater is retrogressing to a more primitive time and I can only hope this is a temporary madness.

And what about the non-music? There's been talk about non-books (and there is a bit later in this chapter.) So why not non-music?

Non-books (an expression invented by *Time* magazine) have been described as anything tape-recorded, pasted together, or told to Gerald Frank. So much for non-books at the moment. Non-music is anything played in a supermarket or emanating from a concealed loudspeaker in an elevator or the armrest of your chair on jet airplanes.

Non-music, even when they're playing pretty good tunes, is background music. The volume is kept low so that you can't quite hear it and yet you can't quite not hear it, either. It's there, pulsating its not-quite-melodies, softly, unemphatically, monotonously. I have made a little poll of people in supermarkets and other spots that have this background non-music on all the time. "What's it like having music thrust into your ears all day?" The answer invariably is: "I don't even hear it any more." But then what's it for?

It's a sedative, gradually taking over the drugstores, department stores, buses, restaurants, massage parlors, and even the chapel at Forest Lawn. It's a blotter-out of thought, and especially of emotion, without stimulating any thought and emotion of its own. That takes some doing, but they've managed it by making the arrangements almost mechanically inoffensive. In fact, they all sound like the same arrangement—all violins and muted brasses, suspended in the same beat.

But is this what our ears are for? The ears were put there originally to warn us that danger lurked—the snap of a twig, the snarl of beasts, the rattle of rattlesnakes. It's a fortunate thing the dangers have dwindled in modern life, because we'd never hear them.

What's the matter with the ordinary sounds that are being drowned out—the chatter of people, the laughter of children, the songs of birds, the wind in the treetops? So, all right, there are no treetops to listen to in elevators. Just the same, elevators used to make a nice natural sound of their own—the whoosh of air whooshing by in the shaft. But you can't hear it now for the "happiness music."

You get into an old-fashioned DC-3-type airplane and you can hear talk and laughter, the rattle of newspapers, human sounds. But those new shiny monsters blot out all those things. One sits to the sound of mood music designed to calm the nerves. Calm *my* nerves? Why do my nerves need calming? You suppose there's something about those airplanes they're not telling? I have a friend who is jittery about airplanes under any circumstances. She sat there having her nerves calmed by—she swears it—"I've Got a Feeling I'm Falling." She got right off the airplane.

I prefer those three sad-faced, proud old men, playing beside the cracked fountain, behind the potted palms in hotels and restaurants all over Europe. At least the music has passed through their fingertips, their emotions, their souls. This empty homogenized non-music sounds as if it were manufactured by automatons and played by an orchestra run by air pressure, oil, and electricity like that mechanical band in Disneyland. ■

■ Once upon a time in the recent memory of men, *Time* magazine had a very cute and astringent article in its book section, about what it called non-books, written by non-authors for non-people, a long-overdue little burst of indignation.

Year in, year out, the best-seller list is as fine a collection of utter tripe as can be found on television. We have some very bad writing on TV. But certainly nothing any worse than that in *Advise and Consent.* That book was at the head or near the head of the best-seller list for months, and it reads like a bad first draft of a bad first novel by a man who shouldn't have attempted literature in the first place.

Time's piece was not directed at slipshod novels like *Advise and Consent* so much as at the real non-books such as those by Art Linkletter, which have hardly any business existing between hard covers. Perhaps the most conspicuous example of a non-author is Rona Jaffe, who was more or less invented by Jerry Wald and the late Jack Goodman. Her book *The Best of Everything* was the brainstorm of Goodman and Wald, who were already planning the movie before the book had been written or even before an author had been found to write it.

My late dear friend Richard L. Simon, former president of Simon and Schuster, was the first man to sell a pocket book in this country. Dick took books out of the bookstores, where reading was almost deliberately confined to members of a small exclusive club, and put books in the supermarkets and the drugstores. This opened reading to millions of people who wouldn't ordinarily buy books. It was a great push forward for people and for publishing.

But now books, it seems to me, are *all* aimed at and written for the drugstore trade. They're not written tc be read; they're written to distract. In addition, there is an enormous and profitable traffic in Christmas books that are not meant to be opened at all. These are designed not for reading, but simply for purchase: books with titles like *The Civil War in Pictures,* with 7,000 color prints, weighing 12 pounds, and costing $12.60. The man who buys it has no intention of reading it, only of giving it away. The man who gets it never opens it but puts it directly on the end table where it looks mighty handsome. Actually that's what it was designed for—just to lie there, looking handsome and giving a little fillip to the owner's culture status. ■

■ There have been times when I've had a horrible feeling that in a few decades all literature will be contained in balloons issuing from the mouths of comic-strip drawings. The nuances of the printed word, which allows the writer some depth of penetration into a character or into a situation, will be confined to the dialogue he can compress into those small areas in the drawing not occupied by breasts or muscles. It's pretty confining.

This is the picture age—moving pictures on the TV set in the living room, still pictures in the books—and the printed word, which requires an exercise of the mind considerably more powerful and subtle than that of a comic book, is having a tough time all over. My friend Jim Hurlbut, when he was in South America, even sent letters to his wife by ad-libbing into a tape recorder and sending her the tape, which she then played back. These letters had some of the sprawling prose style of the commentators at fights killing time on the air before the contest begins. "Well, dear, the cleaning woman is now working outside my door, and it's five minutes to seven and I think I'll get on to breakfast."

Love letters of this nature have, I must admit, a certain air of immediacy and closeness and warmth about them, but there is an enormous amount of unnecessary detail and an almost total absence of style. I'm glad that Robert and Elizabeth Barrett Browning didn't correspond via tape recording; their letters would hardly have survived. But perhaps that's the way collected love letters will be gathered together in another decade or so. "Give me the collected taped love letters of (some future) George Bernard Shaw to (some future) Ellen Terry," you'll ask the librarian, and then go home and listen to the old windbag and wonder what the devil she saw in him. ■

■ As I've said, this is the picture age, and I'm reminded of a minor controversy that was taking place in Rio de Janeiro not long ago: the battle of the picture magazines, which might have been subtitled "Your slums are worse than our slums—so there."

The war of the picture magazines started when *Life,* in June, 1961, ran a picture essay showing how horrible life was in the *favelas* which climb straight up the hills around Rio. These are supposed to be the world's worst slums—though that's a sweeping statement. They are certainly the world's most picturesque slums, and everyone will tell you that no other slum dweller the world over has such a marvelous view of sea and sky. *Life* made the existence of the favelas one of appalling degradation. "Foul!" cried *O Cruzeiro,* which is a sort of Brazilian *Life* magazine.

O Cruzeiro immediately invaded our own Harlem, which has some fairly unsavory slums of its own, and did its own picture feature, centering around the Puerto Rican Gonzales family, whose degradation—cockroaches crawling over the face of a child and all that—was just as great as *Life*'s favela degradation. "Foul!" cried *Time* magazine. *Time* charged that the Gonzales family had been paid to pose for their degradation, that the cockroaches were dead cockroaches carefully placed there by the *O Cruzeiro* photographer.

"Ho!" screamed *O Cruzeiro* in reply to *Time, Life* and the whole Luce empire. *O Cruzeiro* charged *Life* made up the whole favela story. A picture of a boy crying because a mad dog had bit him was phony, said the magazine. The boy had been slapped by his father for being naughty. Another picture of a supposedly dead girl, arms crossed, candles at her feet, in a coffin, was equally phony, an *O Cruzeiro* reporter charged. He said the girl is still alive and walking around Rio and he knows where the *Life* people bought the coffin.

So it went.

Frankly, I think it a risky business for one picture magazine to start questioning the truth of another picture magazine's photographs. I have been watching news photographers (who are among the world's fearless, energetic and creative human beings) at work, lo, these many years, with the growing suspicion that comparatively few news pictures except maybe that of Mickey Mantle sliding into second base are entirely unposed. Or entirely honest. The degree of dishonesty mounts sharply when you get into any kind of photographic essay such as *Life* or *O Cruzeiro* runs. If they start out to find squalor, they'll find squalor if they have to get the Warner Brothers prop department to construct it for them.

Parenthetically, while I'm talking about magazines, I might mention these "all about" monkeyshines that have been the latest lunacy of the periodicals. "All about Puerto Rico." "All about Detroit." "All about Labor." Then they give you 324 pages (with color prints) about something you don't—like the little girl and the penguins—want to know that much about. I think it was *Life* that started this nonsense. I wish they'd all get over it. ■

■ Meanwhile, the architects are not letting the art or music or literature worlds get too far out in front of them in the field of general looniness. No chimpanzees, so far as I know, have designed any of those glass buildings, but—well, how else are we to explain the Summit Hotel? Actually the Summit Hotel was designed by Morris Lapidus, of whom *The Nation*'s architectural critic, Walter McQuade, has said, "He is an interesting architect with a strange specialty—bad taste."

My conviction that architects know about everything expect architecture was reinforced when I was in Brasilia, the new capital of Brazil that was carved into the bleached forest plateau at a cost of roughly $1 billion that the Brazilians could ill afford.

The city was designed by Oscar Niemeyer and Lucio Costa, and its ultramodern buildings sit astride the landscape awkwardly. I drove past acres of superblocks—each containing identical six-story buildings containing thirty-six three-bedroom apartments. They're all glass on one side and all fretwork in the back so you can hang the wash out of sight.

The apartments are quite roomy and comfortable with big combination living room–dining room, one-and-a-half baths, three big bedrooms, maid's quarters, nice kitchen and a nice balcony off the kitchen (which is quite common to most Brazilian apartments and a very good idea). But the residents will tell you these are much too noisy, letting in all the racket from the busy roads. One of the great failures of modern buildings is the absence of soundproofing.

The low-cost apartments, built for the typists and secretaries, are tiny rooms, hot, ugly, noisy, badly designed, but cheap.

I visited the Assembly hall, which has a visitors' gallery in a kind of saucer, and then the Senate, which has the same saucer overturned. These are of marble with great use of the beautiful Brazilian wood, jacaranda. I visited the offices of the majority leader and of the Senate secretary. They are handsome offices but both are hot and stuffy. The buildings are built without air conditioning. The majority leader has his own air-conditioning unit but power failures are frequent.

The Senate offices are too small and all of them, glass-fronted as they are, heat up frightfully. So do the Ministry buildings—one side becoming an inferno in the morning, the other in the afternoon. There's a story that an infuriated Minister called Niemeyer to his sweltering office at its worst hour and lectured him for two hours—just to show him what it was like. This is planning but it's bad planning. Like so much modern architecture, these buildings are designed to be looked at from the outside rather than lived and worked in from the inside. (Niemeyer himself, incidentally, is building himself an old-fashioned colonial house designed strictly for comfort. Modernism is for the people.)

As for the plan of the city, buildings are hundreds of yards from their neighbors, and even if you wanted to walk somewhere, there are no sidewalks. A terrible mistake.

"What do lovers do in the evening?" a Brazilian woman, like myself a visitor, said to me. "Where do they stroll?"

Already people are getting killed on the highways trudging to the bus station because there are no sidewalks. "Brasilia, the only city in the world without crossroads," trumpets a brochure. It's all cloverleafs and underpasses, originally meant as safety measures. Still, people get killed.

"The cloverleafs are numbered but they all look alike and if you miss your cloverleaf after a couple of drinks, you have to go through the most elaborate backtracking to get back where you started," a guy told me.

One of the biggest complaints is that Niemeyer designed a series of ghettos. Nice ghettos but, nevertheless, ghettos where one is segregated with one's own kind. Americans live with Americans, French with French, British with British. If you're in the Air Ministry, you not only work together all day—you live in the same compound at night.

Brasilia was designed for automobiles, but badly designed. There aren't nearly enough parking places in front of the huge capitol building with its combined Senate and Assembly chambers. Already there are traffic problems in the main street, which is not wide enough.

"The people are constantly crossing up the city planners," my guide told me. "None of these streets have names, just numbers. But the people call this one the street of the little church because of that little church up at the head there. Niemeyer planned this as the service entrance, strictly for the trucks to make deliveries. The people were supposed to enter the stores from that side. But the people like this street. So they've changed the stores around. The front is the back and the back is the front."

I have an idea the people will modify Brasilia a lot more drastically before they are finished with it, putting the stamp of their individuality, their cussedness and their humanity on the marble.

There are good things to be said for Brasilia, principally the climate; the city is 3,000 feet high, and its dry and sparkling air and fresh breezes and moderate temperatures are going to be its greatest asset. Time and people may improve it. But when I drove to the airport in the cool of the dusk—the horizon stretching to infinity, like Wyoming, in the clear air—I saw the lights in the monotonous rectangular buildings begin to wink on in the distance, and it occurred to me again that the first modern architect to discover a curved line is going to make a fortune.

In Europe today there is a huge pool of what you might call American remittance men of the arts. Because of the vicious inequities of the tax laws, particularly their terrible discriminations against writers, we are driving creative people out of America to Europe, where they can get a little tax relief, mostly writing in or acting in or producing or directing movies, but also writing novels or producing TV series or painting pictures.

There have always been expatriate artists and writers, including some very good ones. But the new kind of expatriate writer is a different article from, say, Henry James and T. S. Eliot, who went to England because they felt more at home there.

Today the John Hustons and Yul Brynners are in Europe mainly to get some relief from a tax system that is so unfairly rigged against artists and in favor of anyone in business. James wrote about life in English country houses because that was his chosen field of battle among the people he chose to write about. Today's writers move to Paris (apart from the tax angle) almost in the spirit of moving to Westport on a somewhat larger scale. You can live better on the money. It's prettier. The air is better.

This has seriously affected the quality of their work. After the last war Hemingway wrote *The Sun Also Rises* in Paris, a book that was to open a whole new age and act as a beacon for writers the world over. Fitzgerald wrote almost all of *The Great Gatsby* in Paris. Edith Wharton wrote *The Age of Innocence* there and Stephen Vincent Benét *John Brown's Body.*

Have any novels of comparable stature been done by our expatriates after this war? I doubt it. One reason, I'm convinced, is that the writers, far from being in the heart of things, feel actually cut off from the center of things, removed from the roots of their existence, living, as it were, in a sort of cultural suburb, and this has taken some of the freshness and vigor out of their work.

There has been talk for years about "plugging the loopholes" in the tax laws to bring our writers home. I put that in quotes because I feel strongly that this will solve nothing. The problem is to provide some tax surcease in this country so that writers and artists are not so persecuted by the government—while oil millionaires from Texas or gas men from Oklahoma or real estate men from Kansas have it so easy, taxwise.

In most countries, writers and artists are given special dispensation in the tax laws. The Soviet Union taxes its writers only 13 per cent. I think all major works—and by that I mean books or plays—should be considered capital and taxed accordingly. Many writers have only one book or one play in them that they spend a lifetime formulating—even if they write it in three weeks.

Across the board, culture in this country is in the brick-and-mortar phase, or halfway toward the Museum Epoch, or, I'd say, one-third of the way toward fossilization, which is where it is in Europe. In Asia, of course, they're even farther ahead of us, being, in fact, in the Age of Crumbling Ruins into which archeologists peer and wonder how those primitive peoples got such huge stones into such interesting positions and what it all meant.

We're well behind Asia in this matter. We haven't even built the temples to fall into ruins yet. But we're sure trying. In New York the Lincoln Center for the Performing Arts is having its first season, and in Washington, where President Kennedy threw his own prestige into the breach, the National Cultural Center, which will eventually coalesce into a $30-million Pantheon of the performing arts, opened a fund-raising drive. Both these splendid edifices—Lincoln Center and National Cultural Center on the Potomac (if they ever get it built, which is by no means certain)—will one day make terribly interesting Crumbling Ruins over which archeologists will speculate, "How on earth do you suppose those primitive people built such an enormous arch and what do you suppose they did in there?"

The Cultural Center in Washington is now in the hands of what I like to think of as "the fund-raising people," notably Roger L. Stevens, a great expert in these matters, who, when asked what would go on in this immense and beautiful shell, instantly suggested Leonard Bernstein and the Philharmonic.

Everyone does. Whenever a new temple to culture is erected in Houston or Milwaukee, they think instantly of Leonard Bernstein and the Philharmonic. I yield to no man in my admiration of Leonard Bernstein, but I don't think we need another stage for him to operate from. In fact, I think he already operates from maybe too many. What we need, in fact, is more Leonard Bernsteins, not more stages.

These are, I recognize, subversive sentiments in a capitalist democracy, and I shall now proceed to be even more subversive and suggest that what we really need in this country is a subsidy for the arts, all of them, as is given in just about every civilized country in the world. Subsidy has been a dirty word for a hundred and fifty years in the culture dodge in this country, but it is my feeling (and my hope) that if we just put it on paper often enough it'll lose its shock value.

President Kennedy is the best friend culture (another dirty word) has had in the White House since Thomas Jefferson. He feels strongly that the country owes a debt of gratitude to its artists. He even feels that these people will loom larger over the decades than the politicians and the businessmen—an heretical thought, if ever I heard one. In a brief but spirited talk to the advisory council and trustees of the Cultural Center, the President slyly pointed out that the Soviet Union has made "a major effort" in supporting the arts. If there's one sure way to get dough out of the populace or out of Congress in this country, it is by suggesting that the Soviet Union got there ahead of us. ■

Hollywood

■ When, in 1952, I first saw Marilyn Monroe at truly close range, she was—next, possibly, to Adlai and Ike—the hottest topic of conversation in Hollywood. She was twenty-four years old and a very likable—is that the word I want exactly?—girl. One thing that rather astonished me about Marilyn Monroe was that the wives—those, at least, who had met the girl—liked her just as much as their husbands did, though in a somewhat different way.

"Everyone loves Marilyn," said Dinah Shore. "How can you help it? She's so honest."

But Marilyn didn't think so. "I've had friends tell me, 'I had to defend you last night against the women.' So I say, 'What did the men say?' Then my friends tell me, 'The men just sit there, grinning a little.' That makes up for it—a little."

And, she smiled. When Marilyn smiled, she smiled all over. Her lips parted, her eyes narrowed, her eyebrows shot up, and the whole vastly publicized body moved around a little bit. I suppose that would be the definition of a lot of other smiles, but Marilyn did it more expertly than anyone else. Watching her, I remembered what Joseph Cotten had told me just after he'd finished a picture with her: "Everything that girl does is sexy. She can't even light a cigarette without being sexy. A lot of people—the ones who haven't met Marilyn—will tell you it's all just publicity. That's malarkey. They've tried to give the same publicity buildup to a hundred girls out here. None of them took. This girl's really got it."

I thought I'd better test Mr. Cotten's cigarette theory and I offered her one. She had only recently learned to smoke, having been required to do it in *Don't Bother to Knock.* She did it as if she had been at it for years, and after watching her for a while, I decided the Cotten theory was sound, very sound.

"I haven't heard anything but the kindest things about you since I've been here," I said.

"Oh, you are very nice to say so. But I know what they say, the women. I get letters from the women. 'What are you trying to do?' they say. 'Put the country in a worse state than it's in?' Now it's my fault—the state the country's in. They accuse me of starting all the rapes. Rapes went on long before I came."

This girl, I thought, is a very interesting bundle of neuroses. "Crank letters," I said. "Everyone gets them. What the hell do you care what a few cranks say? You're the hottest thing in pictures. You've got the country at your feet. Why worry about a few cranks?"

But she did worry. Some of the Hollywood hatchet girls—and the place abounds in them—had given her the full treatment at parties. This had cut deep. And the critics, who had had a field day with her acting, had wounded her to the marrow. "They are so cruel, the critics. Sometimes I think they just take out their frustrations on other people."

She spoke in a low, throaty murmur, the sound coming from far back in her throat. Both her inflections and the structure of her sentences were more European than American, which was odd because Marilyn had been born and brought up in Los Angeles.

"My wardrobe mistress says that, too. She is a Hungarian and she is my closest friend. She says I am more like a European girl because I enjoy being a woman." She thought a moment, the lips moving a little; the face was never quite still. "I don't know where I picked it up. I was born on the wrong side of the tracks, you know, and I used to play with a lot of little Mexican boys. Perhaps there."

"When did it start, the sex appeal?" I was beginning to use the same sentence structure, the delayed subject.

"I think I was about twelve when things changed—radically. The boys didn't have cars. They had bicycles. They'd come by the house and whistle or they'd honk their little horns. Some of them had paper routes. I'd always get a free paper."

Marilyn's childhood was shrouded in contradictions. She said she saw her parents but rarely. This has been disputed and it's hard to know what is true. But it wasn't a happy childhood.

"Ever since I can remember, I've wanted to be a movie star. I loved the movies. When I was a little girl, it seemed like the only time I was alive was when I was at the movies. The movies were much more real to me than my life."

Well, she'd got there, all right. How was it, being a star?

"Well—it's exciting. The first time I saw my name in lights, I just stopped the car and stared at it for twenty minutes. I thought, this is some kind of ultimate. But, of course, you never quite get everything, do you? I want to be a great stage actress. No, honestly, I do."

Then there were the unkind critics. One critic, in particular, said all she could do was "wiggle my fanny," the unkindest cut of all.

"I know what I'm doing," she said fiercely, "I know I can act. I can play Gretchen in *Faust,* or Teresa in *The Cradle Song.* I know I can." But she never did. ■

■ When I first went to Hollywood there were giants in that land, and Hollywood giants were considerably more gigantic than ordinary giants. There were, too, as there were and are everywhere, the midgets striving for gianthood, and in the early 1950s I ran into several of them.

We had got about five minutes away from the hotel, the driver and I, when he handed me a script, his own. What did I think?

It was, he admitted, rough. He wasn't really a writer. He just liked to play around with it, he said, but he thought this might be of interest to *Suspense.* I read it and I said that, well, it needed work, quite a lot of work.

"That's what they all tell me," he said somberly and fell back to driving, which was his primary but not chosen occupation.

The second driver who piloted me barely got the car out of second before he announced belligerently, "This is just an in-between job." He drove a moment and then asked if I knew of the Benbow in San Francisco. No, I said, I didn't. "It's one of the best nightclubs up there. I just finished a two-week engagement—emceeing and singing."

Ticker Freeman, Dinah Shore's arranger, once walked into an office building. The doorman handed him a song he'd just written; the elevator operator handed him his latest song. Two songs in twenty feet.

There is as much drudgery around Hollywood as anywhere else, but the people who perform it have their minds on the higher glories of show business. They are actors or writers or composers—or they'd like to be. ■

■ If you collect people as I enjoy doing, you haven't really rounded out your library until you encounter a movie starlet. The particular starlet I had under observation was blonde as paper, saucer-eyed, momentarily (and perhaps permanently) unemployed in pictures, and full of talk. Brother, you haven't lived until you've heard a starlet talk.

"Hollywood men," she said, "are the way they are because of the sun. They're all oversexed. Because of the sunshine, you know. I'll show you what I mean. Feel my skin." I felt her cheek. "It's cool. Because the sun has gone down. But inside, I'm terribly warm. Because of the sun. I'm just stored-up sunshine inside."

She moved away from Hollywood men to her one other topic of conversation—Hollywood women. "A girl has a difficult time out here," she observed. "She can go out with an older man. But that's not very satisfactory because he is older. Or she can go out with a married man but that's not very satisfactory because he's married. Or she can go out with a young man. And that's not very satisfactory either. Because they haven't any money. They may drive up in a Cadillac but they really haven't got any money. They live by their wits, the young ones. And that's terribly unsatisfactory."

I never found out what was satisfactory. I suppose nothing really is. ■

■ The tribal customs of Hollywood, which are somewhat different from those anywhere else on earth, have fascinated me from the first. They will probably survive as long as the place and the idea do.

The salutations in Hollywood, for instance, have always baffled and confused me. I've always been a straight "Hello" man in the greeting department, but that's much too uncomplicated for the movie capital. Not so long ago the greeting out there was (and it may still be) "How do you feel?" I would have been only too happy to trot out all my symptoms, but I didn't really think they wanted to hear them. Just the same, if one more guy had pulled that "How do you feel?" line on me, he would have got the full prognosis.

The "How do you feel?" bit is symptomatic of a town that is incessantly feeling its pulse and morbidly examining its motives, which are never simple. If you think a producer makes a picture simply to make money, then you haven't talked to one recently. A great opening line in Hollywood is: "I had to make this picture because . . ."—and the twenty-five words or less with which that sentence is finished are likely to be full of the producer's childhood insecurities, his feelings about race relations in the South, or his guilt complex for all humanity. Never have I heard a producer say, "I had to make this picture because I needed the money."

The place teems with psychiatrists, probably the greatest concentration of headshrinkers in the world, and producers, directors, writers, and actors are lying on their couches by the hundreds at any hour of the day. Why do people who make so much money and live so opulently feel compelled to do this? James Mason has an interesting theory. Everyone there feels incessantly compelled to explain how he felt about his last picture, his innermost spiritual torments about his current role, or his tremendous emotional frustrations about his present job.

After a bit he runs out of people to tell these things to. Everyone has heard it and nobody wants to hear it again. The place abounds in talkers—and some very brilliant talkers, too—but there is a terrible scarcity of listeners. Hence, the psychiatrist's couch.

The psychiatrist's couch and the frenetic urge to explain are part of the self-dramatization which is so inherent in Hollywood that you find yourself doing it when you're there. It takes place at all levels of society from the executive producer's house down to the cabdrivers. Now, in New York we have some really screwball cabdrivers, God knows, but I never met one who felt he had to explain to me why he was a cabdriver.

Everyone, in short, is on stage at all times. You can't buy a package of cigarettes without getting a flourish of skirts, a smile, and an act that would do great discredit to a B-picture. I've always loved listening to the loudspeaker at the swimming pool which announces telephone calls. "Mr. Arnold J. Gladewater," the girl will say briskly, "telephone."

But then, a moment or two later—same girl on the public address system—there will be a husky whisper: "Mr. Clift—Mr. Montgomery Clift"—then a long sigh—"long distance!"

I love all the tribal customs, really. Except one which had grown up the last time I was there and which I hope has been extinguished by now. They were all blowing kisses when they left the party—men blowing kisses to men, women to women. I saw a guy blow a kiss to the cabdriver one day.

They opened with "How do you feel?"; they closed by blowing you a kiss. Aw, come on, fellows, I wanted to say; there are a couple of old Anglo-Saxon words I'd like to introduce—"Hello" and "Good-by." ■

■ In the late forties I have observed something pretty close to a panic in Hollywood. Warner Brothers was closed tight without a camera stirring. Contract players who had been extracting several hundred dollars a week for sitting around movie studios could be found selling cars on Wilshire Boulevard or real estate in Palm Springs. There was widespread unemployment, especially among technicians—the cameramen, lighting experts, stagehands and the like. The picture folk had been publicly talking tough and privately scared blue about television.

Well, things certainly changed. When I was there in 1952, the movie folk had learned to live with television to the extent that they didn't talk about it or even think about it very much. Three years before, if you'd asked a movie star about television, you'd have heard a half-hour talk about how people would always go out nights because married folk couldn't stand the sight of each other every night. They can't hurt us, he'd have told you, because we have the stars, the know-how and the money. Then you'd get a lecture on economics, proving TV couldn't conceivably fill all that time and the home folks would eventually be driven out of their homes in despair and probably take up residence in movie theaters. It was all very entertaining.

In 1952 you asked a movie executive about TV and he said, "Well, I don't look at it much any more," and passed on to more fruitful discourse like sex and politics. Today NBC and CBS have built huge, menacing structures to house their live shows, and every available lot is bustling with television activity.

I walked down the street with an actor. Every time he passed anyone, he'd smile, hold his fingers in an *O* sign and say, "Great! Very funny!" The others would beam at him and nod back.

"What's very funny?" I asked.

"You're the first one who's asked," he said. "Everyone here is shooting comedy shows. You can say, 'Great! Very funny!' to anyone here, and he thinks you're talking about his show. Actually, we're all so busy shooting for television here, none of us has time to look at it very much." ■

■ The advantages of filmed TV shows are manifold to everyone except those of us who have to look at them.

"Why film?" an inksmeared collection of some forty radio and TV editors asked as early as 1952.

Hollywood was stuffed with brains and experience, but the end product as seen in our living rooms was pretty bad. It was generally agreed among these forty-odd that the most exciting moments we had ever seen on television were live. Why, then, this passion for film, which is always three or four thousand dollars more expensive than live television?

Al Simon, the associate producer who was taking the brunt of these churlish questions at a Hollywood conclave, explained that television was going on film largely because it was less of a strain on the actor: "The actors brought it about. The actors forced us into film and will continue to insist on it."

About this time the announcement came that Queen Elizabeth's coronation would be filmed for television. No live television. Her Majesty might be discovered picking her teeth or something. Everything else was already going on film. With Queen Elizabeth joining the lists, practically nothing live remained. ■

■ By 1954 the air of prosperity in both TV and movie industries was overwhelming. Movies perhaps were not better than ever, but they were certainly bigger than ever, and they were making as much money as ever. In sheer size and splendor, there hadn't been anything like the premiere of *A Star Is Born* in Hollywood for years. The excellence of the movie didn't match the opulence of the opening, but that detail was slightly lost sight of in the general fanfare. The following night came the opening of Chrysler's *Shower of Stars,* which may have been the most plush television opening to come along so far.

The smell of money, in short, was overpowering and it was everywhere. Movie stars who had for years turned down television because their marquee value was still strong were succumbing fast because there seemed to be no limit to the amounts of money offered them. If they turned down one sum, the offer was upped another ten thousand dollars the next day. Eventually the price was right.

Well, I enjoyed seeing the actors get rich, but it led to some special problems. I bumped into one director freshly arrived in Hollywood from New York where he directed TV dramas. He was slightly dazed by it all. "In New York," he explained, "we'd get a script we thought was pretty good. Then we'd scout around for the actors we thought best suited for the roles. Out here, you come to work and they've already hired some big-shot actor for about forty thousand dollars—or maybe two big shots—and you got to go look for a script that will make some sense—and will also please the big shots."

This was the star system with a vengeance, something even the movies had pretty well outgrown, and it led to such strange matings of talent as Mario Lanza, Betty Grable, and Harry James in one show.

God knows, the color spectaculars, the hour-long dramas with their all-star casts and the other extravaganzas have not all been unqualified successes. And with this emphasis on bigness, I sometimes get to thinking that it seems like only yesterday that the biggest stars on television were Kukla, Fran and Ollie, who are only about a foot high.

As for bigness in the movies, LOVE IS BETTER ON OUR COLOSSAL MIRACLE SCREEN, I once read in an ad. Now, there's an interesting, if slightly frightening, possibility. I expect it's true, too. Love on a colossal miracle screen is undoubtedly better as well as bigger and tastier and probably milder.

A movie critic I know, who had just been to see *How to Marry a Millionaire,* was telling me about that vast experience with some relish. "In this one scene, Marilyn Monroe was stretched out on a sofa. She was forty-two feet long, and I loved every foot of her."

Well, I decided not to see the picture. A five-foot-seven-inch Marilyn Monroe was unsettling enough. Forty-two feet I wouldn't have been able to stand. Maybe not even twenty-two feet.

And what would happen when you went home and were confronted by your five-foot-four-inch wife? How was a man expected to readjust his scale of values so rapidly?

Love is undoubtedly better on colossal miracle screens, but can the average man stand all that outside emotion? As a matter of fact, the whole problem of scale bothers me. It took me five years to get used to an eight-inch Ed Sullivan.

Twentieth Century-Fox had a movie, *The Robe,* which was the greatest thing to date, largely because the screen was roughly the size of Rhode Island. A man could take his family for a picnic on Mt. Sinai on this screen and never encounter a single actor.

But this passion for bigness has left some of the folks behind, notably me. I saw *The Bandwagon* twice. This is a rather odd thing, because there aren't many movies I see even once, much less twice. This was more or less an experiment in bigness. The first time, I saw the picture in a screening room at Loew's State. There were about eighty people in the audience and it was a hip crowd. I can't recall having had a better time at a picture in years.

The Bandwagon had about everything you ought to require in a picture. It had some of the best tunes Arthur Schwartz and Howard Dietz had written over a couple of decades. It had some of the best dancing you could find around. It had a very fine and very funny script by Adolph Green and Betty Comden. It had—if you go for this sort of thing—a delectable form, in Cyd Charisse. The Technicolor alone—the brilliant interplay of the costumes against the scenery—was worth the price of admission.

That was the first time. The second time, I saw *The Bandwagon* at the Radio City Music Hall. The screen was the size of Yankee Stadium. There were five thousand people there, muttering, falling asleep in the comfortable chairs, laughing now and then—a little late—at the jokes. They seemed to be enjoying themselves, this mob, but everyone seemed to be enjoying himself separately, like a crowd at a ballroom.

The intimacy of the theater was gone. Much of the fine detail in the script or in the dancing or in the settings was missed entirely. Everything—the screen and the crowd—had just got too large. And it wasn't even a colossal miracle screen. It was just the same old Music Hall screen, the size of Yankee Stadium.

Perhaps I'd just been ruined by television, but I decided then and there that it would be a long time before anyone lured me into the Music Hall again. I preferred that eight-inch Ed Sullivan. ■

■ Have you taken a walk down Broadway recently? I'm an old marquee-reader from way back—and, brother, the marquees are gamy. I can't remember the beginning of this trend, but in 1960 I made the following report, which shows that the current situation is nothing new:

> *Love by Appointment*, whispers the marquee over the Rialto, where they got a dandy double feature held over for the ninth smash week. *Unmarried Mothers* is the other one. "Call me anything but call me often," runs the caption under a half-dressed girl. "First New York Showing." "Most daring scenes ever shown. A story of unbridled passion and wanton love. Behind the scenes of a call-girl racket: The girl who can't stop and the ones who won't." The plug for *Unmarried Mothers* is rather mild: "A searing indictment of today's moral standards."
>
> Presently comes the Paramount, which is featuring a con-

fection called *Desire in the Dust.* It's kind of hard to say what that one's all about. "They whispered about the Colonel and his daughter. No one knew about the mother and the son. A challenging insight into the human hungers and the fires of the flesh." What are they hinting at, anyway—incest? "Just a quiet Southern town—until its hidden shames exploded into the light of day. Kin by kin or sin by sin, their hidden desires rocked a town!" *Just* the thing for the kiddies.

So—on we go across the street to the Globe, where you'll find *The Naked and the Wicked.* ("No woman was safe with this brute. She was too much in love to realize she was doing wrong.") In the same theater: *Las Vegas Strip.* ("Never, no never before such scenes! A volcano of smouldering passions. Hours of ecstasy, months of regret. So what goes on—and comes off—at the strip joints, and dice parlors.") And plodding up the avenue you come to *Expresso Bongo* ("Real! Raw! Racy!").

Up the block is *Hell to Eternity.* ("On the beachhead or in the beach house, Bill always made a perfect score. They said Sheila was cold to Marines—but Guy knew her boiling point. The big one that goes all the way.")

Man and boy, I've been walking under Broadway marquees for a long time now, and I can't say that sort of teaser was a new trend even in 1960. Hollywood has been boasting a long time about how it was going to lay my emotions bare with its searing flames, about the picture I dared them to make. (I did not ever dare them to make a picture. I've dared Hollywood not to make some pictures.)

But it does seem to me that sex has never been so naked and unashamed (gee, Mannie, that's a great title for our next picture) or so blatantly the only reason they make so many pictures. I have several objections to this besides the obvious one that it's awfully hard to find a picture to take the kiddies to. For one thing, they're going to take all the novelty out of sex. For another, sex, when I was a kid, wasn't considered a spectator sport. It was meant to be played, not looked at.

Back in 1960 I noted that the storm clouds were gathering. NEW THEMES BEG CENSORIAL FROWN, said *Variety*. "All indications are that the motion picture industry will face one of its most crucial legislative sessions in years."

An adjoining story in the same paper opened with: "Whether it's organized or unorganized, the fact remains that there is a distinct campaign against skid row morality in recent pictures and perhaps some of these upcoming." Classification laws were pending in several states. These were to require films to be labeled, as in England, for adults only or for the whole family. In addition, the Catholic Church was beginning to complain again—and small wonder.

But have you taken a walk down Broadway lately? ■

■ Less than ten years ago Hollywood discovered Egypt. Egypt had been lying under a benevolent—though sometimes blistering—sun for some 7,000 years, and Hollywood, during all that time, ignored it. Then one day somebody in Hollywood—Cheops Pincus is the name I've arbitrarily decided to give him—was leafing through some old maps and came across Egypt. Since then Egypt has been crawling with movie stars. A tourist can hardly get to the Pyramids without brushing aside a Hollywood actor or two—distributing, of course, a little *baksheesh* to each.

During the space of a year or so, besides *Valley of the Kings*, Warner Brothers shot *Land of the Pharaohs*, Twentieth Century-Fox *The Egyptian*, and Gregory Ratoff a picture called, in Egypt, *Abdullah the Great*. I happened to be in Cairo when Cecil B. De Mille's henchmen were constructing settings for a reshoot of *The Ten Commandments* somewhere out in the desert.

M-G-M, though, had stolen a march by releasing its *The Valley of the Kings* ahead of the competition, a sumptuous production and the first major picture shot in Egypt to be released there. It was quite a show. Outside the theater M-G-M constructed a

Pharaonic arch, adorned with hieroglyphics shouting the praises of Eleanor Parker, with two terribly Old Kingdom statues of a man and a woman. The statues looked 4,000 years old but were actually constructed at the behest of those great patrons of art, the Warner Brothers, for their picture *Land of the Pharaohs*. Then the M-G-M boys there michievously bought those massive *objets d'art* and were using them to plug a competing picture. Aaah, the wily Near East!

The Egyptians are pretty good moviegoers, but they have their own strong tastes. They love spectacles with a strong story line—*Scaramouche, Quo Vadis, Ivanhoe,* that sort of thing. The sort of thing they don't like is *Philadelphia Story,* which they considered just a lot of talk.

An appreciative audience, the Egyptians. They howled with laughter at even the smallest witticism in *Valley of the Kings,* and also at some spots where they were not supposed to laugh at all. From time to time during the picture Robert Taylor would shout something in Arabic in what my Egyptian friends confided to me was an atrocious accent. The house would break up. Taylor could easily be the Jackie Gleason of Egypt. He could just walk out on a stage there and say "*Salaam aleikum*" (Peace be with you) and he'd have 'em rolling in the aisles.

One thing the Egyptians don't care about much, though, is kissing scenes. When Miss Parker and Mr. Taylor finally fell into each other's arms, the crowd stirred restively, muttering, "*Bass, bass*" (Enough! Enough!)—and I was with them all the way.

I wonder what the Egyptians will make of *Cleopatra*. ■

News on the airwaves

■ The greatest thing television does is news, and the worst thing it does is news, and all I can say about that is that it should always keep trying. I'd rather Jack Paar made a fool of himself in Berlin (actually I thought he wasn't at all bad) than that television not try at all.

The two most exciting things I ever saw on television, I think, were the hockey game between Russia and the United States, which we won, and the first flight into space by our very own homegrown astronaut. I almost had a heart attack each time.

There have been some real dull news events on TV too. Nearly ten years ago, there was a loud noise out West. "Well," said a voice to the television audience, "it went off."

He was speaking about the atom bomb which had, indeed, gone off. It looked like a small sun in eclipse. Very odd, very disappointing. The picture had been breaking up—tearing, as they say in television—ever since the broadcast started at noon.

"Owing to technical difficulties," said somebody, "we are having difficulties bringing you the picture."

This was an understatement. Even when the picture arrived—which was a sometime thing—it was the dullest possible picture. There was a babble of sound, the dullest possible sound.

"Signals are sent out by switches manually," declared a man who sounded as if he were an expert reading from a paper to a small group of fellow experts. "They are tested electronically by various instruments and are furthermore mounded by earth."

I have no idea what the sentence meant, but it had an authoritative sound. It sounded like experts talking double-talk and hating the rest of us.

"Owing to technical difficulties," came booming out again. "Ladies and gentlemen, please stand by for the telecast of an atomic-bomb explosion," said the invisible man. The phrase "ladies and gentlemen" seemed anemic, inadequate.

At a time like this, I said to myself, you should say "men and women." And you shouldn't say "stand by." Come to think of it, we'd all been standing by for the sound of an atomic explosion since Hiroshima.

We were viewing the thing—in those brief intervals when the scene came through at all—from forty miles away. There is probably nothing duller than Yucca Flat from even two inches away. From forty miles Yucca Flat reaches a pinnacle of dullness which has to be seen to be believed. The announcer spoke briskly but hopelessly about the size of the surrounding mountains, a brace of statistics which didn't exactly tear me screaming from my chair.

"This will be a visual drop. The target is a seven-hundred-foot affair. Black and white stripes. So the bombardier will have a perfect target."

This made me feel very nice. Black and white stripes. They'd never hit me; I'm sort of pink and white stripes. They'd never hit me with an atom bomb in my lifetime.

"We have all been given black glasses because the original flash is so bright. The first flash would definitely injure the eyes."

The picture broke up again. A man was reassuring me that I would not go blind looking at television's atomic bomb.

"That will certainly brighten up your screen. But there is no danger of radiation blindness."

"Thirty seconds," said somebody. "Ten, fifteen, twenty. . . ."

There was nothing on the screen except a sign: "You and the Atom." Even Yucca Flat, that endless nothing, had disappeared.

"Oh, no!" said somebody. "All the money they spent! No picture!"

But there was a picture. Ten seconds before the bomb went off, the picture—a shaky, unsteady picture—came back. There was good old Yucca Flat, miles of just nothing (which is the sort of scenery we're all headed for in this atomic age). The bomb went off—a small bright sun which seemed terribly ineffectual, at least from forty miles away. It awed the announcers, who said exactly nothing.

"The orange and black cloud—a beautiful, angry spectacle in this wasted desert."

It looked like a cloud, nothing more. It stood there, unchanging in the still air, looking like all the still pictures you ever saw of that famous mushroom. The cameras kept ogling it for half an hour, this anticlimactic cloud.

They brought on the Director of Civil Defense, Millard Caldwell. "We know they [Russia] have exploded at least three. We know they have the bombers to bring them here. We know they'll get through our defenses."

It was a real cheerful program. ■

■ Along about the same time, in Foggy Bottom down the road a piece, there was a long fizzle (something that will be called in later history by the same term I would use if this were a novel). It was not an explosion.

I did a fair amount of coverage of the McCarthy hearings, as televised. They were nauseating, but they were news.

It was the twenty-fifth day at the Army-McCarthy hearings. At five hours a day, that meant a hundred and twenty-five hours of bumbling Joe. I fell to thinking. Probably never before had Abraham Lincoln's dictum—you can't fool all of the people all the time—ever really been put to a test. This certainly was such a test.

One hundred and twenty-five hours is not all the time, but it is certainly a great deal of time, and, of course, the hearings were not over yet. The question before us was simply this: could a very skillful demagogue—and McCarthy was certainly that—play on our fears, confuse issues and evade facts successfully over a period of a hundred and twenty-five hours as well as he could over, say, about two hours?

Years ago, when television was in swaddling clothes, this issue had been debated on purely theoretical grounds much as Einstein arrived at his theories by pure mathematics. Television, it was argued, was God's gift to the demagogue. Or, on the other hand, television would murder the demagogue because its pitiless eye would unmask his phoniness.

Neither theory is quite correct. It's not that simple. If you are totally unscrupulous, if you have as little regard for facts as McCarthy had, if you are arrogant enough and clever enough to keep the cameras on you while proclaiming your patriotism (and impugning everyone else's), you can make quite a score on an impressionable audience. For a while.

But there comes a day of reckoning when the wheel comes full circle. Such a day, for example, as that when Army counsel Joseph Welch asked Senator McCarthy, in his brief tenure on the witness stand, "When you took it [the oath], did you have some mental reservation, some Fifth or Sixth Amendment notions, that you could measure what you would tell?"

"I don't take the Fifth or Sixth Amendment," snapped the junior Senator.

"Have you some private reservation when you take the oath that you will tell the whole truth?"

"The answer is that there is no reservation about telling the whole truth," said McCarthy.

"Thank you, sir. Then who delivered the document to you?"

"The answer is no," said old Fifth Amendment McCarthy. "You will not get that information."

There was something richly comic about McCarthy's declining to give information while insisting that everyone else's secrets, including those of the Chief Executive, belonged to him. Much later, on that twenty-fifth day, McCarthy rumbled, "I'm getting awfully sick—sick way down deep inside—about these innuendoes from this clever little lawyer." And this was pretty funny, too. For four years millions of Americans had been sick—way down deep inside—at the innuendoes of this clever little demagogue who had made a career of innuendo and who had not managed to catch a single spy.

On the same day, McCarthy said that he was "sick of people making charges with nothing to back them up"—which is what McCarthy did all the time. Equally comic was McCarthy, who shockingly browbeat one of the Army's best officers, when he complained that his terribly evasive secretary—who, at the urging of Roy Cohn, could recall absolutely nothing about anything—was being browbeaten by the courtly Mr. Welch.

McCarthy methods, it seemed, had caught up with Senator McCarthy—and in full view of the cameras.

Future demagogues, it would seem to me, would use television but would not let television use them. The comedians—Milton Berle and Red Skelton, to name two—discovered that too much television can wreck a man's career very fast. ■

■ At the time McCarthy was flourishing for his brief season, I happened to have occasion to make a trip to Hollywood, and I observed that organized bigotry probably was nowhere so well organized as in California, where Gerald L. K. Smith had taken root. Los Angeles especially was—and is—the seat of more organizations committed to the enjoyable task of suppressing everything they disagree with than any place I know.

In Los Angeles the pressure groups have concentrated their venom on one type of program—the news field. This is, to my knowledge, fairly unique.

News programs on the two big networks, NBC and CBS, are the property of the network. While an advertiser can sponsor a program, he can't bring in his own news commentator and he has no control over the content of the program—beyond the indirect threat of cancellation, which sometimes can be pretty effective. This is a healthy thing. If the pressure groups started dictating the makeup of radio or TV news, as they have succeeded so well in imposing their will on the content and personnel of entertainment programs, the country would indeed be in terrible shape.

In Los Angeles some years ago, they were trying hard. There are dozens of pressure groups out there—the Gerald L. K. Smith group, the Liberty Belles organized by Vivian Kellems, the Freedom Clubs organized by the Rev. James W. Fifield of the enormously rich Congregational Church; the Pro-American League, the Wage-Earners Committee and many others.

Their membership is largely interchangeable, a great many members belonging to two or three of the organizations. A typical member is a man or woman (especially a woman) about fifty-five or sixty years old who has retired and moved there from Iowa. He lives on a small fixed income and, having nothing to do with his time and energy, he exists in a ferment of protest. He is easily organized, easily frightened, and he has a lot of time on his hands to listen to the radio and make denunciatory phone calls.

His objections, you understand, are not against the opinions of the newsmen; radio or TV newsmen generally are not permitted the luxury of opinion. They just tell the news as they see it. The object of the pressure groups is to make the news conform to their own myopic views. Right there they are monkeying dangerously not only with the freedom of the press but their own precious freedom to be informed.

As an example of their activity, there was once a discussion program in Los Angeles called *America Votes Tonight.* One topic discussed was the proposition "Should Red China be admitted to the United Nations?" A storm of protest arose, not because the panel members wanted Red China in the UN but simply because they discussed the problem at all. The program soon lost its sponsor and went off the air.

Another local news show had the practice of interviewing anyone who happened to be prominent in the news that day. Well, when a city official was ousted for refusing to answer questions about his alleged left-wing affiliations, his ouster was the lead story in many Los Angeles newspapers and he was accordingly interviewed on this program. The protest groups instantly raised an outcry over the fact that he was allowed to appear at all.

In other words, certain areas of news are considered untouchable: the reporter can dwell on some facts, not on others. This puts a ridiculous and dangerous limitation on a reporter's duties and obligations. The Radio and Television News Broadcasters Club of Southern California was fighting any such limitations to the best of its ability and in general succeeding in reporting the news honestly.

But there's no denying that the pressure groups were—and still are—doing some damage, and it's quite possible they will do much more. There are some thirty AM radio stations in Los Angeles, all fighting for the dwindling advertising dollar. The competition situation being what it is, the stations are more than prone to give in at the very threat of a sponsor dropping a program. And the sponsors are pushovers in the face of any sort of organized letter-writing campaign.

Since the objectivity and honesty of radio news coverage is one of the most admirable accomplishments of the industry, this attempt to encroach on and to intimidate newsmen is a thoroughly alarming situation, and one that I hope will not crop up anywhere else. ■

■ The television coverage of ceremonies of state—like inaugurations and other launchings—has become more and more detailed. And more and more the same. Presidential inaugurations especially.

Now, I have perfectly good traditional precedent for pointing out that if you've seen one inaugural parade, you've seen all inaugural parades. Romans of distinction are on record as saying the same thing a couple of thousand years back about chariot races and boxing matches, and they probably said it about those triumphal returns after the battle.

Anyway, in our time, we go through the same routine every four years. Periodically the star billing and most of the supporting cast changes, and there are slightly different bits of stage business.

The old saying goes that one picture is worth ten thousand words. But ten thousand pictures, I kept thinking while watching a Presidential inaugural parade as broadcast over three networks through the eyes of sixty-one cameras, to the chattering of twenty-odd commentators, are not worth one well-written paragraph.

On the screen at the time, an arrowhead of motorcycles pushed slowly up drenched Pennsylvania Avenue.

"The outriders are in view," declaimed a CBS commentator. "The Presidential car *makes the turn!*"

And there, by George, it was—a car.

"The Presidential car followed by those of the others makes its way past the crowd that is assembled," continued the voice in what may easily have been the most obvious and unnecessary comment I'd heard in years. "Everyone has turned to watch it."

So it went. Shots of cars, shots of motorcycles, shots of the crowd, shots of cops, while the commentators told you—in case your mind was wandering—that those were cars and motorcycles and people and cops you were watching.

Just for the devil of it (and because I have never really believed that business about the one picture being worth ten thousand words) I turned to a bit of the description of another cavalcade, that of the funeral procession of his father by Sean O'Casey from his autobiography: *

> Hearse, mourning-coach, cabs, and cars threaded their way through the tenement-hedged streets where swarms of boys and girls played and fought in front of the gloomy

* *Mirror in My House* by Sean O'Casey, 1956–1958. Macmillan (N.Y.).

> houses that had once, his mother told him, sheltered all the great lords and ladies of the land. Round into Cavendish Row where the houses were high and still mighty, with stately doors and flashing windows. Outside of some of them maids, with black or blue dresses and white aprons and caps with floating streamers, were polishing brass plates, letter-box flaps and heavy knockers of bronze or brass.

As pictures go, I think I prefer the words to the electronics as infinitely more revealing. The trouble in Washington was there was just too much electronics, too many cameras, too many commentators at too many vantage points. More darned facilities to take a picture of some automobiles from above, from the side, from the front (where it was very funny and wobbly indeed). The trouble with the whole show was a total lack of editing. Just as a writer searches for the right word and then uses that one and that one alone, the TV people ought to seek the one shot—and then use it once, not forty-five times.

To turn again to Mr. O'Casey: *

> The coffin was placed on a low car covered with flowing black draperies, and pulled by a well-groomed gentle black horse, enveloped in a black gown heavily embroidered with silver, so that only the eyes, the ears and the feet of the animal were visible. A tall black plume rising from his forehead made him look like the nag that the Black Prince rode at the battle of Crecy. Overhead, in a gray sky, spotted with timid-looking blue patches, dark heavy clouds were being tossed and pushed along by a northerly wind blowing steadily and reasonably, except that now and again it gathered strength and swept by fiercely, filling the cemetery with a mad rustle and a cold swish-swish from the bending branches of the trees.

As pictures go, I wouldn't trade that one for any number of live TV shots. ■

* Ibid.

■ The mania for detail has spread into almost every nook and cranny of television—including the deodorant ads. Alongside it came a real genius for dispensing swatches of minor information—generally useless and seldom fascinating.

Take weather. I was staring steamy-eyed at the weather chart on *Today* one grisly midsummer New York morning. 85 in Houston. Poor Houston! 77 in New Orleans. New Orleans is lying, I said to myself. 77! In August! In New Orleans! 34 in Omaha. Hmmm, cold in Omaha.

I don't know why I was doing all this. I don't know why we're all doing it. You see it on television sets all over—people in Topeka learning about the weather in Dallas. Wherever you go around the country, you'll find a local TV show with that man standing in front of a map of the United States. "Cold front edging down from Canada," he'll say, and draw a bold chalk line across twelve Midwestern states. That means rain in Wisconsin and high winds in Tulsa—and all for the edification of me on Lexington Avenue in Manhattan.

Back in the dear old days of radio, the weather, which has always commanded fascinated attention, was pretty well confined to the local area. Over in Brooklyn, they sometimes pinpointed it to Brooklyn alone, ignoring the other four boroughs.

Of course, back in those dear old days we did have an early-morning weatherman named Charles F. McCarthy, whose weather chats pulsated with such wondrous prose that some of his listeners regularly dived right back into bed and pulled the covers over their ears.

"Here in midtown Manhattan," Mr. McCarthy was quite likely to say, "it's a rare and lovely November morn. An enchantingly beautiful robin's-egg sky with a lacy pattern of woven wisps of wondrous white. A glowing golden gleam from old Sol adds the touch of a picture-postcard sky. The air is savory and delightful. All makes for a top-drawer, four-S day—succulent, sunny, semi-summery."

(Well, there hasn't been any savory air in Manhattan since the Indians owned it. As for those "woven wisps of wondrous white," if he'd looked again he would have discovered that lacy pattern spelled out Pepsi-Cola.)

Then came television—sight as well as sound—and right away they put a map there to give us something to look at. Then, of course, they had to fill the map with wind currents and cold fronts from Maine to Florida in order to justify its being there, and now we're all weather experts. ■

■ The guys putting chalk on their maps don't have any monopoly on the weather, though. The sports-announcing fraternity —a screwy lot, God knows—fall back on the weather bit more often than Milton Cross does on the gold-curtain bit in his Saturday-afternoon obbligatos to whatever is being sung at the Met.

Take Sammy Renick as a prime case in point. Renick is an ex-jockey who still bears unmistakable marks of his profession but abandoned his honorable trade some years ago and went wrong. He became a sportscaster, if there is such a word. At any rate, he was the guy whom you could see on television when any of the big races came along, standing in the infield with a microphone in his hand and talking a blue streak.

"Oh, it's a great day, folks! A great day for this great race! Oh, a great day!" In short, a weather report. Renick has been clocked on the "great day" department at something like one every fifteen minutes, which may be a world's record for enthusiasm about the elements. Even the weather reports are only five minutes, and they're full of things about low-pressure areas and cold fronts and other nonsense that Renick eschews.

Renick, in fact, was a throwback to the old, old days of sports broadcasting when the whole idea of sitting in New York and listening to a football game in California was sufficiently novel almost to demand this sort of reporting. Graham McNamee would say, "Oh, it's a great day out here, folks. The sun is shining. The band is playing. And there goes Radowski eighty-eight yards for a touchdown. And what a nice colorful crowd this is—the boys in their raccoon coats and the girls waving the red and blue of old Ipswich. And there's a pass to Owaski. No, he didn't get it. Thirty-three thousand people here, folks, and the weather is crisp but not too cold."

Of course, in those days the event rather overshadowed the game itself. It was a spectacle rather than a sport. But those days have long gone.

Apparently somebody got to Renick in time for the Flamingo Stakes, and he switched strategy. He dropped weather and took up flamingos, which are pink, ungainly birds that inhabit the infield at Hialeah by the hundreds. He told about their mating habits, their nesting habits, their molting habits. I hadn't learned so much about birds since the last time I was in the Museum of Natural History.

I could just visualize horse players all over the country sitting before their sets, feeling nonplussed. "Hey, Mac, what's with the television? What you got on there—*Zoo Parade* or something? Let's switch over to the race."

Mr. Renick passed from ornithology to horse racing in one of the most remarkable *segues* I ever heard. He was talking about the fact that flamingos liked to stand in water because it calmed them: "When flamingos get too nervous, they calm them by placing their feet in warm water the horses are on the track." All one sentence. Well, it was good to know, but I wasn't going to need the information. I wouldn't give a nervous flamingo house room.

That's O.K., I guess, for a sport that involves birds and horses and a few jockeys. But in the sports in which the players are more likely to ride each other—football, for example—the sports announcers probably would think twice before saying anything about a nervous player. For some time, in fact, they have avoided unpleasantness, controversy or anything hinting unsportsmanlike conduct to the point where they don't tell the viewers the story.

The situation came to a splendid boil one Sunday during a professional football game between Chicago and Detroit, which developed into a Donnybrook involving players, fans and the police. Just when this brawl began to be interesting the TV cameras shifted elsewhere.

"I'm just very much pleased at the way things are trying to be held down," said the announcer.

Television tried hard to pretend that nothing untoward was going on, a pose that fooled absolutely no viewers.

I don't know exactly when the sweetness-and-light convention became standard practice among sports announcers, but I suspect that the late Ted Husing's crack about Harvard's football team—which got him banned from Cambridge—had something to do with it.

There is much to be said in defense of the avoidance of the seamier aspects of sports over the air, particularly on television. At every sports event, there are the drunks, the profane and the exhibitionists. Editing these folks, both their pictures and voices, out of the broadcast is highly sensible. But when the carnage becomes general, then news is being made and it ought to be reported.

I respect the sports announcers' insistence that all athletes are paragons of sportsmanship and all umpires are lynx-eyed dispensers of exact justice—until the camera clearly shows they aren't. During a red-hot National League pennant race, Roy Campanella was called out at second when the cameras had shown the second baseman was a foot and a half in the air when Campanella slid into second. Since everyone at Ebbets Field had seen the flagrant miscall, too, and roared their displeasure, it's reasonable to suppose that Vince Scully, a very observant sportscaster, had not missed it either. But then the umpire is always right. At least on the air he is.

This kind of reporting—or lack of reporting—has led to a sort of understatement which can be very funny. I remember Dennis James reporting a televised hockey game, in which a couple of players started to brain each other with their sticks. "Little bad feeling there," explained Mr. James.

This kind of elaborate circumlocution provoked Jim Fleming to vent a slightly different and equally worthy protest.

"More than ever," complained Fleming, "they're indulging in what I'd call character evaluation. They say things like this: 'Here's So-and-so batting, batting .284 and a good family man.' In the same vein I've heard: 'Well liked in Louisville, where he sets a fine example for young men,' 'a serious guy—you can trust him,' 'four fine kids at home—but you'd know just by the way he stands up there.'

"Those players who receive no such endorsements are presumably bounders. It wouldn't do to say, 'Here's Smathers, batting .325. Don't know how he does it, the way he drinks,' or 'Another double for Zeke Perch—and him behind in his alimony, too.' "

No, I guess it wouldn't do. ■

■ During a good many years of reporting pretty strictly on the fearsome and once-in-a-while wonderful world of TV, I listened to a lot of death-rattles and was bystander at more than my share of demises. I attended few enough of the wakes.

But in 1958, two historic occasions in one week moved me to a joint obituary. One was the end of Edward R. Murrow's *See It Now* after seven years of distinguished history. The other was the end of Elfrida Von Nardoff after twenty-one weeks on *Twenty-One*. At the time the events appeared more or less complementary. Later, of course, an unexpected autopsy revealed how fierce a cancer *Twenty-One* had been nourishing.

See It Now was born in the early days of television, when it was thought that TV was a tremendous new medium for the exchange of information and ideas. *Twenty-One* came along in the later phase when it was discovered that television was far better suited to play parlor games and give away money. *See It Now* enlightened us. *Twenty-One* stupefied us. One used television more or less as a public service on behalf of the viewers; the other used it solely to sell as much of the sponsor's product as possible.

The last of the *See It Now* programs was one of the best of them, and it exemplified why the program was the greatest prize-winner of television. It tackled an enormously important subject, the rebirth of an immensely powerful and prosperous West Germany. It examined the subject sensibly, critically, fearlessly. It employed the best of pictures with powerful prose. It called on the top experts who could add information or opinion.

See It Now went down the drain because it had had trouble attracting sponsors and because it was expensive. Yet when you saw Ed Murrow and Fred Friendly, by means of prestige alone, attracting to their cameras the top leaders and industrialists of Germany and all for free, you began to wonder at the economics of television. CBS could afford to pay Hal March any amount of money. It could not afford to pay a cameraman to take a picture of Chancellor Adenauer whose own services were free. I don't understand it and, even if I did, I would never forgive it.

The rebirth of Germany was both an inspiring and slightly frightening spectacle. This show dealt with both aspects. Dick Hottelet, then CBS man in Germany, queried the manager of the mighty Krupp works, who said smoothly, "Our experience at producing arms is so bad that the workers wouldn't produce arms, I think." An industrialist feared inflation. A trade-union leader feared the Communists. No one seemed to fear the arrival of another Hitler.

Yet the old Hitler pervaded the program. Most powerful moment of the show was a succession of shots of the audience watching, tense and almost knotted with concentration, a performance of *The Diary of Anne Frank*. "Yet the guilt is not universal," commented Murrow, as the picture moved abruptly, almost shatteringly, from *Diary of Anne Frank* to a German beer hall where the Germans roared out a drinking song. There were shots of the new *Bundeswehr*, which was supposedly democratized and humanized. Even in American-type uniforms, the Germans couldn't avoid that superman look.

Ludwig Erhard, who may or may not be the successor to Adenauer, a bland, confident, fat-faced giant of a man, chided America for "losing faith" in itself. A bunch of teen-age kids had a perfectly wonderful bull session on the reunification of Germany, showing themselves to be marvelously erudite. And Murrow closed it all off with the words: "Their future is uncertain—a position they share with every other nation in the world."

Murrow's own future was just as uncertain when the show went,* but *See It Now* was finished and with it an era ended. I remember the first *See It Now,* in November, 1951, when Murrow, seated in a control room, ordered Camera 1 to "bring in the Atlantic Ocean," then ordered the crew in San Francisco to bring in the Pacific. "We are impressed by a medium in which a man sitting in his living room has been able for the first time to look at two oceans at once."

Later the program almost ruined Senator McCarthy—long before the Army-McCarthy hearings—by simply showing the man in his full flavor. It inspected the integration problems of Clinton, Tennessee, with agonizing humanity; it roamed through Korea; it dwelt on a major land scandal in Texas and the Texas editor who dug it up. There were some dull *See It Now* shows, and some were better than others, but it was by every criterion television's most brilliant, most decorated, most imaginative, most courageous and most important program. The fact that CBS could not afford it but could afford *Beat the Clock* is shocking. ■

* Murrow began distinguished and dedicated service as the head of the United States Information Agency in 1961.

Clichés of drama

■ I have always been amused by the clichés of drama; I've sometimes been accused of liking bad movies better than good movies. This isn't true, but it is possible to take a malicious joy in an absolute stinker.

In a television play in this category—called *Malay Incident*—Ann Sheridan, playing a real tough bad girl, looked the handsome rubber planter in the eye and said, "*Rubber!* Is that all that counts in this stinking jungle? Don't people count, too?"

A little while later we heard Miss Sheridan exclaim, "I'm afraid you know rubber better than people, Mr. Hunter!"

Later on in this same confection she opined that she was a bad girl because—well—men had made her that way, and now that she had met the first good man of her life (Hunter, the guy who was long on rubber and short on people), he failed to understand the one decent thing she had ever done. Oh, brother!

Malay Incident was a jungle story, but somehow they left out a line—maybe it landed on the cutting room floor—without which no jungle picture can long endure: "Those drums! They're driving me mad, MAD!"

One of these fine days the TV people will get music in their blood like the movie folk and then you can expect this little interchange:

"Who is that rude young man who plays the piano so badly?"

"That is Frédéric Chopin."

We've seen the religious dramas—"I think that God will understand, son. Why don't you have a talk with Him about it?"

And there will always be the westerns:

"And who are you, anyway?"

"My name is [pause] Simkins."

"Simkins! Not the man who tamed Dodge City!"

The psychological thriller: "Why do you—look at me like that?"

And I can't wait for television to rediscover the mysterious East. Then we can expect:

"And how are you feeling, Fu Chan?"

"When the honorable dragon's shadow falls across the grave of venerable ancestor, it darkens the lives of rich and poor alike."

Or perhaps we're in for a run of sociological drama about our juvenile delinquents and then—"Listen! Either a girl is decent or she's not. There's no halfway business about it. If Cynthia is such a good girl, what is she doing out with Rodney Penthouse?"

The Wound Within, which became a fairly successful play called *The Far Country,* appeared first as a United States Steel Hour television show back in September, 1958.

In *The Wound Within,* Farley Granger, playing a rather unlikely and hysterical Sigmund Freud, is railed at repeatedly by his wife Martha to leave the "unknowable" alone, to stop monkeying around with the mind and get back to acceptable nerve practice where a doctor can clean up.

This is an arrant libel on Martha Freud, but it is, of course, standard behavior for all wives of scientists, explorers, or adventurers in all dramatic stories of this sort.

"Why can't we live like the other explorers?" wails the wife. "Do you have to discover the North Pole?"

A variant on this: "Why does it have to be you who has to break the sound barrier?" whimpers the wife who is almost certainly played by June Allyson. "Why can't somebody else's husband break the barrier?"

Besides fending off his own wife, the scientist is beset on all sides by the fat cats in his dodge who assure him there is no such thing as radium. Or: "Damn it, Pasteur! What is this nonsense about germs?" In this case, the head of the medical society (or some such thing) sneers: "So now you're delving into a wound in the soul, my dear Freud.... This is medicine, not witchcraft. Once you open the doors of the human soul, God knows where it will all end!"

That speech, too, is sort of standard operating procedure. The crustly old medical reactionary first denies the existence of germs and then says it would be a terrible idea to discover them anyhow. This speech, with the change of a word or two, can be made to fit almost any number of dramas: "Chris, give up this madness about discovering a New World! Besides you might run into Indians, and they're dangerous." Or: "Split the atom? In the first place, it's impossible and in the second place, who wants to open that can of peas?"

"A wound in the mind," says Freud at the closing. "We found it and opened it and drained the poison from it. What happened today is not the end but the beginning. You can't imagine how they're going to fight it."

"They," of course, are the reactionary medical element who said, in Jack Lescoulie's immortal words, it couldn't be done. I suppose they did fight it, but analysis got accepted and even made the United States Steel Hour, which means it's about as controversial as the American flag.

In fact, now the mossbacks in the medical profession are likely to be psychiatrists and analysts whose procedures have hardly improved in fifty years, whose treatment still takes years and years and endless money and is still marked by an unholy incidence of total failure or at best very incomplete success.

And yet, if you should whisper that perhaps their antiquated methods might be speeded up, or perhaps there might be whole new avenues of psychiatric exploration that ought to be looked into, you know what would happen? "They" would sneer at you: "So you think there's another way to cure neuroses? What are you—a Communist or something? This is medicine, not witchcraft. Besides, if you did find a speedy way to cure emotional illness, God knows where it would all end."

Well, I know where it would all end. Warner Brothers would make a picture of it with Paul Muni—and I could write the script right now.

The profession of medicine, as portrayed on radio and in television and movies, shares some of the stratospheric respect and well-nigh-universal popularity of Abraham Lincoln's dog's mother (maybe it's the other way around). Nursing, being a normally feminine adjunct to medicine, is certainly right out in the front among the stereotypes. Radio, in fact, could hardly get through the day without the nurses. In the old days you could tune in at ten in the morning and go right through to eight at night without ever getting out of the hospital. Now television is loaded with doctors, nurses and unlikely ailments.

Janet Dean, Registered Nurse, arrived with some impressive endorsement from the National League for Nursing and the American Nurses Association. The NLN, as a matter of fact, said that it hoped *Janet Dean* would be an important "asset in increasing the public's understanding of modern nursing."

Well, I hoped it would, too, but, brother, if that was modern nursing, the profession has got a lot harder than it used to be. Janet was quite a girl. She not only had to put the thermometers in their mouths but also placate the relatives, psychoanalyze the husbands and run down the clues.

On the last case I saw, Janet was laving the brow of a man who had fallen or jumped off the scaffolding of a building. After tucking him in comfortably, she had to reassure the guy's distraught wife: "They do wonderful things with brain surgery now." Then she shooed away the insurance adjuster who had a lot of nasty questions to ask about the husband's proclivities toward suicide. And finally, after the insurance people decided that it was a suicide attempt and not an accident—which meant that the poor wife wouldn't get any money—Janet tore off her nurse's uniform, donned civvies and went prowling around the saloons in order to get to the bottom of this thing. After hours. On her own time. She broke the case, too.

The actress who played Janet Dean, Miss Ella Raines, declared that in undertaking this series she hoped it would demonstrate that the nursing profession was interesting, vital, perhaps even attractive. Well, it was all that, all right. It just wasn't very medical. ■

■ Now, don't misunderstand me. I adore teen-agers. All I'm saying here is that the little monsters kill each other on the streets with the greatest enthusiasm, but on the TV screen they don't behave like that at all. No siree bob.

I was in the shower the other day singing "When a girl changes from bobby sox to stockings, then she starts trading her baby toys for boys," when it occurred to me that the little female goslings on television are all alike. They are so soggily sentimental about their parents, their girl friends, and themselves that my blood sugar count rises dangerously. Are teen-age girls really this gooey over each other? Perhaps I know an unusually tough-minded crowd.

I feel strongly—I might almost say violently—that the Understanding Father bit on television has got out of hand, too. I once watched the father in *Peck's Bad Girl* tell his little monster of a daughter, "If you did that, I'd be mighty proud of you."

Then he tiptoed out, closing her bedroom door softly after him. By George, she turned herself in for the crime of trespassing on the grounds of old Coogan—while the whole family was wreathed in understanding smiles. The week before it was Mother who did the understanding. Mother came in and found the little Peck girl impaled on the horns of a dilemma, and she uttered the kind of line that makes Big Daddy throw up: "I find," said Mother Peck softly, "when I think people don't like me, it's because I don't like myself."

It's good sound psychology, that line. It's just revoltingly sweet, is all. As an old student of American parenthood as depicted on television and, before that, radio, I must point the finger of accusation at Robert Young of *Father Knows Best* for starting all this. Robert Young revolutionized fatherhood on television and, at the time, it was a good thing.

Before Young, all fathers were All-American dopes, outwitted by their wives, their children, their neighbors, their dogs, even their goldfish. Then Young, the original Understanding Father, came along. He was the first one to open the son's bedroom door—this became standard operating procedure—to dispense wisdom to his sprout, who was wrapped in perplexity.

This sort of parenthood may not seem like a step forward to you now. But you probably have forgotten the *Life of Riley*-type father who was incessantly rescued from his own folly by his own small children. Originally, the Understanding Father—Young had the field all to himself for a while—was quite a guy: human, normal, and reasonable.

But over the years, the quality of understanding has got almost unbearable. In the first place, the problems Father has to understand on television are of a nature that would have driven Solomon out of his mind. The kids in these things don't cheat on the examination just because they want to pass their grades. Nothing is ever that simple in television domestic comedy. They're cribbing the answers in order to give them to little Patty Pranglepuss, who couldn't study up for her own exams because she was taking care of her sick grandmother, and if she doesn't pass, her father will lose his post as head of the orphanage. In other words, the kids, while committing grave breaches of decorum, are always supplied with motives shining with innocence.

This means that Father, sitting down to untangle the messes the children get into on television, not only has to separate the innocent from the guilty; he has to pick his way through a web of justification that would have given pause to Brandeis. It makes slobs out of the rest of us fathers. Frankly, I belong to the Jean Kerr school of justice. Just belt everyone within a reasonable distance of the scene of the crime and you're bound to hit the guilty party.

However, don't get the idea that I'm complaining about the TV brand of fatherhood simply because it's unworkable in the home. (If you look to television for guidance in running your life, you'll wind up machine-gunning the cop on the beat.) I object to it solely and quite properly on the grounds that it makes me sick to look at it. ■

■ And now let's look at westerns. The popularity of westerns, like the movement of the stars, is one of the fixed and changeless laws of the universe. At least that's what I was taught at my mother's knee and I have never quarreled with anything I learned at my mother's knee, at least not publicly.

However, while the box office of westerns is immutable, the nature of the beast has changed so radically that the whole theorem seems pretty useless as a barometer to lead our lives by.

I was watching *Bonanza,* one of the newer crop of westerns at the time, with my twelve-year-old son Michael, who always gave me expert guidance in these matters.

"Is this the hero?" I asked when some lug about eight feet tall showed up.

"There are a whole family of heroes," said Michael. "Name of Cartwright."

We watched the story as it settled down to two sisters, dance-hall hostesses—one aging and a little weatherworn, the other young and pretty.

"She'll be killed," said Michael.

"Why?" I inquired in my innocence.

"The pretty girls always get killed," my son informed me. It sounded a little sweeping, that statement, but I wouldn't have dreamed of arguing, because Mike was a very great authority in these matters.

Five minutes later a shot rang out and the young and pretty one sank to the ground, blood oozing all over her pretty dance-hall dress. One of the young Cartwrights had been sparking the girl, but he didn't take on none when the girl handed in her chips. Just squared his jaw and waited to be accused of the murder, which he was. Unjustly, of course.

"The sheriff did it," said Mike.

"Now, how in tarnation [you get to talking that way if you see enough of this stuff] do you know that?" I asked. There'd been absolutely no indication the sheriff was anything but a law-abiding, upstanding citizen.

He couldn't explain. (It's a sort of instinct you develop after you see a trillion of these things, I gather.) I frankly had my doubts. The evidence pointed pretty strongly to the older sister. Well, time passed. They threw young Cartwright into jail. The lynch mob began building up a head of steam outside the jail. (Even I had seen enough of these things to know that a lynch mob gathers outside every jail after every homicide as regularly as flowers bloom in May.)

Young Cartwright broke jail and began to feel his way along the wall outside the jail.

"See that globe above his head?" said Mike. "The bad guy is going to shoot at Cartwright and miss him and hit that globe." Seconds later, that's what happened.

"Now, how . . . ?" I began.

"They only hang those globes up to shoot out," he explained to his dimwitted father.

I don't suppose it will come as any surprise to learn that it was the sheriff who done the filthy thing. He hadn't meant to do that at all. He was in love with the girl and jealous of Cartwright. It was Cartwright he was shooting at. Missed. Then missed him again and shot out that light. Rotten shot for a sheriff.

What are we to deduce from this? Well, first, that the general tenor of events in westerns is predictable to someone who sees a lot of 'em but rather astonishing to those ordinary citizens who might expect the violence to be a little less neurotic, a little more like the shoot-em-ups of my youth when there was no blurring of values. Second, when twelve-year-old boys say things like "The pretty girls always get killed," then the thing has gone too far.

The only thing I really felt at home with was the card game

that went on in the sheriff's office. That card game has been going on since the days of William S. Hart. Nobody ever picks up any money in these games. The door bangs open. A guy always bangs in and says, "Carruthers has escaped and he's heading for the hills." Everyone gets up and straps on their guns and off they gallop, leaving the money and the cards in a heap. All these years, I have been waiting for some guy to bleat, "Aw, let's finish the hand! I got three queens!" ■

■ And then there's the lady of ill fame. Since the world began, she has been presented on the stage as the true philosopher—open-hearted, gay, kind, generous, loving, true—advising us to *Live, live, live!* She's a cliché, in the running for entertainment's greatest and most venerable. And never in my memory, which extends almost back to the time of George III, have the light ladies run quite so amok in the plays and all over the screen as they have during the past couple of years.

On Broadway—let's see now—we had *The Hostage,* Brendan Behan's lusty tale of a latter-day Irish rebellion, set in a brothel; *Irma La Douce,* an utterly charming confection about a Paris streetwalker; and *Tenderloin,* about the red-light district, which the critics universally deplored. Off-Broadway, there was *The Balcony,* also set in a brothel. In the movie palaces *Never on Sunday,* a story of a Greek bawd, was doing excellent business. Then came *Suzie Wong,* the story of a prostitute in Hong Kong, which was a book and play before it was a movie. And in the bookstalls we had the memoirs of Virginia MacManus, a schoolteacher turned call girl.

All of them open-hearted, gay, kind, generous, loving, true.

There have been on the air since time immemorial (this has been established as the First Punic War) two guys who wreak absolute and delicious havoc with clichés, always, almost, in the quietest possible tone of voice. They'll take *any* cliché from the outhouse garden, any hackneyed situation—*even* from daily human experience—and go to work on it.

Bob and Ray, whose last names are immaterial, irrelevant, and probably false, were selling their home taxidermy course on their morning radio show.

"You can be a home bird-stuffer, too."

"Just write STUFFY, NBC."

"And say . . ."

"I'm strictly for the birds."

That's fairly typical of Bob and Ray's sensational free trial offers, which attract a hell of a lot of mail from hopeful listeners who wish they were true. Mostly the boys ask for the mail to be sent to whichever network or station they're appearing on at the time. Sometimes they have it shipped elsewhere, usually with disastrous results. For the Handy Bob and Ray House Wrecking Kit, we were advised to write the Smithsonian Institution, which got one thousand letters asking for it. The Smithsonian requested, boys, for heaven's sake, don't do it again. (The home-wrecking kit, if you still want one, contains house-wrecking tools, two hundred termites, a trained live mouse, a CONDEMNED sign to hang outside, and a guaranty to make your ugly new house over into a smart antiquated barn within two weeks.)

At various other times the two zanies have offered to give away any state (except Rhode Island) to the winner of a contest for the completion of "I'd like to own a state because. . . ."

Then there was the time they offered sweaters with *O* on them.

"If your name doesn't begin with *O* we can have it legally changed for you. Sweaters come in two styles—turtleneck or V-neck. State what kind of neck you have."

Always there are these two deadpan voices, expounding on these great free trial offers in the language of pure radio cliché. Few people have so keen an ear for the most tired phrase, and no one can make such complete nonsense out of the messages that assault us on radio and television every day.

Once they were giving away a ranch home: "Box hedges made of real boxes."

They have cheerfully offered to give away a twenty-five-foot shelf of fake books (with room for tennis rackets under Tennyson), a ten-day course in how to become a ninety-seven-pound weakling, and untinted sun glasses for cloudy days.

When they're not giving things away, they're satirizing about every other type of voice you will ever hear on the air. There is Mary McGoon, for example, who gives tips on—I believe the word is—homemaking.

"No, friends, beer should *not* be served in fingerbowls. For quiet elegance, serve it in demitasse cups."

Their interviews are classics which should give pause to everyone in the interview racket—uh—profession. They have a nice one with a real stupid ballplayer named Dazzy Very.

"I'd like to fire away."

"Well, fire away."

"The real lowdown from behind the scenes. Well, you've caught about every pitcher in the major leagues. Who would you say was the best, Dazzy?"

"I'd say they were all good. I couldn't single one out. If they're pitchers in the major leagues, they've got it."

"Make a note of that, sports fans."

Sounds like all the sports figures I ever heard interviewed on television. ■

Lines written in anger

■ Some mornings I've sat down at the typewriter and begun to bellow in rage and despair. It isn't always an important matter that has stirred me to anger; my threshold varies.

I was listening to the radio one day and I heard a commercial from FBI Director J. Edgar Hoover which went: "The onslaught of crime is today at an all-time high. Law enforcement is everybody's business. The ever-increasing surge of crime costs the American taxpayer $32 billion a year. You are one of the taxpayers sharing this cost. The front line of defense in this matter is your local police officer, but he needs the supporting element of you, the citizens, to continue to do his job. Get interested in law enforcement. Support good government. Expect and demand efficient law enforcement and do your part to get it."

Get interested in law enforcement? Mr. Hoover, I *am* interested in law enforcement. I know that the onslaught of crime is at an all-time high. In fact, crime in this country has made its most substantial gains in the thirty-six years you have been head of the FBI. Under your benevolent eye, the crime syndicates are now rolling in wealth and respectability.

Get interested in law enforcement! I am, indeed. But when are *you* going to get interested in law enforcement, Mr. Hoover? Ours is the only country in the world with organized crime on such a huge scale, and we are one of the few countries without a national police force. Every time someone suggests a national police force for this country, you shoot it down, and so well organized are your press relations and so docile is the press at accepting your word on police matters that all attempts to grapple with organized crime on a national level have been successfully throttled. I wonder if the FBI wants the job, or wants anyone else to have it for fear of dimming its glory.

"I was seriously concerned with organized crime before I took office," said Attorney General Robert F. Kennedy in April, 1961. "In the past two-and-a-half months, I have become even more aware of how far racketeering has infiltrated our society. Racketeers have moved in from illegal enterprises to infect legitimate businesses, labor unions and . . . sports. At the same time, the racketeers have tightened their hold on bookmaking, narcotics, extortion, prostitution, the numbers game and other gambling."

Meanwhile, what were you up to, Mr. Hoover? You issued a stirring warning to housewives to be careful of baby-sitters. You also called for a relentless campaign against child molesters. I also have here your coloring cartoon ("Boys and girls—Color the picture and memorize the rules. Turn down gifts from strangers. Avoid dark and lonely streets. Know your local Policeman. J. Edgar Hoover"). You called for a crackdown on "smut salesmen." You warned the nation's shopkeepers, as you do every year, to beware of shoplifters. You proposed a new name for juvenile delinquents ("teenage brigands"). You deplored violence on television.

The number of arrests made by the FBI, in light of its nine-figure budget and in light of its own massive crime figures, is rather modest. Only 12,391 convictions in 1961. How many big shots of organized crime has the FBI arrested in the last five or ten years? Are they looking for any? Has the FBI any program for trapping any of those well-organized and enormously rich racketeers Mr. Kennedy talks about?

The FBI leaps into action with great speed at kidnapings. And, of course, it keeps the Communists in check. Or says it does.

But, Mr. Hoover, you ask me to expect and demand efficient

law enforcement. Of whom? If you're afraid to tackle the crime syndicate, do you think my local police officer supported by me, the citizen, can do it? Nowhere in the world is crime more profitable, better organized or less bothered by law enforcement than in the United States, and you have been the top cop in this country for thirty-six years. Crime has flourished under you as it has never before flourished in the history of the world.

How do you explain that? ■

■ A few years ago the Guatemalan Ambassador to Belgium and The Netherlands was captured with 116 pounds of heroin worth $4 million (or $20 million, depending on which newspaper you read). This was chiefly shocking for a reason that generally escaped notice—the fact that 116 pounds of heroin is worth $4 million (or $20 million). All the news stories I read neglected to point out one thing: that the United States is the only country in the world where that amount of heroin would bring that amount of money or, in fact, any sizable amount at all. In Britain, where narcotics addiction is treated—as it ought to be treated here—as a medical problem, heroin is legal and British addicts (for some reason) don't like it and don't use it. We have created a vast market for heroin here by making it illegal. We have built a huge and prosperous crime cartel out of the illegality of narcotics that is doing terrible social damage.

This is in the great American tradition. Appetites that we consider deplorable are against the law. Prostitution. Liquor. Gambling. Narcotics. This doesn't terminate the appetites or, it sometimes seems, even curb them. It merely makes them terribly expensive. But, more importantly, it creates a breed of millionaires among the most unsavory elements of our citizenry. We outlawed liquor and we got Capone and gangsterism. Far worse, we lost our respect for law and we never got it back. By the money that Capone made out of beer alone, he corrupted lawyers, legislators, newspapermen, and to some degree, all of us.

Dope addiction is a very large and very complex problem. But the men who are the biggest experts in it have no experience with, or patience for, the very large social problem that is created by the huge amount of money in illegal narcotics.

In Britain, for instance, where there is no criminal addiction, a medical addict can get what in this country would amount to a fix for fourteen cents. Here it's thirty dollars. An addict on CBS's *Twentieth Century* once explained that he and his partner were forced to steal about $70,000 worth of goods a year or in the ten years of his addiction almost three-quarters of a million dollars' worth of goods.

In addition, there is the vast vested interest among gangsters in pushing dope. Another addict on the CBS show said that he was tired of earning forty or fifty dollars a week when he saw dope pushers riding around in Cadillacs. In the higher echelons, the money from narcotics is corrupting cops, legislators, and children. And it always will—so long as 116 pounds of heroin is worth $4 million (or $20 million). That's a lot of money.

Addiction has shifted from the adult population to the teenagers, who are easier to trap. One thing is indisputable: the Harrison Narcotics Act of 1914 created a huge criminal problem where there had been none at all. If heroin were made legal tomorrow so that it could be obtained at some reasonable price at a drugstore with a doctor's prescription, I doubt there'd be any increase in dope addiction. There wouldn't be—as there now is—a vast network of criminals selling dope in school yards, hospitals, and prisons, because there wouldn't be money in it.

There wouldn't be all that money to seduce our cops, our legislators, and occasional Guatemalan Ambassadors. ■

■ Another increasingly lucrative profession—in what Walter Lippman calls our purposeless society—is time wasting. The great merchant princes of time wasting are Goodson and Todman, who have expended time wasting into a commercial empire. One of the flowers of this great empire is *To Tell the Truth,* which is the very model of a quiz show.

That is: empty-headed. It requires nothing of the observer but the temporary exercise of his eyeballs. It's cheap. That means it can sell cigarettes and other products at a marvelously small cost per thousand. And it occupies a splendid half hour of prime evening time on an important network, thus successfully preventing that half hour from being put to any important use, which is the highest aspiration of the time-wasting profession.

Ah, when you think of thirty million pairs of eyeballs fixed on *To Tell the Truth* successfully getting through another half hour of eternity without a flicker of thought or a motion or the use of a muscle, you realize the superb achievement of the Messrs. Goodson and Todman in the fine twentieth-century profession of wasting other people's time and charging them money for it. Quiz shows, in the opinion of some philosophers, have supplanted the chewing of gum as the great nirvana of the masses.

Now then, *To Tell the Truth* has a somewhat ironic gimmick: the chief ingredient is lying. That is, three people are gathered together, two of them to tell lies about who and what they are to a panel that tries to guess which of the three is telling the truth. Years ago, before Congress took a dim view of the matter, we had schlockmeisters who gathered loot for the giveaway shows. Now we have liemeisters who gather liars for *To Tell the Truth*. I don't know what posterity is going to say about this—that a grown man could earn his living looking for liars. Just as Diogenes went through the streets looking for an honest man with a lantern, the *Truth* people go out looking for liars, but whereas Diogenes couldn't find any honest men, they find lots of liars. There's a commentary on our civilization in there somewhere, but I haven't time to look for it. ■

■ At the University of Michigan, an otherwise splendid factory of learning, I recently read with no little dismay, two rival student groups were doing a brisk business in selling duplicated notes taken at the lectures. Notes were taken by two honor students, then correlated and checked by a committee of three, then sold at ten to fifteen cents a lecture or ten dollars a semester to other students.

This commercialized note-taking was given the reluctant approval of Roger M. Heyns, dean of the Literary College, who, however, castigated it as "lecturing at its worst." It most emphatically is. Taking notes—as opposed to reading somebody else's printed, store-bought notes—is part of the learning process. As the words enter the ears, travel down the right arm and are fixed in some reasonable semblance of order in the notebook, small but important crumbs of learning remain indelibly fixed in the crevices of the brain. That has always been the hope of the educators and the experience of the most rock-skulled students.

This buying somebody else's notes instead of taking your own is one more distressing sample of the increasing fragmentation—I hate to use these big words, but, damn it, there's no better one—of the human being, the increasing specialization of human activity.

In my own profession of journalism, alas, the fragmentation, the specialization of effort, has made deep and utterly deplorable progress. *Time* magazine, to mention one, is the most conspicuous example. One person asks the questions, another person writes it down, somebody else from a different part of the building correlates (lovely word) and assembles this information into Timese, and sometimes still another checks the facts. The result of all this superb pooling of efforts, this marvelous teamwork of brainpower, is that they get the story far wronger than any individual reporter could manage on his own. It takes a lot of reporters—and very bright ones—to get a fact as wildly out of focus as can a *Time* committee.

I think students should read the book themselves and take the notes themselves.

I also think there should be a course in every prep school and in every high school called Virtue I, which would teach simple honesty, candor, courage, and conviction. I am alarmed not only at the prevalence of cheating in the nation's schools but, most importantly, at the fact that no one considers it wrong. No wonder it's so hard to find an honest cop. It's fashionable to say that the cops are on the take because they're poorly paid, and I'm sure low pay is part of the answer. But you could pay every cop in the land $50,000 a year and if virtue has not been inculcated in him at a fairly early age, he'd still be on the take because a fellow can always use a few extra bucks. It takes not laws or money to practice virtue; it takes training and a habit of mind. ■

■ There is no virtue behind the peddling of the books that have moved into the drugstore. They are merchandised exactly like toothpaste—the advertising having no relation whatsoever to the contents. This is an immoral way to sell even toothpaste, but the felony is compounded when books are sold that way. For the first has to do with a substance that is put in the mouth only temporarily; the second has to do with what goes into the mind —and while, God knows, most of it doesn't stay there long, it's difficult to get the trash out of the mind altogether.

This is the age of advertising, whose ultimate triumph is a man named Levine (whose first name I can't remember, and it isn't really worth the trouble of looking up). Levine is the man who unleashed on the world a picture named *Hercules Unchained.* Levine openly boasts that he is more concerned with the advertising of his pictures than the making of them. The picture is so awful that my children came home from it feeling that they'd been robbed of their allowance. This is the first time I've ever denounced a picture without seeing it. But then, if Mr. Levine insists on turning out pictures aimed at twelve-year-old mentality, he mustn't expect and doesn't deserve firsthand criticism. After reading some of Mr. Levine's cold-blooded cynicism about the nature of movie audiences and how to woo pennies from children, I feel no hesitation about printing my children's opinion of his lousy picture.

Rotten TV shows, rotten books, rotten movies—is that as far as it goes? No, it isn't. The decline in competence, the decline in standards of performance seem to touch every line of American endeavor. New cars on the roads are so badly put together the door handles start to fall off in the second week. New apartment buildings in New York are so poorly made you can hear the toilets flush on the next floor. There is no pride anywhere in doing things well. Just get it done, get paid, leave town before the suckers catch on. ■

■ The Kennedy administration's clampdown on expense accounts got a lot of headlines, all right. Undertakers deducting their yachts and all that. It made very interesting reading, and there's not the slightest doubt that there were vast misdealings in the expense account set.

But with all that noise, the expense account clampdown was expected to produce (and it's a wildly optimistic estimate) $250 million, which is chicken feed. A few executives and a lot of writers and artists will have to tighten their belts. It'll probably destroy the theater and ruin the restaurant business. And the oil and gas millionaires will get richer. No one has the guts to tackle the oil depletion allowance which has created many, many Texas millionaires who could pay that $250 million out of their own pockets.

There is an even more important issue at the heart of the tax law than the simple question: how much money will it raise? That is: what kind of country do we want and what kind of citizens do we want in it? There were two self-induced national disasters that have turned us from the path of moral rectitude. The first was Prohibition, which made us a nation of lawbreakers. The second were the tax laws and rulings, which made us a nation of liars.

We need to get rid of the tax lawyers—some of them, anyway—who think solely in terms of loopholes and consult some plain ordinary old-fashioned moralists. What sort of incentives should we build into our tax laws to make decent citizens? To take one tiny specialized example, a writer can work for three years on a novel, sell it to the movies, write his own screenplay—and have it all taxed away. The director and actors will get taxed the same way. But a speculator who buys the completed print can sell it to another guy—neither of whom had anything to do with making the picture—and clean up on capital gains, after the six-month wait.

Why do we penalize hard work, creative endeavor, virtue, in favor of capital? In theory, the capitalist enriches the economy, builds new plants, starts new industries. All to the good. But what about the speculator who buys another work and sells it at a profit, enriching no one but himself?

While we're on the subject, I might as well tell you I ran into William Saroyan, the Armenian pixie, at the theater a while back. First time Bill Saroyan had been in this country in a long time. First time, in fact, since Saroyan fled to Yugoslavia, declaring that he owed the government thirty thousand dollars and had no idea how he could ever pay up.

Danny Thomas used to do a routine which had all the elements of great comedy because it was stark tragedy with laughs. That's the best kind. The routine went like this: "I used to make a hundred dollars a week. But in the last ten years there hasn't been a week I've earned less than three thousand. Today I owe the government a hundred and eighty-eight thousand. How successful can you get?"

Well, I laughed until I cried. Then I kept crying because at the time I owed the government eleven thousand in back taxes and I had no idea how I would ever pay it. (I paid it. Lived off bread crusts for two years, that's how.) Of course, I felt slightly ashamed of myself. Eleven thousand bucks is pretty cheesy stuff next to $188,000 or even thirty grand. How can a fellow face his children when he only owes the government eleven thousand clams? How unsuccessful can you get?

Our tax laws, as one Congressmen has said, are a chamber of horrors. The whimsical idea that Texans are too humorous to be taxed—that the nation needs the Texas jokes more than it needs the money—requires (to use that utterly adorable governmental word) re-examination. I have no intention of re-examining it here, because I have other fish to fry.

I think what the tax laws have done to our writers and our theater and motion-picture industry is a crying cultural scandal. Today any smalltime real estate operator in Kansas City can take a capital gain on any deal that is a few months old. But a writer who has spent three years or ten years writing a novel will get virtually all the profits taxed away from him.

The result has been to send our creative minds fleeing to Europe. And as a writer, I ferociously resent any implication that any of these people are dodging taxes. The people who are dodging taxes are all those real estate men in Kansas City, all those oil operators in Texas.

What are we doing to our writers? Besides driving them abroad, we are driving them out of the business of writing plays or writing novels because both of those things are taxable here. It's much more profitable to write movies which are written abroad and, consequently, not taxed at all. The movies are all pretty lousy. ■

■ Culture isn't the only harassed facet of our age. The iron horse is hobbled, curb-reined, and may well starve.

I love railroads. I remember, when I was a boy, going to meet my father at Gifford Station near Oconomowoc, Wisconsin, every night as he came home from work. The whole family went to meet him. All the families went to meet all the fathers on their way home from work and it was always quite a gabfest on summer evenings, waiting for the train. It still is, I guess, at thousands of commuter stops. But not at Gifford Station. Gifford Station was torn down years ago, and the train hasn't stopped there for ever so long.

In the name of a foolish progress—a word which is getting an increasingly bad name—the railroads have stopped running in thousands of communities. When I was in Wheeling, West Virginia, a few years ago on a lecture trip, I tried to get out of town on the railroad (there was an airline strike), only to be told that passenger trains hadn't run there for a long time.

The Maine Central cut off passenger trains September 1, 1961. Portland's key Union Station shut down in October. The Boston & Maine has killed the famous State of Maine Express. In 1960 the Baltimore & Ohio killed all passenger service between Baltimore and New York and began actually tearing up its tracks. The Pennsylvania has cut way down on its service between New York and Washington. Dozens of stations have become near-ghost camps.

It's all very easy to rail at the railroads for bad management—and heaven knows, some of them are guilty enough—but the public and the Federal government are really the guilty ones for putting the railroads in this pass today. Various governments seem intent on taxing the railroads out of business. Meanwhile the Federal government is shelling out all sorts of help to every other form of transportation. The Federal government paid one-seventh of all transportation expenditures (highways, airways, waterways) as recently as 1955. Today it pays better than a third. No wonder the railroads can't compete with the subsidized highways and airlines.

There is absolutely nothing in this age of progress less efficient than a 300-horsepower automobile taking one person miles to work. Conversely, there's almost nothing more efficient than a Diesel locomotive pulling him to work, provided it pulls enough of him and his friends. Just from the point of view of national efficiency, we can't always afford to have every commuter burning up all those hydrocarbons in his own car to get to work.

Transportation to and from work is getting appallingly expensive. Public transportation costs more than double what it cost ten years ago, and represents the biggest jump in the consumer's budget.

A well-run, well-patronized railroad that was not discriminated against in taxes and subsidies would probably not bring these costs down, but they, at least, would not go any higher. The only way to fight rising costs is by increased efficiency. Mass transportation is efficient. Individual transportation by car isn't. The railroads have hardly advanced an inch technically in the last hundred years but, even then, they are more efficient movers of large numbers of people than cars—and we all know what the cars have done to cities. ■

■ There is a lot of mass misery in this world, and the root of the problem of mass misery is mass. We can open our hearts and open our granaries until the hearts are bled white and the granaries are empty—and still we shall not even begin to approach a solution to the problem of mass misery. There is only one solution and that is population control. And that, in bluntest terms, means birth control. And that, in bluntest terms, is modern contraception, the greatest invention of the nineteenth century.

This planet was not designed to hold three billion people without a vast amount of mass misery. It's even less designed to hold six billion, which will be its population in the year 2000. Just how many people will the planet hold comfortably? It's a moot point. Some say fifty billion—but life would resemble antkind rather than mankind. The fact that this figure is not more openly discussed and studied is in itself a shocking dereliction of public responsibility.

The most forceful opposition to artificial birth control in our half of the planet comes from the Roman Catholic Church. But many are guilty in addition to the Church in this matter. The press itself has dragged one foot in covering this—either the biggest or the second-biggest story of our time—partly because of clerical opposition. That's not the only reason. Like inflation, the population explosion is a tough story to cover, shadowy and hard to report on a day-by-day basis.

President Kennedy talks of mass misery in half the globe, but we'll have the same mass misery here, too, unless unbridled population is checked. The strangulation of our cities—which is already well advanced—the shortages of schools and roads and housing, the taking out of agriculture of a million acres of farmland a year for the private enrichment of real estate speculators to build new suburbs upon, the growing anguish of the suburbanites at traveling farther and farther to work, at the difficulty of finding a parking place when he gets there or a seat on the train—what are all these but aspects of the population explosion?

To the Communist hierarchy the population explosion is the greatest of blessings, increasing mass starvation and mass unrest far beyond their poor powers to stir up trouble. And to Wall Street the population explosion is marvelous news. All those mouths to feed and provide schoolbooks for and clothe and sell soap to. (Here we find the Catholic Church, the Communist party and Wall Street all in the same bed. Dogma makes strange bedfellows.) ■

■ A violent emotion like rage should probably be saved for national scandals and world problems. But I've been known to blow my top over something purely personal.

I'm still seeking a laundry to wash my shirts. Is this asking too much? I mean here it is the 1960s. We've put astronauts into space. We invented the nuclear submarine. Come right down to it, we invented the atom bomb. Why is it my shirts are beyond the technical capability of this country?

The last laundry I tried is a huge chain laundry which has scores of branches throughout New York City. "They does good shirts," said my cleaning woman, whose word has been utterly reliable. Off went a batch of shirts, our hopes high. A week passed. The cleaning woman picked up the laundry, inspected the shirts and immediately called me. The gist of the conversation: they done good shirts once. They doesn't do good shirts now. In short, they have retrogressed in this matter.

I inspected the shirts myself, a heartbreaking experience. The first one had two buttons off, one button broken. Well, I'm a broad-minded man, but not that broad-minded. The collars looked as if they had been ironed by a lunatic chimpanzee.

Never in the long march of history has there been a nation so soap-conscious as ours. ("So join in the chorus for the soap for people who like people.") The air rings with abjurations to buy soap flakes ("So fine! So fast! So mild!") or a detergent ("Cleans clear through").

So why do my shirts come back a dull gray? My own theory is that so much of the national energy has gone into advertising soap we haven't any strength left to wash my shirts.

Aah, me! When I was a child, my family had a laundress. Everyone's family had a laundress. But now that I am a man, I have put aside childish things and I have a Laundromat. Or even better yet, oh joy, oh progress, in this richest of all countries, I can call a national laundry chain and they will smash my buttons, age my shirts, to say nothing of aging me, for as little as twenty cents a shirt.

I have gone 2,000 miles up the Amazon. In the shallows, braving the bites of the piranhas and totally devoid of detergents and automatic washers, are the dusky maidens of some of the most backward Indians on earth, and they're getting their lingerie cleaner than I'm getting my lingerie. You know what they use? *Muscle!* The new miracle ingredient! The all-purpose detergent! And it cleans clear through so fine, so fast, so mild.

This is one of those backward areas into which our money is to be poured to bring the natives up to our standard of living. With any luck, their laundry will be as badly done as my laundry within a decade. Maybe sooner. Aah, lucky brown-skinned maiden!

In Europe, the shirts still come back snowy white, beautifully ironed, arranged almost like a bouquet in a little wicker basket. At least they did a couple of years ago. But since then, they've put the bowling alleys in the Bois de Boulogne. The quick lunch is spreading all over the Continent. Maybe they've even got an American laundry.

The smart thing in Wall Street and on Madison Avenue is to import English secretaries—with their cool, crisp accents and their English ways. You suppose maybe we might import some French laundresses who know how to iron a shirt? Would it be unreasonable to arrange a trade? For all those billions in foreign aid, couldn't we get just a few backward people who are so terribly backward they haven't yet forgotten how to do the work properly?

I'm an ordinary man who desires nothing more than just an ordinary clean, white shirt. But this is not the right age to ask for the ordinary. You'd have better luck asking for a cobalt bomb. But I don't want a cobalt bomb. Just a clean, well-ironed, white shirt. Apparently it's easier to put a man on the moon. ■

Agony on the air

■ I don't know what history is going to make of us, but it's just possible we may go down as the agonized generation. Certainly the amount of agony that has poured out of radios and TV sets would justify future historians in making this judgment. After all, the Romans couldn't get to the Colosseum for their agony shows more than once in a while, but we can get all we want most any time of the night or day.

We got more variety in our agony shows, too. If you collect real hard-luck stories—as who doesn't?—here are a few you may not have heard. To win a "my favorite hymn" contest on the Johnny Olsen show, a woman related how, when she was a child, her mother had been struck and killed by a car while they walked hand in hand. Her only child died in infancy. She adopted a child who died. She had an accident after which the doctor told her she couldn't possibly live. But, if she did live, she couldn't possibly walk. Well, she both lived and walked and later acquired an adopted daughter and grandchildren.

There were, in the fifties, half a dozen shows that specialized in misery; since some of them were on five times a week, it took an awful lot of grief to keep them all supplied. There never seemed to be any shortage. *Welcome Travelers* used to feature child misery, this being considered even more poignant and heart-rending than adult misery. On exhibition was eight-year-old

Richard Fecteau, who was being wined and dined and fussed over. His problem: he was orphaned at the age of four and a half when his mother, father and brother were killed in an automobile crash, and he'd been living on dreams ever since.

This was rather mild stuff for *Welcome Travelers.* Shucks, I can remember back when a couple of hysterical mothers broadcast a plea to a kidnaper to return their children unharmed. Viewers of that show were once shown a piece of paper which contained a pardon from a death sentence, a lovely morbid sight. And a cancer victim told how he planned to spend the last couple months of his life—as millions wept.

Then there was *On Your Account,* which dredged up some beauties. On a nice typical weepy day you'd meet a woman whose only child had set fire to her house and died in the flames; a woman with four children, all of them mentally retarded; and a multiple-sclerosis victim confined to a wheelchair.

I don't know what ever happened to a program called *Wheel of Fortune,* but life hasn't been the same since it went away. This was the one on which the master of ceremonies once cried, "And what would you do if you were a little girl who was attacked by a crazed fox?" And then produced the little girl who had emerged from this ordeal unscathed. (The fox had just chewed up her little brother a bit.)

However, before it died somewhere around 1956 (the end came quickly but not easily; the pain was excruciating) and went to The Great Kinescope Vault, for sheer assorted agony *Strike It Rich* stayed a few yards out in front of the pack. On any good day on that show you were likely to encounter a ninety-three-year-old gold prospector, blinded by cataracts; a father who wanted to win money for a wheelchair for his nine-year-old daughter, crippled by heart disease; a little girl suffering from cancer with only a few weeks to live; or—strictly for laughs—a man who wanted false teeth because his wife called him Hopalong Cavity.

Strike It Rich was an agony show, one of the pioneers in that lush and apparently inexhaustible field. All these shows followed a certain dreary pattern. A woman would appear, looking low in the mouth, and tell Warren Hull (or whoever) all about it. Her husband had Bright's disease and couldn't work; the children were getting rickets from malnutrition, and the woman herself was slowly losing her sight. Whereupon Warren Hull (or whoever) would present the lady with a check so she could feed the children and get the operation which would save her vision. And, theoretically, millions of housewives would feel comforted by the thought that their own afflictions were so relatively minor next to the lady on TV that they had no business being anything but happy as kings. At least that was the theory.

There was a period there when I used to toss and turn in my bed at night worrying whether there was enough misery in the world to staff all the misery shows. I used to have a nightmare—horrible thought—of some dame turning up on *Strike It Rich* and telling poor Warren Hull she hadn't a care in the world.

But that horrid prospect is now safely behind us. There is only one daytime show now exploiting misery; that is good old reliable *Queen for a Day*, where four women show up daily with assorted unhappiness. All the others have quietly expired, not, as I feared, because we ran out of misery, but because people just got sick of listening to it and looking at it.

I was watching *Queen for a Day* one day when out of the bedraggled group of unfortunates, each with her tale of misery, Jack Bailey, that ever-cheerful fast-talking emcee, who in an earlier and probably happier time would be selling the Brooklyn Bridge to yokels and is now in pretty much the same line of work but on a larger and more up-to-date scale, dredged up an unhappy-looking girl who confessed, between long, long, long pauses, to being an out-of-work waitress. Her husband had deserted her and the three kids and she had supported the family. But then the kids came down with measles and her baby-sitter had fled. So she had to stay home and take care of her children, which cost her her job.

Bailey chuckled jovially over this gay little story (he always finds these tales terribly funny) and asked the girl what she wanted. Well, she wanted a used car. She had a car but she lost it. She couldn't remember the ages of her children.

"How do you remember the orders all the way to the kitchen?" said Bailey, chuckling away.

"I can remember when I'm not nervous," she said wanly.

They led her away, looking as if she were about to slip into a coma. For your real *aficionados* of misery, which is what the audience for *Queen for a Day* is largely composed of, this girl was a pretty rare specimen.

Naturally, after Bailey had dispensed with another woman whose husband had died twenty minutes after being stung by a bee, the big daily contest of misfortune was held and the ex-waitress won and was led back to the microphone, looking even more dazed than ever. An attendant kept laving her forehead to keep her from fainting dead away. She looked miserable enough to staff four *Queen for a Day* shows.

"Say something," said Bailey.

She opened her mouth. Nothing emerged. So they started trotting out the loot—the matched luggage, the Westinghouse steam iron, the kitchen range. The audience *oohed* and *aahed,* but the girl stared straight ahead, never cracked a smile and looked actually as if she were on some other planet, a million miles away. The program went off the air that way—the camera still focused on her totally expressionless face, Bailey still yelling his platitudes.

Then, as the light fades and the agony of the day fades into the misery of evening, there's nothing like a good laugh. Well, one night the whole country had a chance to roar with laughter over the misfortunes of Mrs. Gladys Workman on Ralph Edwards' *This Is Your Life* program. Mrs. Workman, who had been dogged by accidents and illness her whole life, led the hilarity, capably assisted by a host of her friends who doubled up with mirth at each misfortune.

I knew it would come to this eventually; there was so much agony on the air that sooner or later we were bound to start laughing at it—but it did come as a shock to hear Mrs. Workman get the giggles about a childhood illness that left her deaf, dumb, and blind. During the years of her affliction, her brothers and sisters used to tease her and wave things in front of her to find out if she could see, and laugh at her. Her parents encouraged this practice, telling Gladys she should be happy she was able to make children laugh. Self-pity, we were told, was not allowed in Oregon.

After a few years sight, hearing and speech were restored, and Gladys, then a young girl, went out to crank her father's Maxwell and broke her arm. Gladys had clean forgotten this, but howled when reminded of it. On her first job, there was a large hole on the premises so—"Well, naturally, Gladys fell in and broke her foot," related a friend, gasping with merriment. The doctors wanted to cut off the foot but Gladys insisted they leave it on. After the foot healed, she got another job but soon broke her neck.

Well, I tell you, it went on like that, just one hilarious incident after another—her husband's dye poisoning, her own heart trouble and sleeping sickness and St. Vitus' dance, floods on the old homestead—until I thought I'd split a gut. And I thought Mrs. Workman would, too. To say nothing of her friends. (I'll just have to skip the bit about the cow with diarrhea. I can't tell it the way Gladys did.)

But then Gladys had to go and spoil it all. Mr. Edwards presented her with a TV and hi-fi set and a thousand dollars' worth of classical records, and she started to cry. One of her pals on the show, Ma Crews, a tough and tiny dame from Oregon—mindful of that rule about self-pity—kept leaning over and whispering, "Stop your bawlin'." But Edwards shoved her aside, shouting, "Let her bawl if she wants to. You just leave her alone, Ma Crews." ■

When commercials strike

■ I guess I'm the only guy in the world who has ever loved a commercial. Over the years I've loved several: the one for Gold Medal flour, for instance—a ballet, of course.

This boy and this girl were bounding around a kitchen, baking a cake, and singing about the cake mix.

Years ago a man would have had to pay his way into the Palace to see such talent, and the choreography wouldn't have been nearly as good. And the subject matter wouldn't have been nearly so original. The guy and the girl probably would have been doing *entrechats* over some tired old subject like love in the springtime.

The splendors and heartbreaks of a cake mix were almost never properly celebrated in song and ballet. Almost never? I think I might be safe in saying cake mixes were never sung about at all at the Palace, more's the pity. The poets and minnesingers and choreographers ignored cake mix entirely for thousands of years until our own enlightened times.

Since television, all sorts of vistas have opened. I've seen tap dances to the glory of Pepsi-Cola. Believe me, it takes ingenuity.

The cigarette people have been particularly ingenious not only in avoiding all that tired old romantic stuff but in actually thwarting it when it raises its silly head.

The Chesterfield people had one about a young couple on a

park bench who are just about to make the serious mistake of kissing each other. Suddenly four cops leap out of the bushes and thrust a package of cigarettes between them, meanwhile singing, "Stop! Start smoking with a smile with Chesterfield," etc.

The nice thing about this commercial was that the park bench couple fell on the cigarettes like Siberian wolves on a spent horse. The implication was clear. The poor things had only resorted to lovemaking because there wasn't anything better to do. Wasn't a cigarette among them. Or any cake mix. Or any Pepsi-Cola. So what else was there to do but fall to kissing, that old thing?

The Lucky Strike people put one on TV about a guy who is trying to paint a bucolic scene. Meanwhile, his wife is singing and dancing about light up a Lucky, it's light-up time. He tries hopelessly for a moment or two to keep on painting, but she finally wrests his attention from that silly easel and gets a cigarette between his lips. The last we see of him he's a good, loyal consumer, puffing away, the easel forgotten.

This is what I like to think of as the interruption commercial—stop what you're doing and go buy something—and I deplore it, especially when employed about love.

Some of the greatest acting on television comes out of the mouths of those little cartoon characters that romp through the commercials. I can remember way back when commercials were silent. The beer cans marched but they didn't talk. But that was long ago. Now the cigarettes talk, sneer, have their own inner reality and sometimes do The Method.

Zel deCyr, a nice-looking young lady, who has made a good living being the voices of Kiwi shoe polish, the Dutch Boy and about a million other voices, projects herself into the part just as if she were playing Camille: "If I'm playing a rose—usually a cartoon rose—I try to think what would a rose be like, what's the purpose of what the rose is saying. I feel the more you're involved, the more you communicate."

Don't think Miss deCyr hasn't played a rose, either, because she has. Her yellow rose—an advertisement for the Yellow Pages of the telephone book—set the yokels on their ear in Sheboygan.

Since actresses these days start out playing trees in all the acting schools, this sort of work is duck soup.

There is enormous competition for such roles, and Miss deCyr has had to use all her Sandy Meisner Neighborhood Playhouse training to wrest some of these roles from competitors. For one commercial, the interests were looking for a croupy cough from a seven-year-old girl, and Miss deCyr found herself up to her ears in seven-year-old children of both sexes, sneezing and coughing their heads off.

"They taped hundreds of coughs," she reported wonderingly, "and darn if they didn't try them all out on a medical board. It turned out I had the most legitimate chronic cough of a seven-year-old girl." ■

■ Reflections on the cancerous growth of childhood all over the world of entertainment have released some long pent-up bitterness among the cash customers. There was an Englishman in town who saw *The Sound of Music,* and it drove him over the thin red line of sanity. He announced to one and all he was going to go straight home to London and strangle his little ones.

It's not that I'm against the little tots. It's just that they've gone too far. And where—I keep asking—did it all start? (I'm a trend spotter by nature and we trend spotters are constantly asking ourselves questions like "Where did it all start?" or, failing that, "Where will it all end?") I think I've pinpointed the exact moment when the little monsters got out of hand. It was when the first little moppet dashed up to a camera and squealed, "Look, Mom, no cavities!"

Of course, there are some scholars who say it started much earlier than that. There are those who trace the beginning of the unrest way back when that little girl pulled out her first Castro bed. Frankly, I find this view extreme; that little girl didn't talk. The trouble started when they wired the little beggars for sound. Reason tottered when the little darlings began exclaiming in their high-pitched voices, "My mommy made me use Ipana." Strong men began coming unglued when that itsy-bitsy girl quavered into the camera, "Hudson paper tissues tear so straight."

Well, of course Hudson paper tissues tear so straight. But do I have to find this out from five-year-old girls? I'm a grown man, for God's sake. Been earning my own living for years. I take subways by myself and everything, changing to the express at Fourteenth Street, and complicated stuff like that. I don't need some five-year-old kid to tell me Hudson paper tissues tear so straight.

Or that little brat who sold Delco batteries while standing on his head. If we have to have a bunch of kids tell us what to buy, the least they can do is stand up straight, take their hands out of their pockets, and talk up.

All over radio and television, children have taken over commercials with their sticky little voices and their sticky little sentiments. If that Englishman is still around, sure as God made little apples, he'll run amok in the nursery when he gets home. ■

■ Out in Hollywood, a man from *TV Magazine* named Frank Orme put a stop watch on a kid's program named *Space Funnies.* Out of one twenty-seven-minute segment of the program, he ticked off twelve minutes and five seconds of commercials. Plugged in that twelve minutes were Monarch bikes, Wenmore airplanes, Automite racing cars, Bat Bat set, Sturdee Gym, Hecht's clock radio, BMC tractor, a camera shop, Ship 'n' Shore blouses, Sioux Bee honey, Bosco chocolate flavoring, Planter's peanuts, Zenith magic set, Dandy barbecue set, Voit basketball kits, a game board, Sculptex paint kit, *Better Homes and Gardens* books, and Super Coola, a canned drink. The station also managed to get in some plugs for its later shows.

Now honestly, fellows! It seems to me that the station representative who permitted that much advertising on a children's program should be compelled by law to go out and buy for his own offspring one Monarch bike, one Wenmore airplane, one Automite racing car and all the rest of it in order to understand what the rest of us have to go through.

And while they're doing all this soul-searching, the ad men might try to find an end to the unfinished comparative which is getting rampant again. BAB-O cleans grease four times as quick, Gem razors are four times as sharp.

As quick as *what*, gentlemen? As sharp as what? Advertising like that is four times as fraudulent as. Or, to put it another way, recent impartial surveys show that our surveys are 50 per cent more impartial than all other leading impartial surveys. ■

■ Weiss and Geller, a Chicago ad agency which has gone overboard on the psychiatric approach to advertising, stuck a panel of social science authorities in front of a television set for fourteen consecutive hours (which is enough to drive even a social scientist out of his wits) and came up with some rather interesting observations. For one thing, after fourteen hours of bright-eyed damsels showing off their new hair rinse, their refrigerators, their ready cake mix, the panel decided that women projecting commercials to other women arouse thoughts of a nagging mother and create resentments. If you remove the psychiatric husk from that kernel of thought, it means that women can be damned irritating when they sell you things.

In fact, I would like to go a little further than the social scientists and say that women can arouse resentments not only among women but among men. It used to seem odd to me that in thirty years of radio there were almost no women delivering commercials. They were all men. Even the soap salesmen were largely men. But the women have taken over TV in droves, generating enough resentment to provide electric light to a small city.

The panel, which, incidentally, consisted of two psychoanalysts, a cultural anthropologist, two sociologists, an experimental psychologist and two professors of social science—altogether an imposing collection of massive domes—pointed out that women have great suspicion of women who know too much. I'm willing to go along with that theory, but I was terribly interested to know where, for God's sake, they found a woman delivering a commercial on TV who looked like she knew too much.

I don't know who they got delivering the spiels in Chicago, but out our way, most of the fillies in this line of work, while undeniably pretty, look as if their lovely noggins had never been defiled by a single thought.

That doesn't mean that men are the answer necessarily. The social scientists declared that the women resented men, too, if they seemed to invade women's domain—the kitchen, say—with any degree of confidence. It's all right for the men to be in the kitchen, but—if I read the scientists correctly—he must not be at ease there and he better not know too much. Tops at this sort of knowing something but not too much was Arthur Godfrey, the tall domes said, which may conceivably be the dimmest compliment ever paid to Arthur.

As a matter of fact, the perfect announcer, the scientists agreed, must be quite a bit of a stumblebum. Not only must he not know too much; he comes across better if he's all thumbs while demonstrating how easy the icebox door swings open and maybe even fluffs a line or two. Next time you demonstrate a can opener, men, cut yourself a little bit. Or maybe you could contrive to slam the deep-freeze door on one thumb. Makes you, according to the scientists, "human and fallible" and, therefore, lovable.

While not quite going so far as to say that American housewives are just a collection of neurotics, the scientists implied it strongly in one of their final recommendations. It was their thesis —and a more debatable one I can't imagine—that the average housewife is not nearly so worried about whether the product is good enough as whether she is good enough for the product.

Frankly, I never met any female who harbored any fears, conscious or subconscious, that she didn't measure up to the soap flakes. But then I move in a limited circle. I do think, though, after reviewing the qualifications, that I'd make one hell of a good announcer. I've never been known to open even a can of coffee without putting at least three fingers out of action for a week, and my diction is so human and fallible that it is almost totally unintelligible, which is to say, terribly lovable. ■

■ Mr. Brooks Taylor does not fit the socal scientists' definition of the perfect announcer, for reasons that should soon be clear. Mr. Taylor, whom we saw extolling aluminum on *Alcoa Presents,* is not a staff announcer (employed by a network) or a commercial announcer (who speaks for many non-competing products)—he is a glittering representative of a brand-new shiny profession in this age of the Organization Man. Mr. Brooks Taylor is a Presenter, which is to say he is the image of a corporation. He doesn't sell aluminum. He *is* aluminum.

But let him speak for himself, which he rarely ever does: "There are only a handful of us in the country. Very small category. Choosing a man for the job, a company looks beyond the man's ability to act or announce. In front of the camera he must project the very image of the corporation. You speak not only for the manufacturers of the product but for the dealers and their families, for everyone connected with the organization."

An awful lot of people for one little man to look like, but I must say he does it well. He's a very conservative-type gentleman, dapper, well-spoken, terribly polite.

"You have to dress to fit the over-all picture; you have to have a businessman-like dignity. You can't wear a severe Madison Avenue suit. My suits are medium-tone gray, single-breasted sharkskin. The shirt has a straight tab collar and I wear a conservative tie." He sighed. "I have a double-breasted suit but I save it for Westhampton. I can't wear a vest. I don't want to look avant-garde." And he shuddered slightly at the terrible thought of an avant-garde corporate image.

"A presenter is not a personality. . . . You see, the whole idea is to present the product so that it and I are the same thing. We are both Alcoa."

What can you say to a man who is Alcoa except, "Mr. Taylor, truthfully, do you take all this seriously?"

Mr. Taylor said, "I take it absolutely seriously."

We left it at that.

There are certain tricks to hiring Presenters. For instance, a male Presenter must be clean-cut, American, and above average height. When you're selling a car, you've got to be tall—makes the car look longer, lower, sleeker. If you're a girl selling refrigerators, you've got to be medium height. After all, you've got to take things out of the box and there must be no bending, no stretching, nothing difficult.

"And another thing," said Mr. Taylor in his magnificently well-modulated, accent-free voice. (Are you ready? Is everybody awake? Everybody alert?) "Don't ever put anything in your pockets. Never look bulky. Only button the center button." Then he added, "I would never represent a product which I wouldn't want to discuss with friends and family."

There was no conflict in Mr. Taylor's personality at all. He was quite patently proud to announce at the end of the program that he was Brooks Taylor speaking not only for Alcoa but for all its distributors, small businessmen, users of Alcoa—and all their wives and children to boot. As I said, that's a lot of people to project out of one single-breasted conservative suit. ■

■ "Our television set's broken, yippee!" a reader wrote me. "And you can bet I didn't miss not seeing Ban's lesson in anatomy while peddling their deodorant, that creep with the stuffed-up nose, Kellogg's giant screaming about eating a bonnie bonnie breakfast and those little people gloating about no cavities! I'd sooner offend my friends with obnoxious armpits and a runny nose than buy any of their products."

Lest we forget, commercials still form one of the largest and most legitimate complaints against television. The Schwerin Research Corporation has revealed the results of an audience sampling on the question: "What is your main criticism of TV today?" Forty-six per cent of the people criticized commercials (as opposed to only 44 per cent who criticized programs). Of that number—now pay attention here, Federal Trade Commission—60 per cent said there were too many commercials, 26 per cent that they were too "long, loud, or annoying" and only 3 per cent that they were false or misleading.

We all remember with mixed emotions the Federal Trade Commission's charge that real sandpaper was not used in shaving-soap advertisements on television. The Colgate-Palmolive Company retorted that scientific research had proved "beyond any doubt" that sandpaper could be shaved. Now, let's all keep our heads. In matters of grave moment like this, there's no sense rushing to conclusions.

I haven't shaved any sandpaper in years. In fact, come to think of it, I've never shaved any sandpaper. Peaches I've shaved. Naturally. Everyone has. If you ask me, the country started to go to hell when people started shaving sandpaper instead of peaches like Grandfather did. This whole controversy would never have arisen if we'd stuck to the old ways.

"This demonstration has been duplicated successfully on many occasions, and most recently to an FTC representative who actually made the sandpaper test himself," the Colgate people declared stoutly. This didn't square with the FTC charge at all. The truth was, cried the FTC sorrowfully, "The supposed sandpaper" wasn't sandpaper at all; it was a mock-up of glass or a "similar substance to which sand has been applied."

Shivers must have rippled up and down all of Madison Avenue when they found out that a three-man commission had been sitting monitoring commercials all day and all night, looking for fraud. No one had ever counted on three sets of beady eyes being fixed on the screen when that little girl rushes up and says, "Look, Mom, no cavities."

"Get a tail on that girl," growls the chief monitor. "If there's a break in her teeth, upper or lower, the president of Crest is going up the river, or my name isn't Tom Swift."

But, seriously though—a phrase I picked up listening to disk jockeys explain that they never took any payola themselves but it's widely known everyone else did—what does all this portend? Honest commercials? Are we ready for honest commercials? "You can wash your hands with our soap and get reasonably clean." Just wait till someone tries to set *that* to music! "Revlon reddens the lips. If you expect gypsies to abduct you, go to charm school."

I can't wait for the FTC to step in and referee that race between the Bufferin and the aspirin. You know—who gets into the blood stream faster? I think the race is fixed. All I ask is an honest count.

But, oh, the disillusionment that lies ahead for all of us! You know that girl that keeps her hands soft and lovely with Jergens for her husband. Well, that guy that bounds in and folds her in his arms—suppose that isn't her husband? My God, the headlines! Suppose it isn't her hands he's so feverishly attracted to and not even legally? What will the church groups say to that?

It's not that I'm *for* false or misleading advertising. But I think it's probably harder to mislead the public than the FTC thinks. I don't really think the populace took that sandpaper shaving very seriously. When Ted Bates & Company bleated in a full-page ad in newspapers that even actors had a different color and flavor in real life than on TV and why not Jello, I sympathized.

The FTC, I feel, missed the crux of the problem: The sheer number of commercials is becoming a strain that may pull commercial television right down on its ear. I watched *Playhouse 90* with a friend from Vienna who was flabbergasted and infuriated by the incessant interruptions of a serious story. It seemed incredible to him that the American public would put up with so much bilge and such constant interruptions.

Well, we put up with a lot, but there is a point when people rebel. Then they turn the set off altogether. For instance, the 1960 Olympics. The praise for CBS's coverage was fairly universal, but the commercials drove everyone dippy. There were just too many.

Also, false and misleading advertising doesn't anger viewers half as much as offensive advertising—liver bile, armpits, and the rest of it. Short of outright fraud, the viewer can watch a certain amount of exaggeration with calm, and he puts it into proper perspective almost automatically. No one expects a man selling a car to be 100 per cent honest, any more than a frontiersman expected 100 per cent honesty from a man selling a horse.

But in the matter of noise, quantity, and taste, commercials are increasingly unpopular with viewers, and one annoyance has led all the rest in the letters I have received. That is that the volume of sound goes up during the commercial. This complaint finally drove *TV Guide* to investigate with an audiometer in four cities. The finding was that volume did *not* go up with commercials but that vocal and recording tricks gave the commercials an urgency and strident quality that just made them sound louder. Well, if the FTC wants to investigate misleading commercials, they might start there. The noisiness of commercials drives viewers nutty. ■

■ When I'm looking for fast, fast, *fast* relief from it all, you know what I do? I turn off the television set. You can get awfully fast relief that way from those nagging commercials. I know a girl who, when commercials strike, runs out of the room. She claims she gets even faster relief than I do, but on the other hand, I point out that she has abdicated her living room to the commercials, a form of defeat.

Speaking of *fast* relief, what I would like to know is: what ideas do you suppose they turned down before they came up with stomach acid? What phrases were tossed out as too rough on you and me before they came up with liver bile, which obviously wouldn't bother your sweet old grandmother?

Well, as I say, I can just see the scene around the conference table. A young man named Crewcut Beaver IV is saying, "J.D., let's put this on the train and see if it gets off at Westport. I see a photograph of a white-haired doctor pointing his stethoscope at you, and the legend underneath says, 'Friends, before leprosy strikes . . .' "

"Now, now, Crewcut," says old gray-haired J.D. in kindly tones, "if I've told you once, I've told you a thousand times, the public isn't ready for leprosy. I tell you, men, there's a revulsion against these gamy commercials. The public is dying to get back to the quiet, good taste of our grandmothers' time. Remember those nice, quiet halitosis ads. Nothing pushy, nothing noisy. Just the suggestion that something wasn't quite right."

"How about this, chief?" shouts Crewcut excitedly. "Here's one you could use on valentines. There's this girl, see, and she's waving at her guy and suddenly a blotch of sweat appears under her arm and . . ."

"Crewcut, you're orbiting! You're in outer space! A beautiful suggestion! So low-keyed! Not a mention of leprosy! Not even a hint the girl has got bubonic plague! Just plain honest American sweat! It may be old-fashioned, Crewcut, but it's got heart!" ■

■ My favorite singing commercial, which I used in the shower, remained for some time "Good-by, Crabgrass, Good-by." It contains those great lines: "I'm going to get you early this spring/ Dow Chemical has the very thing/ Good-by, crabgrass, good-by."

By George, I would say to myself, they don't write lyrics like that any more.

Except that obviously they do. Well, I mean, they wrote that one. "Good-by, Crabgrass, Good-by" is the favorite all up and down my block. Small children sing it much as they would sing

"Oh, we're off to see the Wizard, the wonderful Wizard of Oz." They're both equally fanciful and dreamlike.

Crabgrass?

Why, bless my soul, Dow Chemical, there hasn't been a blade of grass, crab or any other variety, seen in my vicinity since somewhere in the mid-nineteenth century. You got the very best thing, have you, Dow Chemical? Well, we got a better cure for crabgrass. Cement. The crabgrass grows "high as an elephant's eye" but not in Greenwich Village. ■

■ A pernicious trend in commercials became clear during the 1950s: the suborning of actors by the base workings of commerce. I always felt a little aggrieved when I heard Bing Crosby pushing gas ranges. What was Bing Crosby doing that for? Or Frank Sinatra selling Fords on the radio. Frank Sinatra needed maybe the money? He had to be selling cars on the radio?

By the end of the decade the trend had gone farther. In this commercial, Max Shulman was smoking a cigarette and selling it to the people. As if that wasn't bad enough, he also had a sort of column that appeared here and there full of funny anecdotes, which was really one long advertisement.

It's not that I was opposed to funny ads. It's not that these weren't very funny ones. It's just that I was against Max Shulman, one of our funniest writers, getting in the advertising business.

It's got so no actor can get work unless the commercial pitch goes right in with it. But at least writers, I had always felt, put their precious integrity above gold. But now that Max Shulman has let them get their foot in the door, heaven knows where it'll end. Next thing you know, Sir Winston Churchill's face will be seen grinning out of an ad with the words: "All the Nobel Prize winners I know use Munchkin, the tissue with the porous fiber."

Just before women got back into the liquor ads, the hooch manufacturers made me do a double-take on just what they were up to in their advertising. For about a year every time I picked up a magazine I saw—or at least I *thought* I saw—a picture of Maurice Evans about to engage in a duel with Bennett Cerf under an improbable moon. Or maybe some other celebrities—I've forgotten who they were or maybe I just don't *want* to know—sitting in a tree.

In every case, there was a bottle of booze nearby and I could only assume they'd been belting the stuff. As I reconstructed the thing, they got to hitting the stuff they were advertising and you know how one thing leads to another. The next thing you know they have *épées* in their hands and are squaring off in Central Park or wherever they are.

I'm a member of the old school. Sit down, son, and let me tell you about the old days. Back when I was a boy, a whiskey drinker—at least in the advertisements—was a man of distinction. You met him in his own home in front of his Georgian fireplace. He showed you his collection of firearms. Or maybe his old prints.

His name was Rutherford B. Jessup (or something like that) and, by God, he was a gentleman. There was none of this brawling with swords in Central Park, none of this tree climbing. He drank at home in front of a roaring fire. And he knew when he'd had enough.

I can't quite put my finger on the point when the hooch ads got—well—a little too alcoholic. The first one I remember was an ad in which a guy in white tie, top hat and tails was wandering around the Sahara. In the foreground, maybe a hundred yards ahead of him, was an ice-cold, terribly dry martini. It gave me quite a turn. I was once a guest of honor at a little party on the edge of the Sahara and there were no martinis. Just Coca-Cola and hot tea. This ad writer, I thought, has not been in the Sahara; he has been at the corner saloon, and he's been there much too long.

That was just the beginning. After that, the copywriters went berserk. Instead of being invited into the old Jessup mansion, we'd be shown into some saloon with spears on the wall, the floor crawling with live leopards. This was what I like to think of as the Greenwich Village phase of whiskey advertising.

But things rapidly got much worse. For one thing, the drinkers moved outdoors. The Schweppes man came over here and he was photographed drinking gin-and-tonic in swimming pools, at hunt meets and in the darnedest places. Once old Commander What's His Name was handing a gin-and-tonic to a ballerina backstage at Covent Garden. She'd just done, the ad writer said, thirty-two fouettés and was hot, tired, and thirsty. And after that gin-and-tonic, I bet, too drunk to go back on stage and do even one fouetté. Fine thing to do to a ballerina. ■

■ You know something, fellows? I don't really think Madison Avenue especially cares about selling. The idea is to have a Nielsen rating like *I Love Lucy*—which, I believe, never managed to sell many packages of the cigarettes it advertised. This is the perfect Madison Avenue objective.

I tell you, it takes a split personality to live on Madison Avenue. It has always seemed to me in my ivory tower that many of the ads in our magazines are not designed to sell breakfast food to the little old lady in Dubuque but to impress the vice-president down the hall with the ingenuity, imagination, and inventiveness of the guy who thought up the ad.

I'm absolutely enchanted, for example, with all the advertisements for missiles. Have you seen the ad put out by the Raytheon Missile System Division? "Flames swept across the open plains as the Mongol hordes ran in terror from 'arrows of flying fire.' When the smoke had cleared, the Chinese had won the battle with the first rocket." The ad went on to state that modern rockets were "much more sophisticated" than those fifteenth-century bamboo rods, and Raytheon was right there with the leaders in making shining new rockets.

Well, my family is so backward it's been using those old-fashioned Chinese rockets—been using them ever since the fifteenth century—so I went right down to the store to get some new fancy, dynaflow Raytheon rockets. The store didn't sell 'em. Didn't stock missiles at all. They had lots of Dow Chemicals to get rid of the crabgrass I haven't got but no missiles, which are advertised in every magazine and which clearly every growing American boy can hardly do without.

There's not a store on my block that stocks Polaris missiles. Now, why? You can hardly open a magazine without finding marvelous color advertisements of the Polaris, and if they're not trying to sell me one, what *are* they trying to do?

The purpose of these ads, I was told, was not to sell anything. But then what is the purpose of what *The Nation* calls "advertising doomsday"? Well, as I said, it's a status symbol. There's almost nothing more expensive than a nuclear submarine. And the nicest thing about it is that you can't buy one, even if you've got the price.

Any day now I expect to hear the first singing commercial for a missile:

General Electric goes high in the sky;
Its ICBM protects you and I.
Safe in our beds now we can lie. . . .

And these guys are *fast*. The first American astronaut got into outer space on a Friday, and by Tuesday he was enshrined in advertisements. *Time* magazine, for instance, certainly profited heavily from Alan Shepard's five minutes of weightlessness.

"Astronaut probes space in a B.F. Goodrich suit," it said—or rather screamed—on page 9A. "From the moment he was sealed in his tiny space craft until he was fished from the Atlantic, he wore a B.F. Goodrich full pressure space suit. The fully insulated suit kept the astronaut at a comfortable 70-odd degrees. . . ." It was a two-page ad with a picture, a miracle of rapid commercialization.

On pages 42–43 there was another two-page ad: "Northrop's landing system brought him back." Guess who *him* is?

Page 45 was a full-page Allis-Chalmers ad for its "vital link with our man in orbit" (generators used in tracking stations). On page 45B the Rocketdyne Division of North American Aviation boasted of producing the Redstone, which got our fellow into space, and the Atlas engine. On page 69B there was another full-page ad for Chrysler Corporation, extending congratulations to everyone who had anything to do with getting Shepard up there, including themselves for helping develop the Redstone.

Time had roughly six pages of text on Shepard and six pages of ads boasting about the space shot. About the only guy who didn't boast about helping put Shepard into space was me. I tentatively sketched out an advertisement: "Congratulations, team! We did it! You and I and 40,000,000 other taxpayers with our patient, tireless, unremitting contributions to the space age made possible the historic manned flight," etc. The reason I didn't was—well, I can't afford it. Not after paying my taxes.

Senator Howard W. Cannon of Nevada estimates that the defense industry spends more than $500 million a year on this sort of institutional advertising.

That same issue of *Time*, for example, had a good many such ads that had nothing to do with Shepard. The most painful and least edifying of these was a double-page color ad showing a red telephone and looking sinister.

"Why the red phone may never be used," the ad read. "The red phone sits deep in the underground headquarters of the U.S. Strategic Air Command. It is reserved for one fateful message to SAC forces throughout the world: that enemy missiles have been launched against us." Lockheed paid for the ad.

I don't want to abolish advertising. The only newspaper in New York in my time that ever did that was an awful flop because people like advertising. But in my little old naïve way, I think advertising ought to provide a service like telling me where to find the product, how much it costs, and what's new about it. It shouldn't go boasting about space suits that I couldn't buy if I wanted one. ■

■ According to a survey conducted by Gallup & Robinson, admen have a deep-rooted guilt complex. The survey, *Sponsor* magazine revealed, asked one hundred housewives and one hundred admen whether they considered admen respectable, honest, hardworking, neurotic, hard-drinking, and as you probably guessed, the ad guys were a lot harder on themselves than were the housewives. Only four admen figured the housewives would think they were honest; by actual count, twenty of them did, which shows how hard it is to figure a housewife's brain.

Anyhow, *Sponsor* thought it ought to dig a little deeper into the psychological and emotional problems of Madison Avenue, and they found a psychiatrist who has, among his thirty-five patients, seven advertising men. "People who work in television," says the psychiatrist, "tend to be more frightened and anxiety-ridden than people in any other field."

What's the chief cause for anxiety among the ad fraternity, the spadebeard was asked. His answer was both illuminating and, in a gory way, hilarious: "There don't seem to be clear-cut channels of responsibility, so they have a tough time making decisions. Executives in other businesses don't seem to worry as much about a decision; they make it and stick to it more.

"I have a patient from the garment center who's a partner in a big firm. Last year he decided on a revolutionary new way for making buttonholes. He and his partner invested fifty thousand dollars in new machines for making buttonholes, put a big advertising campaign behind the new process and marketed their whole line around these new buttonholes.

"The process flopped. My patient and his partner lost a big chunk of money but he wasn't unduly worried. He'd made a decision and stuck to it. But within two weeks after his advertising campaign was launched, the president of his agency became a patient of mine.

"I think he felt guilty because the money he lost wasn't his. When he was a little boy, he used to play marbles. He told me about one time when he'd lost all his marbles. He didn't cry; he wanted to go on playing. So he got his younger brother to lend him all of his marbles. Within an hour, he'd lost them, too. Then he cried."

And that, friends, is where the expression "He's lost all his marbles" came from. It's a little frightening—isn't it?—when you get to thinking that behind every ad campaign there may be some secret neurosis. I mean a guy gets locked in a closet as a child and twenty-five years later we get the flip-top box.

As a group, the psychiatrist said, admen are covered with guilt over largely imaginary faults. Far from being dishonest, said the psychiatrist, they "lean over backwards trying to be ultra-scrupulous because they think they're suspect." What's more, they enjoy their work and therefore they feel guilty at taking money for it.

Well, the poor slobs really can't do much of anything but keep on making money and feeling guilty. ■

More mint tea, Amanda?

■ Dear me, Amanda, isn't the school news interesting these days? I can't remember a time since I joined the PTA that school news has been so fraught with significance. Hand me my tatting—there's a dear—and do let's talk about it.

Of course, you read that splendid statement by our Secretary of State, that nice Mr. Rusk, that we're going to spend all that lovely foreign-aid money educating Indians in South America and Indonesia and places like that. Of course, it's a shame we can't spend some money educating our own little wild Indians here in America, but that seems impossible, what with the religious issue. I was so hoping Congress would pass just a little teensy-weensy aid to education bill—poor Martha's child Peter can't read at all and he's going on twelve—but President Kennedy says wait until next year. My dear departed husband always used to say that about the Dodgers, remember?

But it is comforting to know that, even though we can't teach little Peter to read, Dean Rusk will be teaching basket weaving to all those underdeveloped Africans with our money. (He has such lovely manners, Mr. Rusk. Doesn't go around brandishing the hydrogen bomb under everyone's nose like that horrid Mr. Dulles.)

Would you like a little mint tea, Amanda? But, of course, all the school news isn't so pleasant. I'm sure you read Dr. Conant's statement. You didn't? Dear me! Well, he said that schools in the slums of our big cities where mostly Negroes live are so bad that the Negroes can't get a job after they get out of school. Isn't that terrible? Dr. Conant also says that suburban schools where all the white folks live are so much better than the city schools and so much richer that . . . that . . . now, let's see, what *did* he say? I have it right here.

"The contrast in the money available to the schools in a wealthy suburb and to the schools in a large city jolts one's notion of the meaning of equality of opportunity." That's what he said.

I heard, Amanda, that the Negroes are leaving the South very rapidly to come up North to avoid discrimination. All that fuss about integrating the schools in the South! They'll just get them decently integrated and there won't be any Negroes left down there to integrate. They'll all be living in ghettos up North going to perfectly dreadful all-black schools in the big cities. And, of course, they can't get into the decent schools out in the suburbs because the real estate people won't sell them houses out there.

I wouldn't be at all surprised, Amanda, if in about ten more years the South won't have any Negroes. Then the South will start a perfectly dreadful clamor about integrating the schools in the *North.* My land, can't you just see the indignation down there, after it's no longer their problem about the way we treat the Negroes? We'll have the Freedom Riders coming from Atlanta to New Rochelle.

But, dear me, how is a poor American Negro to get a decent education now? The only sensible solution I can see, Amanda, is for the Negroes to get out of the developed regions like Chicago and go to some underdeveloped region like Nigeria where Dean Rusk has all that lovely foreign-aid money. I think that's a marvelous solution, don't you, Amanda? Of course, he'll have to rub elbows with those white Peace Corps girls complaining about the living conditions, and making him feel inferior as usual—but we can't have everything, can we? ■

Index

ABOUT THE AUTHOR

John Crosby was born in Milwaukee, Wisconsin, in 1912. He was educated at Phillips Exeter Academy and Yale University, and started work as a reporter for the *Milwaukee Sentinel.* He joined the staff of the New York *Herald Tribune* in 1935. From 1941 to 1946 he served with the U.S. Army, and at the end of the war rejoined the *Tribune* as radio and television critic. His first book, *Out of the Blue,* was a collection of his critical columns and was enthusiastically reviewed. Not long after its publication, he broadened the scope of his writing to include commentary on general topics as well as radio and television, and he now writes his regular column from Paris, where he is stationed as correspondent for the paper.